COMPLETE COOKING WITH JENN-AIR®

What's a cookbook?

• a collection of delectable recipes?
• a series of mouth-watering photographs?
• a fun browsing experience?
• an epicurean adventure?
• a much-used reference work?
• a grease-stained, food-spattered, family-favorite cookbook?

COMPLETE COOKING with JENN-AIR is all of these, and more.

Those of us who have enjoyed cooking with Jenn-Air have discovered how easy it is to prepare a vast array of delicious foods. The versatility of the appliances also makes cooking more pleasurable and a fun-filled experience which can be shared with family and friends.

In developing the concept and contents of this cookbook, Gail Heeb, Jenn-Air's Test Kitchen Home Economist, and I wanted a cookbook that was packed full of tasty ideas, a book that would stimulate your creativity and help you make the most of your Jenn-Air appliance. We also wanted to create a cookbook classic.

We feel fortunate in having worked with the fine, talented staff of Cy DeCosse Incorporated who have produced this book. Our endeavors have resulted in a cookbook of which we are most proud. We also hope you will be just as pleased and that COMPLETE COOKING with JENN-AIR will become a treasured addition to your favorite cookbook collection.

Enjoy!

Ann Vaughan

Ann Vaughan
Director of Consumer Services
Jenn-Air Corporation

Design and Production: Cy DeCosse Incorporated

 ® JENN·AIR

Table of Contents

Introduction

Welcome to the convenience and fun of a complete cooking system. Whether you're the owner of a convertible cooktop, wall oven or grill-range, you're on your way to an exciting cooking adventure.

Why exciting? Because these appliances and the accessories that go with them offer all sorts of new ways to be creative in the kitchen.

The **grill** lets you enjoy the great flavor of outdoor cooking indoors all year around. The **griddle** makes it easy to cook breakfast favorites or grilled sandwiches. The **rotiss-kebab** cooks roasts, poultry or shish kebabs to perfection. The **French fryer/cooker** is ideal for deep-fat fried foods or large-quantity soups and stews. And the **wok** does everything from stir-frying to popping corn!

The **radiant bake oven** is a traditional oven, offering all the advantages you have enjoyed over the years. The **convection oven** cooks many foods faster and better by constantly recirculating the hot air. Meats stay juicier when roasted in the convection oven, and quantity cooking is possible because you can bake on three racks at once.

Roasted Turkey page 109, White Bread page 153, Popcorn page 65, Fried Egg, Sausage, and Toast Breakfast page 34, Peppered Sirloin Tip Roast page 45, Seafood Kebabs page 58, Beef Stew page 90, T-Bone Steak page 10, Grilled Onion Half and Grilled Green Pepper Ring page 25.

This book is your guide to all the parts of your cooking system. The recipes we've included have been specially formulated and tested for the grill, accessories and oven. Your own favorite recipes will adapt beautifully, too.

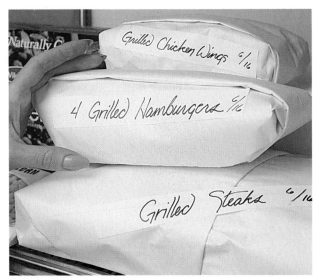

Many foods can be prepared with a combination of appliances. Grill one or two extra steaks or hamburgers, freeze them and reheat them in the microwave oven. Or start ribs or chicken in the microwave and finish cooking them on the grill. The versatility of your cooking system is a big help for working people and others with on-the-go schedules.

Using several different accessories to create an entire meal is both convenient and timesaving. Increase your versatility by adding an additional grill accessory. When entertaining, for example, you can prepare an appetizer on the grill while the roast cooks on the rotisserie.

If you don't have a particular accessory, you can often improvise with another accessory. For example, the wok can often be substituted for the French fryer/cooker. Use your own skewers on the grill if you don't have a rotiss-kebab accessory.

Your complete cooking system is terrific for today's casual entertaining. The fun of grilling, rotissing or stir-frying brings the guests into the kitchen to participate. Gone are the days of the lonely cook. The host or hostess can enjoy the party even while the food is being prepared.

Convenience, speed, versatility, fun—all these are good reasons for planning your meals around your cooking system.

Read the introductory pages to each section before trying the recipes in that section. The tips and techniques will help you achieve delicious results.

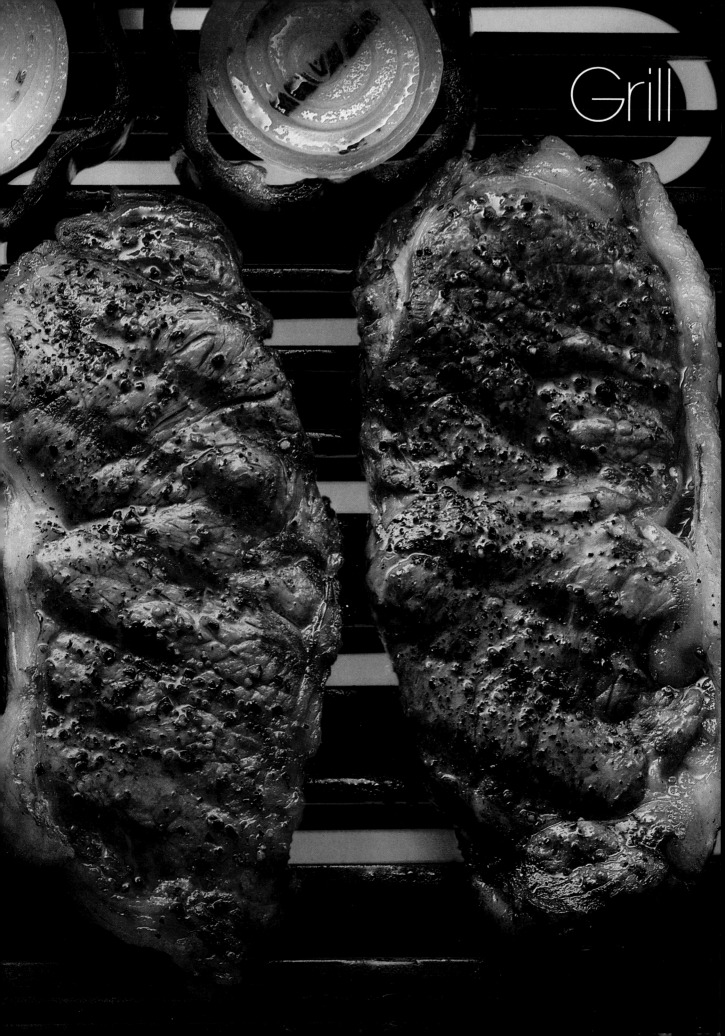

Grill

Grill

Your grill accessory brings the fun and flavor of outdoor grilling indoors. Many of your favorite outdoor barbecue recipes adapt beautifully to the indoor grill.

Try our unique recipes for grilled appetizers, marinated roasts, ham patties, individual meatloaves — even grilled dessert fruits. The chart on page 25 features ideas for grilled breads, fruits and vegetables to serve with your main course.

Use the following tips and ideas for cooking with your grill accessory.

Always preheat the grill on "Hi" for 5 minutes after seasoning grates and before grilling food. Preheating improves flavor and appearance of grilled foods and helps retain juices. Preheat with grill grates in place. The heating element should glow bright red.

Season the grill grates by brushing with vegetable oil or spraying with a non-stick coating, such as Pam®. Seasoning should be done *before* preheating the grill. (Many pastry brushes will melt if they come in contact with hot grates.) Season the grates if the recipe calls for it. Grates should also be seasoned after washing in the dishwasher.

Choose top grade meat. Meat that is at least ¾-inch thick is better for grilling than thinner cuts.

Trim excess fat from meat to reduce smoke and flare-ups. Score the fat on the edges of steaks to prevent them from curling during grilling.

Pictured on preceding page: Peppered Steaks, recipe page 14

Apply sauces sparingly during grilling. Excessive amounts will end up inside your grill.

Turn meat with tongs. Do not pierce with a meat fork; this causes the loss of meat juices.

Place food on the grill with enough space between pieces to allow proper air circulation.

Individual heat controls on certain ranges let you grill foods at two different temperatures at the same time. For example, grill hamburgers on setting "10" on the front grates while you grill green pepper rings on "Hi" on the back grates.

Salt meat after cooking, not during or before. This helps retain meat juices.

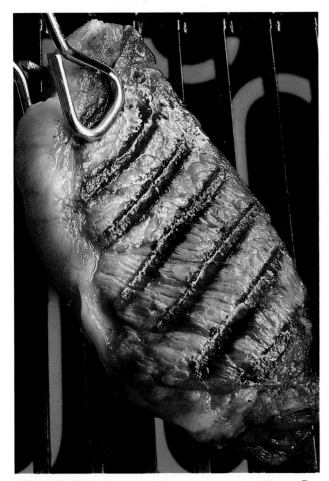

"Branded" look on steaks is easy to achieve. Be sure grill is preheated. Cook one side of meat to desired doneness, or until juices appear on the top surface, before turning. Turn and cook the other side. (It takes less time to cook the second side.)

Prepare an entire meal on the grill by combining foods like pork chops, yams and apple rings. The chart on page 25 helps you time the foods so they will be done at the same time.

Grill Guide Season grill grates. Preheat 5 minutes on "Hi".

Type	Setting	Cooking Time	Procedure
Beef			
Steak (½ to ¾")			
Rare	Hi	9 to 12 minutes	Turn after half the time.
Medium	Hi	12 to 19 minutes	Turn after half the time.
Well	Hi	16 to 23 minutes	Turn after half the time.
Steak (1 to 1½")			
Rare	Hi	10 to 17 minutes	Turn after half the time.
Medium	Hi	19 to 26 minutes	Turn after half the time.
Well	Hi	24 to 32 minutes	Turn after half the time.
Hamburgers (½ to ¾")	10	15 to 25 minutes	Turn after half the time.
Chuck Roast - medium	8	55 to 70 minutes	Marinate roast. Turn and baste occasionally*.
Flank Steak - rare	Hi	5 to 7 minutes	Score flank steak with diagonal cuts. Baste occasionally, if desired*. Turn once.
Pork			
Pork Chops	9-10	30 to 40 minutes	Turn occasionally. Baste, if desired*.
Fully-cooked Smoked Pork Chops	Hi	10 to 15 minutes	Turn once. Baste during last 5 minutes, if desired*.
Ham Slices	10	15 to 20 minutes	Turn once. Baste during last 5 minutes, if desired*.
Pork Spare Ribs	10	50 to 60 minutes	Turn occasionally. Baste during last 15 minutes*.
Sausage			
Precooked Hot Dogs, Brats, Polish	Hi	5 to 10 minutes	Turn once.
Links (uncooked)	10	10 to 15 minutes	Turn occasionally.
Patties	9	20 to 25 minutes	Turn after half the time.
Italian Sausage, Ring Bologna	9	20 to 25 minutes	Pierce casing with fork. Turn occasionally.
Lamb Chops	9-10	25 to 35 minutes	Turn occasionally. Baste if desired*.
Chicken			
Pieces: Bone-in	10	45 to 60 minutes	Turn occasionally. Baste if desired*.
Boneless Breasts	10	25 to 35 minutes	Start skin side down. Turn occasionally. Baste if desired*.
Wings	10	20 to 25 minutes	Turn frequently. Baste during last 5 minutes, if desired*.
Fish and Seafood			
Small Whole Fish 1½ inches thick	9	20 to 25 minutes	Baste occasionally with butter or marinade*. Turn after half the time.
Salmon Steaks 1 inch thick	9	25 to 30 minutes	Baste occasionally with butter or marinade*. Turn after half the time.
Fillets ½ inch thick with skin on	9	10 to 15 minutes	Baste flesh side with butter. Start flesh side down. Baste and turn after half the time.
Lobster Tails	8-9	20 to 30 minutes	Baste with butter. Turn occasionally.
Shrimp	9	10 to 15 minutes	Turn and baste frequently with butter or marinade*.

*See pages 97-101 for Marinade, Sauce, Baste and Glaze ideas.

Barbecued Rib Appetizers

2½ to 3 pounds beef chuck short ribs*
1 recipe Barbecue Sauce, page 98

Cut ribs into individual pieces. Season grill grates; preheat grill on "Hi". Reduce heat to setting "9". Grill ribs 30 to 35 minutes, or until fork tender. Turn frequently and brush with Barbecue Sauce.

*Ask butcher to cut ribs in half crosswise so that bones are about 2 inches long.

About 24 appetizers

Onion and Bacon Appetizers

7 slices bacon, cut into thirds crosswise
1 recipe Teriyaki Marinade, page 97
21 cocktail onions, drained and patted dry

Place bacon pieces in baking dish or plastic food storage bag. Pour marinade over bacon. Cover dish or close bag. Refrigerate at least 2 hours.

Wrap each bacon piece around 1 onion. Secure with wooden pick.

Preheat grill on "Hi". Reduce heat to setting "8". Grill appetizers 20 to 25 minutes, or until bacon is crisp. Turn after half the time.

Water Chestnut and Bacon Appetizers: Follow the recipe above, substituting 1 can (8 ounces) water chestnuts, drained and patted dry, for cocktail onions. (Large water chestnuts should be cut in half.)

Pineapple and Bacon Appetizers: Follow the recipe above, substituting 1 can (8 ounces) pineapple chunks, drained well and patted dry, for the cocktail onions.

Cocktail Wiener and Bacon Appetizers: Follow the recipe above, substituting 21 cocktail wieners for cocktail onions.

TIP: Speed cooking time by partially cooking bacon after marinating.

21 appetizers

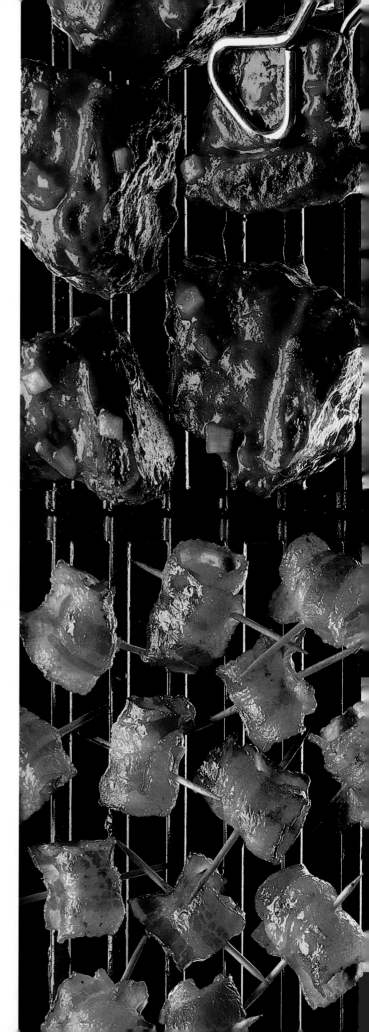

Barbecued Rib Appetizers, Onion and Bacon Appetizers

Marinated Shrimp Appetizers, Spicy Pork Appetizers

Spicy Pork Appetizers

2 pork chops, ¾ inch thick (1 pound), trimmed of excess fat

Marinade:
1 large red onion, grated
¼ cup water
¼ cup soy sauce
3 tablespoons lemon juice
2 tablespoons packed brown sugar
2 cloves garlic, minced
2 tablespoons ground coriander
2 teaspoons chili powder
1 teaspoon salt
1 teaspoon coarsely ground pepper
⅛ teaspoon crushed red pepper

Cut chops across the grain into thin strips. On each of twelve 6-inch skewers thread strips accordian-style to within 1 inch of skewer ends. Arrange kebabs in baking dish. Set aside.

For marinade: In small mixing bowl combine remaining ingredients. Pour marinade over kebabs. Cover dish. Refrigerate at least 2 hours, turning kebabs occasionally.

Season grill grates; preheat grill on "Hi". Reduce heat to setting "10". Grill kebabs 15 to 20 minutes, or until meat is fully cooked. Turn frequently.

12 appetizers

Marinated Chicken Wings

1 to 1½ pounds chicken wings (about 9 or 10 wings)
1 recipe Teriyaki Marinade or Curry Marinade, page 97

Cut wing tip at joint. Discard tip. Cut remaining wing into two pieces at joint. Place pieces in baking dish or plastic food storage bag. Pour marinade over chicken. Cover dish or close bag. Refrigerate at least 2 hours, turning chicken occasionally to coat all pieces.

Season grill grates; preheat grill on "Hi". Reduce heat to setting "10". Grill chicken 20 to 25 minutes, or until thoroughly cooked. Turn frequently. Brush with marinade occasionally, if desired.

18 to 20 appetizers

Marinated Shrimp Appetizers

1 pound medium-size raw shrimp, shelled, deveined and cut in half lengthwise
1 recipe White Wine Marinade (Shrimp Variation), page 97, salt omitted

Place shrimp in medium bowl or plastic food storage bag. Pour marinade over shrimp. Cover bowl or close bag. Refrigerate 1 hour, turning shrimp occasionally.

Thread each shrimp on wooden pick. Season grill grates; preheat grill on "Hi". Reduce heat to setting "9". Grill shrimp 5 to 10 minutes, or until firm and opaque. Turn frequently and brush with marinade.

About 24 appetizers

Stuffed Bacon Appetizers

15 slices bacon, cut in half crosswise
1 recipe Teriyaki Marinade, page 97

Filling:
1 can (6 ounces) crab meat, rinsed, drained
    and flaked
¼ cup fine dry bread crumbs (unseasoned)
1 teaspoon freeze-dried chives
⅛ teaspoon pepper
2 tablespoons butter or margarine, melted

Layer bacon pieces in baking dish or plastic food storage bag. Pour marinade over bacon. Cover dish or close bag. Refrigerate at least 2 hours.

For filling: In medium mixing bowl combine crab meat, bread crumbs, chives and pepper. Blend in melted butter. Spread about 1 teaspoon crab mixture down center of each bacon piece, pressing lightly. Roll each slice jelly roll fashion. Secure with wooden pick.

Preheat grill on "Hi". Reduce heat to setting "8". Grill appetizers 20 to 25 minutes, or until bacon is crisp. Turn after half the time.

TIP: Speed cooking time by partially cooking bacon after marinating.

30 appetizers

Stuffed Bacon Appetizers

How to Assemble Stuffed Bacon Appetizers

Layer bacon pieces in baking dish. Pour marinade evenly over bacon. Cover and refrigerate at least 2 hours.

Spread about 1 teaspoon crab filling down center of each bacon piece, pressing lightly with back of spoon.

Roll each slice jelly roll fashion. Secure with wooden pick.

Marinated Chuck Roast

3 pound beef chuck roast, about 2 inches
   thick, trimmed of excess fat
1 recipe Red Wine Marinade, page 97

Place roast in baking dish or plastic food storage bag. Pour marinade over roast. Cover dish or close bag. Refrigerate at least 8 hours or overnight, turning roast occasionally.

Season grill grates; preheat grill on "Hi". Reduce heat to setting "8". Grill roast 55 to 70 minutes, or until desired doneness. Turn every 15 to 20 minutes. To serve, cut into thin slices.

4 to 6 servings

Peppered Steaks

4 Beef T-bone, rib eye or New York strip
   steaks, about ¾ inch thick
2 teaspoons coarsely ground pepper
½ cup dry red wine

Sprinkle both sides of steaks with pepper. Press pepper lightly into meat surface.

Arrange steaks in baking dish or plastic food storage bag. Pour wine over steaks. Cover dish or close bag. Refrigerate overnight, or let stand at room temperature 30 minutes, turning steaks once.

Season grill grates; preheat grill on "Hi". Grill steaks according to chart on page 10. For steaks marinated at room temperature, reduce cooking time by 1 to 2 minutes per side.

4 servings

London Broil

1 to 1½ pounds beef flank steak
½ recipe White Wine Marinade, page 97
   (optional)

Make diagonal cuts, ⅛ inch deep, in each side of flank steak to form diamond pattern.

Season grill grates; preheat grill on "Hi". Grill steak 5 to 7 minutes, or until rare or medium-rare. Turn once and brush frequently with marinade. To serve, cut into thin slices diagonally across grain.

4 to 6 servings

Marinated Flank Steak

1 pound beef flank steak

Marinade:
¼ cup chopped onion
¼ cup chopped celery
2 tablespoons vegetable oil
½ cup water
¼ cup red wine vinegar
1 teaspoon salt
1 teaspoon sugar
¼ teaspoon dried thyme leaves
¼ teaspoon ground allspice
⅛ teaspoon ground cloves
⅛ teaspoon coarsely ground pepper
1 bay leaf

Make deep cuts, 1 inch apart, diagonally across the grain in one side of flank steak to form diamond pattern. Place steak in baking dish or plastic food storage bag.

For marinade: In small saucepan sauté onion and celery in oil until tender. Add remaining ingredients. Heat to boiling. Cool slightly.

Pour marinade over steak. Cover dish or close bag. Refrigerate at least 8 hours or overnight, turning steak occasionally.

Season grill grates; preheat grill on "Hi". Place steak scored-side down on grill. Grill steak 5 to 10 minutes, or until rare or medium-rare. Turn after half the time. To serve, cut into thin slices diagonally across the grain (for meal servings) or into 1-inch cubes (for appetizers).

4 servings or about 50 appetizers

London Broil

Bacon-Wrapped Meatloaves

Sesame Beef and Mushroom Kebabs

1½ pound beef boneless sirloin, trimmed of excess fat and cut into 1½-inch cubes
1 recipe Teriyaki Marinade, page 97
3 tablespoons sesame seeds
9 medium-size fresh mushrooms (1 to 1½-inch diameter)
  Vegetable oil

Place beef cubes in baking dish or plastic food storage bag. Pour marinade over beef. Cover dish or close bag. Refrigerate at least 3 hours, or let stand at room temperature 1 hour, turning beef cubes occasionally.

In small skillet place sesame seeds. Cook on high heat, stirring constantly, until golden. Set aside.

On each of four 12-inch skewers alternately thread beef cubes and mushrooms. Brush mushrooms with vegetable oil. Sprinkle toasted sesame seeds over kebabs.

Season grill grates; preheat grill on "Hi". Grill kebabs 15 to 25 minutes, or until desired doneness. Turn after half the time. For kebabs marinated at room temperature, reduce time by 5 minutes.

4 servings

Bacon-Wrapped Meatloaves

1 pound lean ground beef
1 slice white bread, torn into small pieces
¼ cup milk
1 egg, slightly beaten
2 tablespoons minced green pepper
1 tablespoon minced green onion
1 tablespoon steak sauce
½ teaspoon dried marjoram leaves
¼ teaspoon dried summer savory leaves
⅛ teaspoon pepper
4 slices bacon

In medium mixing bowl combine all ingredients except bacon. Divide mixture into 4 equal portions. Form each portion into about 4 × 2½-inch loaf. Wrap slice of bacon around each loaf. Secure with wooden pick.

Preheat grill on "Hi". Reduce heat to setting "10". Grill meatloaves about 25 minutes, or until bacon is crisp and meatloaves are of desired doneness. Turn after half the time. Remove wooden picks before serving.

4 servings

Italian Hamburgers

1½ pounds lean ground beef
2 tablespoons minced onion
1 to 1¼ teaspoons dried Italian seasoning
¾ teaspoon Worcestershire sauce

In medium mixing bowl combine all ingredients. Divide mixture into 6 equal portions. Form each portion into 3½-inch diameter patty.

Preheat grill on "Hi". Reduce heat to setting "10". Grill patties 15 to 25 minutes, or until desired doneness. Turn after half the time.

Stuffed Italian Hamburgers: Follow the recipe above, except form hamburger mixture into twelve 3½-inch diameter patties. Sauté ¾ cup chopped fresh mushrooms in 1 teaspoon butter until just tender. On each of 6 patties place 2 teaspoons cooked mushrooms and 1 scant tablespoon shredded mozzarella cheese, leaving ½ inch around edges. Top with remaining patties. Pinch edges together to seal. Grill as directed.

6 servings

Chili Hamburgers

1½ pounds lean ground beef
2 tablespoons minced onion
1 tablespoon chili powder
½ teaspoon dried oregano leaves
½ teaspoon hot pepper sauce
⅛ teaspoon garlic powder

In medium mixing bowl combine all ingredients. Divide mixture into 6 equal portions. Form each portion into 3½-inch diameter patty.

Preheat grill on "Hi". Reduce heat to setting "10". Grill patties 15 to 25 minutes, or until desired doneness. Turn after half the time.

Stuffed Chili Hamburgers: Follow the recipe above, except form hamburger mixture into twelve 3½-inch diameter patties. On each of 6 patties place 1 tablespoon shredded Cheddar cheese, leaving ½ inch around the edges. Top with remaining patties. Pinch the edges together to seal. Grill as directed.

6 servings

Italian Hamburgers

Vermouth Burgers

1 pound lean ground beef
⅓ cup minced onion
¼ cup dry vermouth
2 tablespoons fine dry bread crumbs
  (unseasoned)
1 teaspoon dried bouquet garni
½ teaspoon salt
⅛ to ¼ teaspoon garlic powder

In medium mixing bowl combine all ingredients. Divide mixture into 4 equal portions. Form each portion into ¾-inch thick patty.

Preheat grill on "Hi". Reduce heat to setting "10". Grill burgers 15 to 25 minutes, or until desired doneness. Turn after half the time.

4 servings

Smoky Hamburgers

1 pound lean ground beef
3 slices bacon, partially cooked, cut into small
   pieces
¼ cup barbecue sauce
3 tablespoons fine dry bread crumbs
   (unseasoned)
¼ to ½ teaspoon liquid smoke
4 thin slices smoked Cheddar cheese (optional)

In medium mixing bowl combine all ingredients except cheese. Divide mixture into 4 equal portions. Form each portion into ¾-inch thick patty.

Preheat grill on "Hi". Reduce heat to setting "10". Grill patties 8 minutes. Turn patties. Top each patty with 1 slice cheese. Grill patties 7 to 12 minutes longer, or until desired doneness.

4 servings

Ham and Olive Burgers

1 pound lean ground beef
¾ cup finely chopped fully-cooked ham
½ cup chopped pimiento-stuffed olives
¼ teaspoon pepper
4 slices Swiss or mozzarella cheese

In medium mixing bowl combine all ingredients. Divide mixture into 4 equal portions. Form each portion into ¾-inch thick patty.

Preheat grill on "Hi". Reduce heat to setting "10". Grill patties 10 minutes. Turn patties. Top each with 1 slice cheese. Grill patties 5 to 15 minutes longer, or until desired doneness.

4 servings

Glazed Pork Chops

4 fully-cooked smoked pork chops* (about 1½
   pounds), trimmed of excess fat
1 recipe Apricot Glaze, page 100
   Apricot halves (optional)

Season grill grates; preheat grill on "Hi". Brush one side of chops with glaze. Place brushed-side down on grill. Brush other side with glaze. Grill chops 10 to 15 minutes, or until heated through. Turn after half the time and brush with glaze. Garnish with apricot halves. Serve with any remaining glaze.

*If smoked pork chops are not fully-cooked, cook as directed to internal temperature of 165°F.

4 servings

Smoky Hamburgers

Pineapple Ham Patties

1 pound fully-cooked ground ham
½ pound unseasoned ground pork
1 can (8 ounces) crushed pineapple, drained
1 egg, beaten
½ teaspoon pepper
¼ teaspoon ground ginger

In medium mixing bowl combine all ingredients. Divide mixture into 6 equal portions. Form each portion into ¾-inch thick patty.

Season grill grates; preheat grill on "Hi". Reduce heat to setting "9". Grill patties 15 to 20 minutes, or until thoroughly cooked. Turn after half the time.

6 servings

Marinated Spareribs

4 pounds pork or beef spareribs, cut into 2 or 3-rib portions
Double recipe Curry Marinade, Teriyaki Marinade or Polynesian Marinade, page 97

Arrange ribs in baking dish or plastic food storage bag. Pour marinade over ribs. Cover dish or close bag. Refrigerate at least 2 hours, turning ribs occasionally in the marinade.

Season grill grates; preheat grill on "Hi". Reduce heat to setting "10". Grill ribs 50 to 60 minutes, or until meat is fully cooked. Turn occasionally and brush with marinade.

4 servings

Tangy Mustard Ribs

3 to 3½ pounds pork spareribs, cut into 2 or 3-rib portions
1 medium onion, cut into quarters
1 cup water
1 teaspoon salt

Sauce:
¾ cup butter or margarine
½ cup fresh lemon juice
¼ cup vinegar
2 teaspoons all-purpose flour
1 teaspoon cayenne
1 teaspoon pepper
2 to 3 teaspoons dry mustard
1 clove garlic, minced
½ teaspoon sugar
½ teaspoon salt
¼ teaspoon liquid smoke

In wok or Dutch oven combine ribs, onion, water and salt. Heat to boiling. Reduce heat to setting "3" or "4". Simmer, covered, 1½ to 2 hours, or until ribs are tender.

For sauce: In small saucepan melt butter. In small mixing bowl combine remaining ingredients. Stir mixture into melted butter. Heat on setting "7", stirring constantly, until mixture thickens and just comes to boil.

Season grill grates; preheat grill on "Hi". Reduce heat to setting "10". Brush ribs with sauce. Place brushed-side down on grill. Grill ribs 10 to 20 minutes, or until browned. Turn frequently and brush with sauce.

2 to 4 servings

Marinated Spareribs

Brats in Beer

Stuffed Polish Sausage

¼ cup chopped onion
¼ cup chopped green pepper
 Dash garlic powder (optional)
 1 tablespoon olive oil
⅓ cup sauerkraut, undrained
 4 fully-cooked Polish sausages
 4 hot dog buns, split

In small skillet sauté onion, green pepper and garlic powder in olive oil until vegetables are tender. Stir in sauerkraut. Set aside.

Split sausages lengthwise, but do not cut all the way through. Preheat grill on "Hi". Place sausages split-side down on grill. Grill 5 minutes. Turn sausages. Top each sausage with one-fourth of sauerkraut mixture. Grill sausages 3 to 5 minutes longer, or until heated through. Serve in hot dog buns.

4 servings

Glazed Lamb Chops

8 lamb loin chops (about 2½ pounds), trimmed
 of excess fat
1 recipe Orange Glaze, page 100, or Mint
 Sauce, page 99

Season grill grates; preheat grill on "Hi". Reduce heat to setting "10". Grill chops 25 to 35 minutes, or until desired doneness. Turn every 10 minutes. Brush occasionally with glaze.

4 servings

Brats in Beer

1 can (12 ounces) beer
1 teaspoon caraway seeds
4 whole peppercorns
4 uncooked bratwurst (1 pound)

In wok or medium saucepan combine beer, caraway seeds and peppercorns. Heat to boiling. Add bratwurst. Reduce heat to setting "4" or "5". Simmer, covered, 15 to 20 minutes.

Preheat grill on "Hi". Grill bratwurst 5 to 10 minutes, or until browned. Turn occasionally.

4 servings

Herbed Lamb Patties

½ pound ground lamb
½ pound ground beef
 1 egg, beaten
¼ cup fine dry bread crumbs (unseasoned)
¼ teaspoon dried basil leaves
¼ teaspoon dried rosemary leaves, crushed
⅛ teaspoon pepper

In medium mixing bowl combine all ingredients. Divide mixture into 4 equal portions. Form each portion into ½-inch thick patty.

Season grill grates; preheat grill on "Hi". Reduce heat to setting "10". Grill patties 10 to 20 minutes, or until desired doneness. Turn after half the time.

4 servings

Herbed Cornish Hens

Smoked Turkey

½ turkey (about 5 to 6 pounds)*, defrosted
10 cups hot water
1 cup salt
¼ cup packed brown sugar
1 tablespoon liquid smoke
Vegetable oil

Place turkey half in large oven cooking bag or very large glass dish. In wok or large saucepan heat water, salt and brown sugar, stirring constantly, until salt and sugar are dissolved. Stir in liquid smoke. Pour salt mixture over turkey. Close bag or cover dish. Refrigerate 4 days, turning turkey occasionally.

Season grill grates; preheat grill on "Hi". Reduce heat to setting "9". Brush turkey with vegetable oil. Place turkey on grill. Cover turkey and grill with large sheet of heavy-duty foil, leaving an opening on vent side of grill. Grill turkey 20 to 30 minutes per pound, or until juices run clear and meat thermometer registers 180° to 185°F in several places. Turn and brush with vegetable oil occasionally. Serve as snack or in sandwiches.

*Ask butcher to cut 10 to 12 pound turkey in half lengthwise through breast and back. Remaining half of turkey (with giblets) can be kept frozen for use in other recipes.

Herbed Cornish Hens

Baste:
¼ cup butter or margarine
¼ cup lime juice
3 tablespoons dry white wine
2 teaspoons freeze-dried chives
1 teaspoon dried parsley flakes
½ teaspoon dried tarragon leaves
½ teaspoon dry mustard
¼ teaspoon salt
⅛ teaspoon pepper

2 Cornish hens (about 24 ounces each), thawed if frozen

For baste: In small saucepan melt butter. Add remaining ingredients. Heat to boiling, stirring constantly. Set aside.

Cut each hen in half lengthwise (through breast and back bone). Season grill grates; preheat grill on "Hi". Reduce heat to setting "10". Place hen halves on grill, skin-side down. Grill hens 35 to 40 minutes, or until meat is no longer pink. Turn frequently and brush with baste.

4 servings

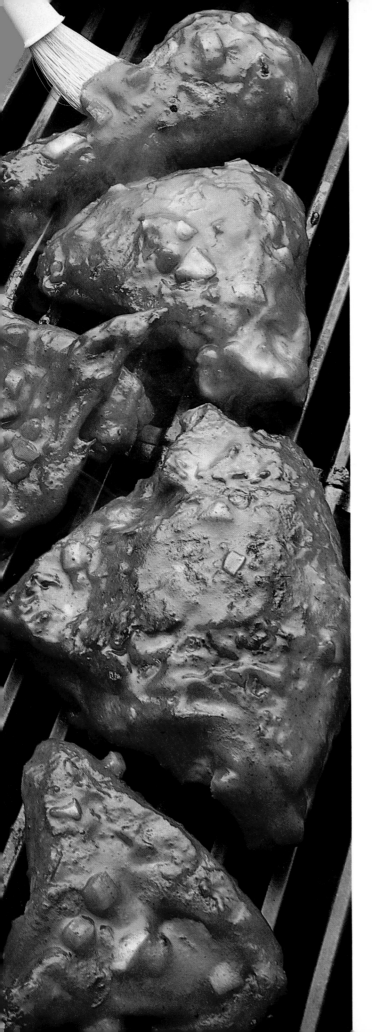

Barbecued Chicken

2 to 2½-pound broiler-fryer chicken, cut up
1 recipe Barbecue Sauce, page 98

Season grill grates; preheat grill on "Hi". Reduce heat to setting "10". Grill chicken pieces 45 to 60 minutes, or until juices run clear. Turn frequently. Brush with sauce during last 15 to 20 minutes.

4 servings

Marinated Chicken Breasts

4 boneless chicken breast halves, (about 1½ pounds)
1 recipe White Wine Marinade (Chicken Variation), page 97

Arrange chicken in baking dish or plastic food storage bag. Pour marinade over chicken. Cover dish or close bag. Refrigerate at least 2 hours, turning chicken occasionally.

Season grill grates; preheat grill on "Hi". Reduce heat to setting "10". Place chicken skin-side down on grill. Grill chicken 25 to 35 minutes, or until meat is no longer pink. Turn every 8 minutes.

4 servings

Glazed Chicken Breasts

4 boneless chicken breast halves, (about 1½ pounds)

Marinade:
⅓ cup maple syrup
¼ cup soy sauce
¼ cup catsup
2 cloves garlic, minced
¼ teaspoon ground ginger

Arrange chicken in baking dish or plastic food storage bag. For marinade: In small mixing bowl combine all ingredients. Pour over chicken. Cover dish or close bag. Refrigerate at least 1 hour, turning chicken occasionally.

Season grill grates; preheat grill on "Hi". Reduce heat to setting "10". Place chicken skin-side down on grill. Grill chicken 25 to 35 minutes, or until meat is no longer pink. Turn every 5 minutes.

4 servings

Barbecued Chicken

Herb-Filled Chicken Thighs

Herb-Filled Chicken Thighs

4 to 6 chicken thighs (about 1¾ pounds)

Filling:
- 1 tablespoon Dijon-style mustard
- 2 teaspoons minced onion
- 2 teaspoons dried parsley flakes
- ½ teaspoon dried rosemary leaves, crushed
- ¼ teaspoon dried marjoram leaves
- 1 clove garlic, minced

   Vegetable oil (optional)

Loosen skin from chicken to form a pocket. For filling: In small bowl combine all ingredients. Spread about ¾ to 1 teaspoon filling mixture under skin of each thigh.

Season grill grates; preheat grill on "Hi". Reduce heat to setting "10". Place chicken skin-side down on grill. Grill chicken 45 to 55 minutes, or until juices run clear. Turn every 10 minutes and brush occasionally with vegetable oil.

2 to 4 servings

How to Fill Chicken Thighs

Loosen skin from each chicken thigh (with fingers) to form a pocket.

Spread about ¾ to 1 teaspoon filling in pocket under skin. Replace skin over filling.

Grilled Salmon Steaks

4 salmon steaks, about 1 inch thick
1 recipe Garlic Dill Butter or White Wine
    Marinade (Fish Variation), page 97

Preheat grill on "Hi". Reduce heat to setting "9". Brush one side of salmon with desired marinade. Place brushed-side down on grill. Brush other side. Grill salmon 25 to 30 minutes, or until fish flakes easily. Turn and baste after half the time. Serve with any remaining marinade, if desired.

4 servings

Grilled Fish Fillets

1½ pounds fresh fish fillets, ½ inch thick, with
      skin on
1 recipe Garlic Dill Butter, page 97

Season grill grates; preheat grill on "Hi". Reduce heat to setting "9". Brush flesh side of fillets with butter mixture. Place flesh-side down on grill. Brush skin side with butter mixture. Grill fillets 10 to 15 minutes, or until fish flakes easily. Turn and baste after half the time. Serve with any remaining butter mixture, if desired.

4 to 6 servings

Grilled Dessert Fruits

24 dark sweet pitted cherries (canned or fresh)
 4 peach halves (canned or fresh), each cut
      into 3 pieces
 2 pear halves (canned or fresh), each cut into
      3 pieces
 2 large bananas, each cut into 6 pieces
 1 medium apple, cored and cut into 12 pieces
⅓ cup orange-flavor liqueur
      Pound cake (optional)
 1 recipe Lemon Cream Sauce, page 99
      (optional)

In medium bowl or plastic food storage bag combine fruits and liqueur. Cover bowl or close bag. Let stand at room temperature 30 to 60 minutes, turning fruit occasionally. Remove fruit. Reserve liquid to use as marinade.

On each of six 10-inch skewers alternately thread fruit pieces.

Season grill grates; preheat grill on "Hi". Reduce heat to setting "10". Grill kebabs 8 to 12 minutes, or until heated through. Turn occasionally and brush with reserved liquid. Serve fruit over pound cake. Top with Lemon Cream Sauce.

6 to 8 servings

Meal Accompaniments

Item	Ingredients and Procedure
Breads	
Garlic Bread 4 servings	4 to 8 thick slices bread, 4 to 7 tablespoons softened butter or margarine, garlic powder.
	Preheat grill on "Hi". Spread both sides of bread with butter. Sprinkle with garlic powder to taste. Grill 4 to 6 minutes, or until browned. Turn after half the time.
Texas Toast 4 servings	4 thick slices bread, 6 to 8 tablespoons melted butter or margarine.
	Preheat grill on "Hi". Spread both sides of bread with butter. Grill 4 to 6 minutes, or until browned. Turn after half the time.
Toasted Hamburger Buns 6 buns	6 hamburger buns, split.
	Preheat grill on "10". Grill buns split-side down 1½ to 2 minutes, or until browned.
Fruits	
Grilled Apple Rings 4 to 6 servings	2 tablespoons butter or margarine, 1 tablespoon packed brown sugar, 1 teaspoon lemon juice, ¼ teaspoon ground cinnamon, dash ground allspice, 1 large apple, cored and cut into ½-inch rings.
	In small saucepan combine butter, brown sugar, lemon juice, cinnamon and allspice. Heat, stirring constantly, until sugar dissolves. Set aside. Season grill grates; preheat grill on "Hi". Brush one side of apple rings with butter mixture. Place brushed-side down on grill. Brush other side with butter mixture. Grill apple rings about 4 minutes, or until fork tender. Turn after half the time.
Grilled Pineapple Rings 4 servings	8 pineapple rings, butter (optional).
	Preheat grill on "Hi". Grill pineapple rings 8 to 10 minutes. Turn after half the time. Brush with butter, if desired.
Vegetables	
Grilled Glazed Carrots 4 to 6 servings	12 ounces pared baby carrots, 1 tablespoon packed brown sugar, 3 tablespoons orange juice, 3 tablespoons butter or margarine.
	Trim tough ends from pared carrots. Parboil carrots 5 minutes. Drain and set aside. In small saucepan combine brown sugar, orange juice and butter. Heat, stirring constantly, until sugar dissolves. Set aside. Season grill grates; preheat grill on "Hi". Grill carrots 15 to 25 minutes, or until fork tender. Turn frequently and brush with glaze. Serve with any remaining glaze.
Grilled Onion Halves 4 servings	2 medium onions, melted butter.
	Parboil onions 2 minutes. Drain and cut in half. Brush with melted butter. Preheat grill on "Hi". Grill onions 10 to 15 minutes. Turn occasionally.
Grilled Green Pepper Rings 4 servings	1 medium-size green pepper, seeded and cut into ½-inch rings.
	Preheat grill on "Hi". Brush one side of pepper rings with vegetable oil. Place brushed-side down on grill. Brush other side with oil. Grill pepper rings 7 to 9 minutes, or until fork tender. Turn after half the time.
Grilled Squash 4 to 6 servings	2 medium-size yellow or zucchini squash (about 1 pound), cut lengthwise into ½-inch slices, 2 tablespoons melted butter, salt, pepper, Parmesan cheese.
	Preheat grill on "Hi". Brush one side of squash slices with butter. Place brushed-side down on grill. Brush other side with butter. Grill squash slices 8 to 12 minutes, or until fork tender. Turn occasionally and brush with butter. Before serving, sprinkle with salt, pepper and Parmesan cheese.
Grilled Yams 4 to 6 servings	2 medium yams (about 1 pound), pared and cut crosswise into ½-inch thick slices, 2 tablespoons melted butter, salt, pepper.
	Preheat grill on "Hi". Brush one side of yam slices with butter. Place brushed-side down on grill. Brush other side with butter. Grill yam slices 15 to 25 minutes, or until fork tender. Turn occasionally and brush with butter. Before serving, sprinkle with salt and pepper.

Griddle

Griddle

Your griddle accessory makes many favorite foods easier to fix. Its large surface lets you cook several pancakes, hamburgers or grilled sandwiches at a time. Breakfast is ready on the double when you cook eggs, bacon and hashed browns on the griddle all at once. And excess fat drains for easy cleanup.

Page through our recipes for delicious foods you can cook on the griddle. You'll find appetizers, sandwiches, ethnic specialties, even homemade English muffins. The tips below will help you make the most of your griddle accessory.

Preheat griddle for 5 minutes at the setting specified in the recipe or chart. Do *not* preheat or cook on the "Hi" setting. Be sure to reduce the heat after preheating if the recipe calls for it.

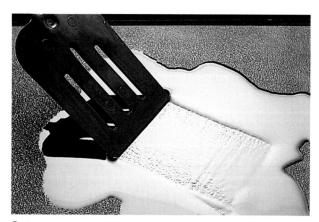

Grease the griddle lightly *after* preheating. Utensils made for use with non-stick skillets are least likely to damage the surface.

Pictured on preceding page: Eggs and Bacon, chart page 28

Clean the griddle after each use to properly maintain the finish. After the griddle has cooled, wash with detergent and hot water. To avoid damaging the finish, use a plastic scrubber to remove cooked-on residue.

Check the grease collection container frequently. It fills up quickly when cooking fatty foods such as bacon. Be sure to wait until all grease has drained before removing the container.

Cooking Times for the Griddle

Item	Control Setting	Cooking Times (min.) (1st Side)	(2nd Side)
Eggs*	5 - 6	2 to 3	(1)
Pancakes*	9 - 10	2	1 to 2
French Toast*	9 - 10	3	2 to 3
Bacon (regular sliced)	8 - 9	3	1 to 2
Sausage Patties	8 - 9	8	6
Ham Slice	8 - 9	6	5 to 6
Grilled Sandwiches	8 - 9	4	3
Hamburgers	7 - 8	6	5
Hot Dogs	8 - 9	5	5
Fish Sticks	6 - 7	5	3 to 4
Buns	8 - 9	3	

*For best results, preheat for 10 minutes.

NOTE: These are suggested guides for control settings and times. Settings and times may vary due to factors such as low voltage.

Mexican Cheese Appetizers

4 flour tortillas (8-inch diameter)
1 cup shredded Cheddar cheese
1 cup shredded Monterey Jack cheese
¼ cup chopped green onion
¼ cup chopped pitted ripe olives
　Sour cream or taco sauce

Preheat griddle on setting "8". Lightly grease griddle with vegetable oil. Place 2 tortillas on griddle. Top each with one fourth of cheeses, onion and olives. Cook tortillas 1½ to 3 minutes, or until cheese melts. With pancake turner, roll each tortilla jelly roll fashion. Remove from griddle. Cut crosswise into 4 pieces. Repeat with remaining tortillas. Serve with sour cream or taco sauce.

Deluxe Mexican Cheese Appetizers: Follow the recipe above, except add 1 cup refried beans and 1⅓ cups shredded lettuce. Spread each tortilla with ¼ cup refried beans. Place on lightly greased griddle. Top with ¼ of cheese, onion, olives and shredded lettuce. Cook as directed. Fold each tortilla in half and cut into 4 wedges.

16 appetizers

Seasoned Hashed Browns

2 pounds white potatoes (about 6 medium), pared
¼ cup minced onion
1 teaspoon garlic salt
½ teaspoon fennel seed (optional)
⅛ teaspoon pepper
3 tablespoons butter or margarine

Shred potatoes into large bowl of ice water. Drain potatoes, pressing out excess moisture. Transfer to large mixing bowl. Blend in onion, garlic salt, fennel seed and pepper. Mix well. Set aside.

Preheat griddle on setting "8". Melt butter on griddle, spreading over surface as it melts. Spread potatoes on griddle to within ½ inch of sides and 1½ inches of ends. With pancake turner, gently press down potatoes. Fry potatoes 12 to 15 minutes, or until set and golden brown. With edge of pancake turner, carefully cut potatoes into 6 equal portions. Turn each portion. Cook potatoes 8 to 10 minutes longer, or until golden brown and fork tender.

6 servings

Nutty Burgers

Nutty Burgers

Patties:
- 1 pound lean ground beef
- ½ cup minced walnuts
- ¼ cup chopped green onion
- 1 teaspoon sesame seed oil

- 4 sesame seed hamburger buns, split and toasted

For patties: In medium mixing bowl combine all ingredients. Divide mixture into 4 equal portions. Shape each portion into ¾-inch thick patty.

Preheat griddle on setting "7". Lightly grease griddle. Cook patties 9 to 11 minutes, or until desired doneness. Turn after half the time. Serve in hamburger buns.

TIP: Grilled onions make a good addition to Nutty Burgers (or other burgers). Slice 1 large onion (about ¾ pound) crosswise into ¼-inch slices. Cook on griddle along with burgers until golden brown. Turn occasionally.

4 servings

Liver and Onions

- 1½ pounds calves' liver, 2 × 2-inch slices
- ½ cup wheat germ
- ¼ cup butter or margarine
- 8 to 10 green onions, thinly sliced

Coat liver slices with wheat germ.

Preheat griddle on setting "9". Reduce heat to setting "6". Melt butter on griddle. Add liver. Turn when coating is lightly browned.

Add onions. Sauté about 4 minutes. Stir and turn to cook evenly.

6 servings

Seasoned Cubed Steaks

- 1 teaspoon onion powder
- ¼ to ½ teaspoon garlic powder
- ¼ teaspoon pepper
- 4 beef cubed steaks
  Worcestershire sauce

In small bowl combine onion powder, garlic powder and pepper. Set aside.

Preheat griddle on setting "9". Lightly grease griddle. Brush one side of steaks with Worcestershire sauce. Sprinkle lightly with half of seasoning mixture. Place seasoned-side down on griddle. Brush other side of steaks with Worcestershire sauce. Sprinkle with remaining seasoning mixture. Cook steaks about 7 minutes, or until desired doneness. Turn after half the time.

4 servings

Tarragon-Basted Lamb Chops

Baste:
- ¼ cup butter or margarine
- 1½ teaspoons dried parsley flakes (or 1 tablespoon snipped fresh parsley)
- 1 tablespoon honey
- ¼ teaspoon salt
- ¼ to ½ teaspoon dried tarragon leaves
- ⅛ teaspoon dried thyme leaves
- ⅛ teaspoon pepper

- 4 rib or loin lamb chops (1 inch thick)

For baste: In small saucepan melt butter. Add remaining ingredients. Heat, stirring constantly, until hot. Set aside.

Preheat griddle on setting "7". Brush one side of lamb chops with baste. Place brushed-side down on griddle. Brush other side with baste. Cook chops 8 to 12 minutes, or until desired doneness. Turn frequently and brush with baste.

2 to 4 servings

Tangy Veal Cutlets

- 1 cup dry white wine
- 1 teaspoon grated orange peel
- 1 teaspoon grated lime peel
  Dash ground allspice
- ⅛ teaspoon dried rosemary leaves, crushed
- 1 pound veal cutlets (¼ inch thick)
- 1 egg, beaten
- 1 tablespoon milk
- ½ cup fine dry bread crumbs (seasoned)
- 6 tablespoons butter or margarine

In small saucepan combine wine, orange peel, lime peel, allspice and rosemary. Heat until hot. (Do not boil.) Cool slightly. Place veal in medium mixing bowl or plastic food storage bag. Pour marinade over veal. Cover dish or close bag. Refrigerate at least 3 hours, turning veal occasionally.

In shallow dish blend egg and milk. Dip veal in egg mixture, turning to coat both sides. Dip in bread crumbs, turning to coat both sides. Set aside.

Preheat griddle on setting "8". Melt 3 tablespoons butter on griddle. Cook veal 3 minutes. Melt remaining 3 tablespoons butter on griddle. Turn veal. Cook 2 to 3 minutes longer, or until crisp.

4 servings

Tarragon-Basted Lamb Chops

Breaded Pork Chops

- ½ cup milk
- 1 egg, slightly beaten
- ¾ cup fine dry bread crumbs (unseasoned)
- 2 teaspoons dried parsley flakes
- 1 teaspoon poultry seasoning
- ¼ teaspoon onion powder
- ¼ teaspoon pepper
- 4 pork chops (½ inch thick)

In shallow bowl blend milk and egg. In another shallow bowl combine bread crumbs, parsley flakes, poultry seasoning, onion powder and pepper. Dip chops in egg mixture, turning to coat both sides. Then dip in crumb mixture, turning to coat both sides. Set aside.

Preheat griddle on setting "7". Generously grease griddle. Cook chops 20 to 25 minutes, or until juices run clear. Turn every 10 minutes.

4 servings

Salmon Patties

Salmon Patties

Sauce:
⅓ cup mayonnaise or dairy sour cream
¼ teaspoon grated lemon peel
⅛ teaspoon dried dill weed

Patties:
1 can (16 ounces) salmon, drained, cleaned and flaked
½ cup finely shredded Cheddar cheese
⅓ cup fine dry bread crumbs (unseasoned)
¼ cup chopped celery
¼ cup mayonnaise or dairy sour cream
1 egg
2 tablespoons chopped green onion
½ teaspoon prepared mustard
⅛ teaspoon garlic powder
⅛ teaspoon pepper

4 buns, split and toasted (optional)

For sauce: In small bowl combine all ingredients. Set aside.

For patties: In medium mixing bowl combine all ingredients. Divide mixture into 4 equal portions. Form each portion into ½-inch thick patty.

Preheat griddle on setting "8". Generously grease griddle. Cook patties 8 to 10 minutes, or until browned. Turn after half the time. Serve in buns with sauce.

Tuna Patties: Follow the recipe above, substituting 1 can (12½ ounces) tuna, drained and flaked, for the salmon.

4 servings

Egg Foo Yung

Sauce:
1½ teaspoons cornstarch
1 tablespoon plus 1 teaspoon soy sauce
½ cup cold water
½ teaspoon instant chicken bouillon granules
¼ teaspoon sugar
Dash ground ginger
Dash garlic powder
Dash pepper

Patties:
4 eggs
1½ cups fresh bean sprouts*, rinsed, drained and coarsely chopped
1 can (4 ounces) mushroom stems and pieces, drained
¼ cup chopped green onion
½ teaspoon soy sauce
Dash garlic powder
Dash pepper

For sauce: In small saucepan blend cornstarch and soy sauce until smooth. Stir in remaining ingredients. Heat, stirring constantly, until mixture thickens and boils. Remove from heat and cover to keep warm.

For patties: In medium mixing bowl beat eggs. Stir in remaining ingredients. Set aside.

Preheat griddle on setting "7". Generously grease griddle. Pour egg mixture by ¼-cupfuls onto griddle. With pancake turner, push cooked egg up over bean sprouts to form patty. Cook patties 4 to 6 minutes, or until set. Turn after half the time. Reheat sauce if necessary before serving with patties.

*Or 1 can (14 to 16 ounces) bean sprouts.

4 servings

French Omelet and Bacon Breakfast

4 slices bacon
2 tablespoons chopped onion
1 tablespoon chopped green pepper
1 tablespoon butter
2 eggs
1 tablespoon milk
½ cup shredded Cheddar cheese

Preheat griddle on setting "8". Place 2 bacon slices along each long edge of griddle. Cook bacon 5 to 6 minutes, or until brown and crisp. Turn after half the time. While bacon cooks, sauté onion and green pepper in butter until tender-crisp. Remove vegetables from griddle. Set aside.

In small bowl beat eggs and milk together. Slowly pour egg mixture down center of griddle. Spread egg mixture quickly to form rectangle. Cook eggs 1 to 2 minutes, or until almost set. Sprinkle onion, green pepper and cheese over top of eggs. With pancake turner, gently roll up omelet. Remove from griddle. Cut in half. Serve omelet with bacon.

2 servings

Spicy Brunch Sausage Patties

1 pound unseasoned ground pork
½ pound ground veal
2 teaspoons paprika
¾ teaspoon salt
¾ teaspoon fennel seed
½ teaspoon crushed red pepper
⅛ teaspoon garlic powder

In medium bowl combine all ingredients. Mix well. Divide mixture into 6 equal portions. Form each portion into ½-inch thick patty.

Preheat griddle on setting "8". Grill patties 12 to 15 minutes, or until thoroughly cooked. Turn after 8 minutes. Serve warm.

6 servings

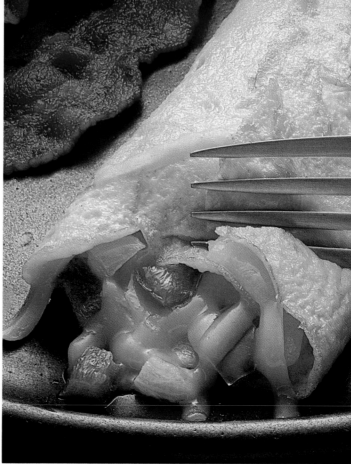

French Omelet and Bacon Breakfast

How to Cook Omelet and Bacon Breakfast

Pour egg mixture carefully down center of griddle. Spread quickly to form a rectangle. Cook eggs 1 to 2 minutes, or until almost set.

Sprinkle with onion, green pepper and cheese. With pancake turner, gently roll up omelet. Remove from griddle.

Fried Egg, Sausage and Toast Breakfast

Fried Egg, Sausage and Toast Breakfast

4 sausage patties, ½ inch thick
2 Texas toast-style bread slices
   Butter or margarine, softened
2 eggs

Preheat griddle on setting "7". Place sausage patties in center of griddle. Cook 7 to 8 minutes, or until first side is browned. Turn sausage.

Spread both sides of bread slices with butter. Place bread on back of griddle after turning sausage. Cook bread 3 or 4 minutes, or until browned. Turn bread.

Lightly grease front of griddle. Break eggs into saucer. Carefully slide one egg at a time onto front of griddle after turning bread. Cook eggs 3 to 4 minutes, or until desired doneness. (Eggs may be turned after half the time.) Remove sausage, toast and eggs from griddle. Serve immediately.

2 servings

Cheesy Omelet Cakes

3 eggs, separated
½ cup cottage cheese
2 tablespoons milk
¼ cup all-purpose flour
⅛ teaspoon salt
   Shredded Cheddar cheese (optional)

In medium mixing bowl beat egg whites until soft peaks form. In another medium mixing bowl beat egg yolks with electric mixer until thick and lemon-colored. Add cottage cheese. Beat until almost smooth. Blend in milk, flour and salt. Fold in beaten egg whites.

Preheat griddle on setting "6". Generously grease griddle. Pour egg mixture by ¼-cupfuls onto griddle. Cook omelet cakes 2 to 3 minutes, or until tops are bubbly and edges are set. Turn cakes and sprinkle with shredded cheese. Cook omelet cakes 2 to 3 minutes longer, or until set.

12 omelet cakes or 6 servings

Toad-in-the-Hole

1 slice white bread
   Butter or margarine, softened
1 egg

Preheat griddle on setting "7". Spread both sides of bread with butter. With 2½-inch round cutter, cut out center of bread slice. Break egg into saucer. Place bread slice on griddle. Carefully slide egg into center of bread slice. Cook 2 to 3 minutes, or until egg is almost set. Turn and cook 1 to 2 minutes longer, or until desired doneness. While egg cooks, place center cut-out on griddle. Cook until golden brown and serve with egg.

TIP: Recipe can be increased for number of servings desired.

1 serving

Pancakes

1¾ cups all-purpose flour
¼ cup sugar
2 teaspoons baking powder
1 teaspoon salt
1⅔ cups milk
2 eggs, beaten
⅓ cup butter or margarine, melted

Preheat griddle on setting "9". In medium mixing bowl combine flour, sugar, baking powder and salt. Stir in milk and eggs. Add butter. Stir just until dry ingredients are moistened. Lightly grease griddle. Pour batter by ⅓-cupfuls onto griddle. Cook pancakes 3 to 4 minutes, or until golden brown. Turn when bubbles appear and edges look dry.

Apple Pancakes: Follow the recipe above, except increase sugar to ⅓ cup. Add 1½ teaspoons ground cinnamon to dry ingredients. Stir 1 cup pared, chopped apples into batter.

Blueberry Pancakes: Follow the recipe above, except stir 1 cup fresh or thawed and well-drained frozen blueberries and 1 teaspoon grated lemon peel into batter.

Carrot Pancakes: Follow the recipe above, except add ½ teaspoon ground nutmeg to dry ingredients. Stir 1 cup grated carrots into batter.

Chocolate Chip Pancakes: Follow the recipe above, except stir ¾ cup miniature semi-sweet chocolate chips into batter.

Orange Nut Pancakes: Follow the recipe above, except stir ¾ cup minced nuts and 1½ teaspoons grated orange peel into batter.

About 12 pancakes

Potato Pancakes

2 cups cold mashed potatoes or cold
    prepared instant potatoes
1 egg, slightly beaten
2 tablespoons finely chopped green onion
2 tablespoons all-purpose flour
2 tablespoons dairy sour cream
1 teaspoon freeze-dried chives
½ teaspoon seasoned salt
    Dash pepper
    Applesauce or dairy sour cream

In medium mixing bowl combine all ingredients except applesauce or sour cream. If mixture is too stiff to press into pancakes, add 2 tablespoons milk. Set aside.

Preheat griddle on setting "8". Lightly grease griddle. Drop 4 to 6 mounds of potato mixture by ¼-cupfuls on griddle. With pancake turner, press down each mound to form a 4-inch diameter pancake. Cook 3 to 4 minutes, or until set and golden brown. Turn after half the time. Repeat with remaining potato mixture. Serve with applesauce or sour cream.

Sweet Potato Pancakes: Follow the recipe above, substituting 2 cups sweet potatoes for potatoes. Omit green onion, chives and seasoned salt. Add ½ teaspoon salt, ⅛ teaspoon ground allspice and dash ground ginger.

9 to 12 pancakes

French Raisin Toast

3 eggs, beaten
½ cup milk
2 tablespoons sugar
1 teaspoon vanilla
½ teaspoon ground nutmeg
    Dash salt
8 slices raisin bread
    Confectioners' sugar or pancake syrup

Preheat griddle on setting "9" to "10". In shallow bowl blend eggs, milk, sugar, vanilla, nutmeg and salt. Dip each bread slice in egg mixture, turning to coat both sides.

Lightly grease griddle. Cook bread slices 4 to 6 minutes, or until deep golden brown. Turn after half the time. Sprinkle with confectioners' sugar or serve with syrup.

4 servings

Sourdough English Muffins

1 cup Sourdough Starter (below left)
¼ cup sugar
1 teaspoon salt
¾ cup warm water (110° to 115°F)
½ cup warm milk (110° to 115°F)
2 tablespoons butter or margarine, softened
4½ to 5 cups all-purpose flour
½ cup raisins (optional)
3 to 4 tablespoons cornmeal

In large mixing bowl combine starter, sugar, salt, water, milk and butter. Gradually beat in flour until a stiff dough forms.

Turn dough onto floured surface and knead in remaining flour until dough is smooth and elastic, about 8 to 10 minutes. Knead in raisins. Shape dough into ball and place in greased bowl. Turn dough greased-side up. Cover. Let rise in warm place (80° to 85°F) until dough has doubled in size, about 1 to 1½ hours.

Punch down dough. Sprinkle cornmeal on bread board. Roll dough to ⅜-inch thickness. Turn dough over to coat both sides with cornmeal. Cut dough into 3-inch rounds. Reroll trimmings and cut again.

Preheat griddle on setting "5". Cook 6 to 8 muffins at a time 20 to 30 minutes, or until firm and golden brown. Turn every 10 minutes. Repeat with remaining rounds. Serve split and toasted.

About 18 muffins

French Raisin Toast

Sourdough Starter

1¾ cups warm water (110° to 115°F)
2 cups all-purpose flour
1 package (¼ ounce) active dry yeast
1 teaspoon sugar

In large glass mixing bowl combine all ingredients. Cover with plastic wrap. Let stand in warm place (80° to 85°F) 3 days, stirring down dough once a day. (Starter should be foamy.)

If not used immediately, store covered in refrigerator. Stir every few days.

Stir starter and allow to come to room temperature before using. As you use the starter, replenish by stirring in 1 cup flour and 1 cup warm water (110° to 115°F) for each cup starter removed.

Whole Wheat-Raisin English Muffins

  1 package (¼ ounce) active dry yeast
  1 cup warm water (110° to 115°F)
  ½ cup warm milk (110° to 115°F)
  ¼ cup sugar
  2 tablespoons butter or margarine, softened
  1 teaspoon salt
  1 teaspoon ground cinnamon
  1 cup whole wheat flour
2½ to 3 cups all-purpose flour
  ½ cup raisins
  3 to 4 tablespoons cornmeal

In large mixing bowl dissolve yeast in warm water. Stir in milk, sugar, butter, salt and cinnamon. Beat in whole wheat flour. Gradually beat in all-purpose flour until a stiff dough forms.

Turn dough onto lightly floured surface and knead in remaining all-purpose flour until dough is smooth and elastic, about 8 to 10 minutes. Knead in raisins. Shape dough into ball and place in greased bowl. Turn dough greased-side up. Cover. Let rise in warm place (80° to 85°F) until dough has doubled in size, about 1 to 1½ hours.

Punch down dough. Sprinkle cornmeal on bread board. Roll dough to ⅜-inch thickness. Turn dough over to coat both sides with cornmeal. Cut dough into 3-inch rounds. Reroll trimmings and cut again.

Preheat griddle on setting "5". Cook 6 to 8 muffins at a time 25 to 35 minutes, or until firm and deep golden brown. Turn every 10 minutes. Repeat with remaining rounds. Serve split and toasted.

About 18 muffins

Whole Wheat-Raisin English Muffins

How to Roll, Cut and Cook English Muffins

Sprinkle cornmeal on bread board. Roll dough to ⅜-inch thickness. Turn dough over to coat both sides with corn meal.

Cut dough into 3-inch rounds, using a floured cutter or inverted drinking glass. Reroll trimmings and cut again.

Cook 6 to 8 muffins at a time 25 to 35 minutes. Turn every 10 minutes. Muffins are done when firm and deep golden brown.

Grilled Vegetarian Sandwich

Sandwich Guide

Type	Ingredients and Procedure
Grilled Vegetarian 4 sandwiches	½ cup mayonnaise, 2 teaspoons Dijon-style mustard, ⅛ teaspoon garlic powder, 8 slices bread, 1 cup alfalfa sprouts, 1 medium-size ripe avocado (thinly sliced), 4 thin slices Cheddar or mozzarella cheese, 4 thin slices tomato, 1 cup sliced mushrooms, 8 thin slices green pepper, 4 thin slices onion, softened butter or margarine.
	In small bowl blend mayonnaise, mustard and garlic powder. Spread generously on bread slices. Top each of 4 bread slices with one-fourth of the sprouts, avocado, cheese, tomato, mushrooms, green pepper and onion. Top with remaining bread slices. Spread both sides of sandwich with butter. Preheat griddle on setting "8". Cook sandwiches 8 to 10 minutes, or until cheese melts and bread is golden brown. Turn after half the time.
Grilled Ham and Cheese Salad 6 sandwiches	1 package (3 ounces) softened cream cheese, 1 tablespoon chopped green onion, ½ teaspoon dry mustard, ½ pound ground fully-cooked ham, 1 cup shredded Swiss cheese, 12 bread slices, softened butter or margarine.
	In small mixing bowl combine cream cheese, onion and dry mustard. Mix well. Stir in ham and cheese. Spread each of 6 bread slices with about ⅓ cup ham mixture. Top with remaining bread slices. Spread both sides of sandwich with butter. Preheat griddle on setting "8". Cook sandwiches 4 to 8 minutes, or until cheese melts and bread is golden brown. Turn after half the time.
Grilled Tuna and Cheese	Follow the recipe above, substituting 1 can (9½ ounces) tuna for ground ham. Substitute shredded Cheddar cheese for Swiss cheese.
Grilled Cheese 1 sandwich	2 bread slices, prepared mustard (regular or Dijon-style), 1 thin slice Cheddar cheese, 1 thin slice Swiss cheese, softened butter or margarine.
	Spread one bread slice lightly with mustard; top with cheese slices and other bread slice. Spread both sides of sandwich with butter. Preheat griddle on setting "8". Cook sandwich 4 to 8 minutes, or until cheese melts and bread is golden brown. Turn after half the time.
Variations	Follow the recipe above, substituting 1 thin slice American and 1 thin slice Monterey Jack cheese or 1 slice Colby and 1 slice mozzarella cheese for Cheddar and Swiss cheese.

Type	Ingredients and Procedure
Grilled Chicken Salad 4 sandwiches	1 cup chopped cooked chicken, ⅔ cup mayonnaise, ½ cup chopped nuts, ¼ cup sweet pickle relish (drained), ½ teaspoon salt, ⅛ teaspoon pepper, 8 bread slices, mustard or horseradish (optional), softened butter or margarine.
	In medium bowl combine chicken, mayonnaise, nuts, pickle relish, salt and pepper. Mix well. Spread bread slices with mustard. Divide and spread chicken mixture on 4 bread slices. Top with remaining bread slices. Spread both sides of sandwich with butter. Preheat griddle on setting "8". Cook sandwiches 4 to 6 minutes, or until bread is golden brown. Turn after half the time.
Grilled Turkey Salad	Follow the recipe above, substituting chopped cooked turkey for chicken.
Grilled Ham Salad	Follow the recipe above, substituting chopped fully-cooked ham for chicken.
Spicy Grilled Cheese 1 sandwich	2 bread slices, 2 teaspoons prepared pizza sauce, ¼ cup shredded mozzarella cheese, softened butter or margarine.
	Spread one bread slice with pizza sauce; top with shredded cheese. Place other bread slice on top. Spread both sides of sandwich with butter. Preheat griddle on setting "8". Cook sandwiches 4 to 8 minutes, or until cheese melts and bread is golden brown. Turn after half the time.
Mexican Grilled Cheese	Follow the recipe above, substituting taco sauce for pizza sauce. Substitute shredded Cheddar or Monterey Jack cheese for mozzarella cheese.
Grilled Peanut Butter and Banana 1 sandwich	2 bread slices, peanut butter, honey, 1 small banana (cut in half lengthwise), softened butter or margarine.
	Spread both bread slices with peanut butter. Spread honey lightly over peanut butter on one bread slice. Top with banana and other bread slice (peanut butter-side down). Preheat griddle on setting "8". Spread both sides of sandwich with butter. Cook sandwich 4 to 6 minutes, or until bread is golden brown. Turn after half the time.
Variation	Follow the recipe above, substituting marshmallow creme for honey.
Grilled Reuben 1 sandwich	2 rye bread slices, 1 tablespoon Thousand Island dressing or 2½ teaspoons mayonnaise plus ½ teaspoon mustard, 2 ounces sliced corned beef, 3 tablespoons drained sauerkraut, 1 thin slice Swiss cheese, softened butter or margarine.
	Spread one bread slice with Thousand Island dressing. Top with corned beef, sauerkraut, cheese and other bread slice. Spread both sides of sandwich with butter. Preheat griddle on setting "8". Cook sandwich 6 to 8 minutes, or until cheese is melted and bread is golden brown. Turn after half the time.
Grilled Deli 1 sandwich	1 thin slice Swiss cheese, 2 bread slices, 1 slice ham, 1 slice bologna, 2 thin slices tomato, 1 slice cotto salami, Italian dressing, 1 thin slice Cheddar cheese.
	Place Swiss cheese on one bread slice. Top with ham, bologna, tomato and salami, brushing with dressing between each layer. Top with Cheddar cheese and remaining bread slice. Preheat griddle on setting "8". Brush top of sandwich with dressing. Place dressing-side down on griddle. With pancake turner, lightly press down sandwich. Brush other side of sandwich with dressing. Cook sandwich 4 to 8 minutes, or until cheese melts and bread is golden brown. Turn after half the time.
Grilled Crab 4 sandwiches	1 package (3 ounces) softened cream cheese, 2 tablespoons chopped green pepper, 1 tablespoon chopped green onion, 4 drops hot pepper sauce, dash pepper, ½ cup shredded Monterey Jack cheese, 1 can (6 ounces) crab meat (rinsed, drained and flaked), 8 bread slices, vegetable oil.
	In small mixing bowl combine cream cheese, green pepper, onion, hot pepper sauce and pepper. Mix well. Stir in cheese and crab meat. Divide and spread mixture on 4 bread slices. Top with remaining bread slices. Preheat griddle on setting "8". Brush griddle generously with oil. Cook sandwiches 4 to 8 minutes, or until bread is golden brown. Turn after half the time.

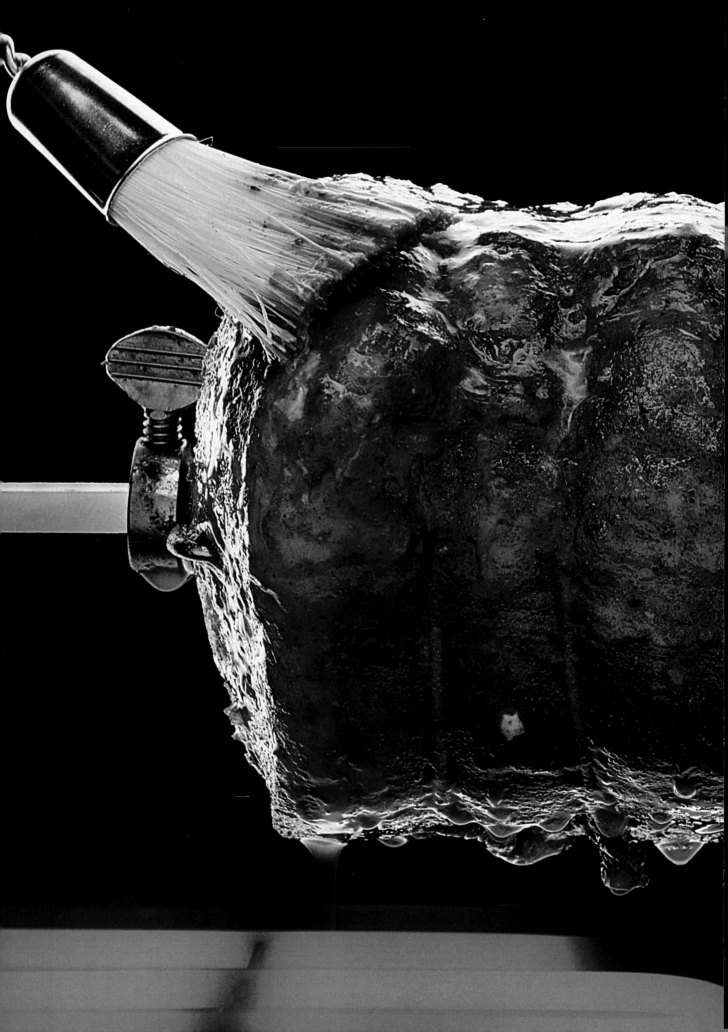

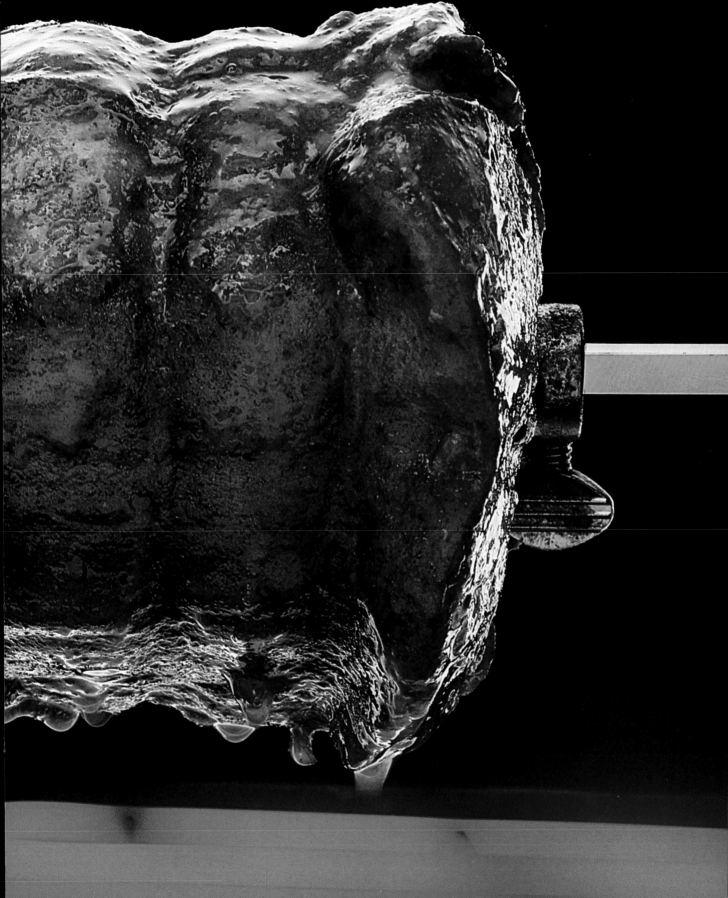

Rotisserie

Your rotisserie attachment gives meat and poultry the old-fashioned flavor of spit roasting. The exhaust system on your range keeps the kitchen from getting smoky while the meat slowly cooks to perfection. Best of all, foods cooked on the rotisserie need very little attention. Try our recipes for beef, pork, veal, lamb and poultry. You'll like the interesting sauces, glazes and marinades that enhance the slow-cooked flavor of meats and poultry. For best results, use the following techniques for cooking with the rotisserie.

Choose evenly-shaped ingredients for even cooking. The best size roasts for rotissing are 3 to 4 pounds. Rolled roasts and other large pieces of boneless meat should be tied firmly at intervals with heavy string.

Cooking Times for the Rotisserie

Meat	Weight in Pounds	Minutes/Pound	Control Setting	Final Internal Temperature
Beef rib eye roast, boneless	2 to 3	30 to 40	Hi	140° to 160°F
Beef eye of round roast	3 to 4	20 to 30	Hi	150° to 160°F
Beef sirloin tip roast	2½ to 3	30 to 40	Hi	140° to 160°F
Beef chuck eye roast (tenderized)	2	30 to 40	Hi	150° to 160°F
Pork loin roast	3 to 3½	35 to 45	10	170°F
Ham, fully cooked, boneless	4 to 5	18 to 20	Hi	140°F
Veal rump roast	2 to 2½	40 to 50	Hi	160° to 170°F
Leg of lamb, boneless	4	30 to 40	Hi	170°F
Lamb shoulder roast, boneless	3 to 3½	30 to 35	Hi	170°F
Turkey breast, boneless	3 to 4	30 to 35	Hi	185°F

Meat	Weight in Pounds	Total Cooking Time	Control Setting	Final Internal Temperature
Chicken, fryer (1)	2½ to 3½	60 to 75	Hi	185°F
Cornish hens (2)	1 to 1½	60 to 70	Hi	185°F
Duck (1)	4 to 5	90 to 100	Hi	185°F
Turkey ham, fully-cooked	4	60 to 70	Hi	140°F

• Above times are approximate.
• Poultry times and temperatures will vary according to placement of meat thermometer.
• Preheating is optional.
• Roasts of 3 to 4 pounds are best for rotissing.

Pictured on preceding page: Apple Cinnamon Pork Roast, recipe page 46

Skewer meat on spit and secure it with the two meat holders. To cook evenly, the meat must be well balanced and centered on the spit. Check the balance by holding the spit across your palms. Rotate the spit; the meat should rotate easily and evenly. If the balance is off, remove meat holders and meat and reposition the spit.

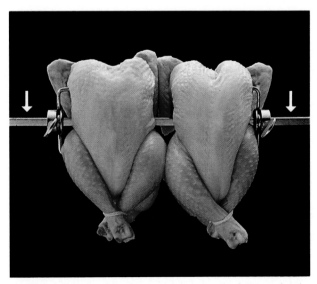

Leave a few inches free at each end of the spit; do not crowd it. This allows space for the meat holders and helps meat cook better. The heating element does not run the entire length of the spit. Skewer Cornish hens or other small birds either sideways or end-to-end, but do not skewer more than two birds at a time.

Use a meat thermometer to determine when meat has reached the desired doneness. First, turn off the heat and rotisserie motor. Insert thermometer in the thickest part of the meat. For poultry, insert the thermometer in the inner thigh. To get an accurate reading, make sure the tip of the thermometer sensor does not touch bone, fat or the spit.

Tie legs and wings securely to the body of whole poultry. Do not tuck wings behind as you would do for roasting. Tie the bird at intervals to form a compact bundle. It is easiest to truss birds before skewering on the spit. Cooking stuffed poultry on the rotisserie is *not* recommended.

Remove meat from the rotisserie when it registers 5 degrees below the desired temperature. Meat continues to cook by conduction after it has been removed from the heat.

Let meat stand for 10 to 15 minutes before carving. Meat is easier to carve and loses less juice if it is allowed to rest before being carved.

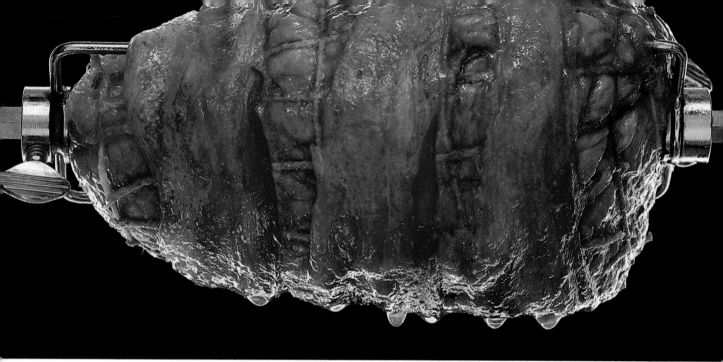

Bacon-Wrapped Veal Roast

Dried marjoram leaves
2 to 2½-pound boneless veal rump roast
3 or 4 slices bacon

Sprinkle marjoram generously over surface of roast. Wrap bacon around roast. Tie with strings to secure bacon.

Skewer roast on spit. Secure with meat holders. Cook on "Hi", 40 to 50 minutes per pound, or until meat thermometer inserted in center registers 160° to 170°F. Remove spit and strings. Let roast stand 15 minutes for easier carving.

4 to 6 servings

Stuffed Flank Steak

1 to 1½-pound beef flank steak
¾ pound bulk Italian sausage

With meat mallet pound steak to flatten slightly. Spread sausage in center of steak to within ¾ inch of edges. Starting with short end of steak, roll meat jelly roll fashion. Tie with strings in at least 5 places.

Skewer steak on spit. Secure with meat holders. Cook on "Hi", 1¼ to 1½ hours, or until sausage is cooked through. Remove spit and strings. Let meat stand 15 minutes for easier carving.

4 to 6 servings

Marinated Eye of Round

3½ pound beef eye of round roast

Marinade:
1 can (15 ounces) tomato sauce
½ cup dry red wine
1 small onion, chopped
¾ cup chopped celery

Place roast in dish or plastic food storage bag.

For marinade: In small saucepan combine all ingredients. Heat to boiling, stirring constantly. Simmer on medium low heat, uncovered, until onion is tender. Stir occasionally. Cool slightly. Pour marinade over roast. Cover dish or close bag. Refrigerate 1 to 2 days, turning roast occasionally. Reserve marinade for basting.

Skewer roast on spit. Secure with meat holders. Cook on "Hi", 20 to 30 minutes per pound, or until meat thermometer inserted in center registers 150° to 160°F. Brush occasionally with reserved marinade. Remove spit and strings. Let roast stand 15 minutes for easier carving.

10 servings

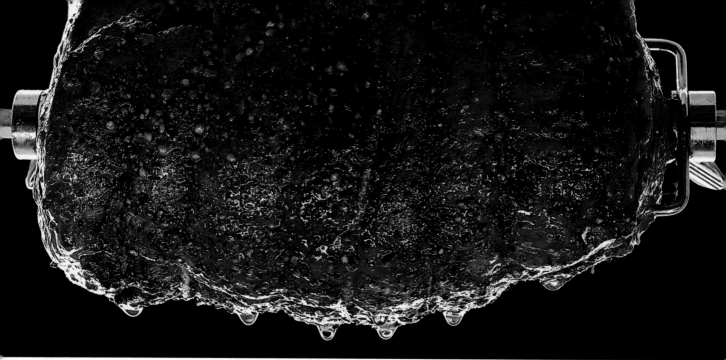

Peppered Sirloin Tip Roast

1½ teaspoons seasoned salt
1 to 2 teaspoons coarsely ground pepper
2½ to 3-pound beef sirloin tip roast

In small dish combine salt and pepper. Rub mixture evenly on surface of roast.

Skewer roast on spit. Secure with meat holders. Cook on "Hi", 30 to 40 minutes per pound, or until meat thermometer inserted in center registers 140° to 160°F. Remove spit and strings. Let roast stand 15 minutes for easier carving.

6 to 8 servings

Lamb Shoulder Roast with Dijon Baste

Baste:
2 tablespoons Dijon-style mustard
1 tablespoon dry vermouth or dry white wine
1 teaspoon dried chervil leaves
½ teaspoon dried thyme leaves

3 to 3½-pound boneless lamb shoulder roast

For baste: In small dish combine all ingredients.

Skewer roast on spit. Secure with meat holders. Cook on "Hi", 30 to 35 minutes per pound, or until meat thermometer inserted in center registers 170°F. Brush with baste during first 30 minutes. Remove spit and strings. Let roast stand 15 minutes for easier carving.

8 to 10 servings

Barbecued Bologna

1 bologna roll (7 to 10 inches long and about 4 inches wide), unsliced
1 recipe Barbecue Sauce, page 98, or prepared barbecue sauce

Remove casing from bologna. With sharp knife, make lengthwise cuts, about 1 inch apart and 1 inch deep around bologna. Then make crosswise cuts, about 1 inch apart and 1 inch deep to form square pattern.

Skewer bologna on spit. Secure with meat holders. Cook on "Hi", 10 minutes, or until juices rise to surface of bologna. Brush bologna with sauce. Cook about 20 minutes longer, or until golden brown. Reduce heat to setting "10". Cook 30 to 45 minutes longer, or until bologna is heated through.

To serve from spit: Insert wooden pick in center of bologna square. With knife cut off a 1-inch cube. Brush remaining bologna with more sauce. Continue to cook on setting "10" until golden brown. Continue to cut and serve cubes until center of bologna is reached.

TIP: Remaining bologna can be cut in slices and refrigerated for future use.

About 100 appetizers

Herbed Pork Roast

3 to 3½-pound boneless pork loin roast
1 large clove garlic, cut in half
  Dried summer savory leaves
  Dried thyme leaves

Rub cut edges of garlic over surface of roast. Cut garlic halves into thirds. Cut 6 slits, about ½ inch deep in roast. Insert pieces of garlic in slits. Sprinkle roast generously with savory and thyme.

Skewer roast on spit. Secure with meat holders. Cook on setting "10", 35 to 45 minutes per pound, or until meat thermometer inserted in center registers 170°F. Remove spit and strings. Let roast stand 15 minutes for easier carving.

8 to 10 servings

Apple-Cinnamon Pork Roast

3 to 3½-pound boneless pork loin roast

Marinade:
1 cup apple juice
1 teaspoon ground cinnamon
¼ teaspoon ground cloves

Place roast in dish or plastic food storage bag.

For marinade: In small saucepan combine all ingredients. Cook until hot to blend spices. Cool slightly. Pour marinade over roast. Cover dish or close bag. Refrigerate overnight, turning roast occasionally. Reserve marinade for basting.

Skewer roast on spit. Secure with meat holders. Cook on setting "10", 35 to 45 minutes per pound, or until meat thermometer inserted in center registers 170°F. Brush occasionally with reserved marinade. Remove spit and strings. Let roast stand 15 minutes for easier carving.

8 to 10 servings

Porketta

3½ to 4-pound boneless pork shoulder roast

Filling:
- ½ cup snipped fresh parsley
- 2 teaspoons minced garlic
- 2 teaspoons dried dill weed
- 1 teaspoon fennel seed, crushed
- 1 teaspoon dried rosemary leaves, crushed
- ¼ teaspoon salt
- ¼ teaspoon pepper

Coating:
- ¾ teaspoon salt
- ½ teaspoon coarsely ground pepper
- ¼ teaspoon dried dill weed

Remove strings or netting from roast. Trim excess fat from surface. Remove any inside pockets of fat.

For filling: In small bowl combine all ingredients. Rub filling into inside surface of roast. Roll roast jelly roll fashion. Retie with strings.

For coating: In small dish combine all ingredients. Rub mixture evenly on surface of roast.

Skewer roast on spit. Secure with meat holders. Cook on setting "10", 35 to 45 minutes per pound, or until meat thermometer inserted in center registers 170°F. Remove spit and strings. Let roast stand 15 minutes for easier carving. Serve meat slices warm or cold in hard rolls, if desired.

TIP: For spicier pork, fill as directed. Retie and refrigerate overnight. Rub coating on surface of roast just before cooking.

10 to 12 servings

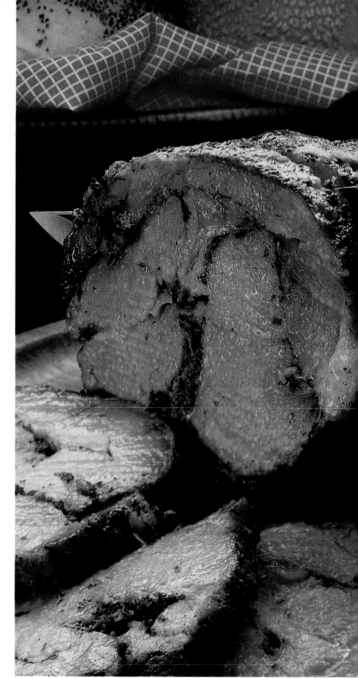

Porketta

How to Prepare and Fill Porketta

Remove pockets of fat from inside roast with sharp knife.

Spread filling evenly with back of spoon. Rub in gently.

Roll, tie and skewer roast. Rub coating on surface.

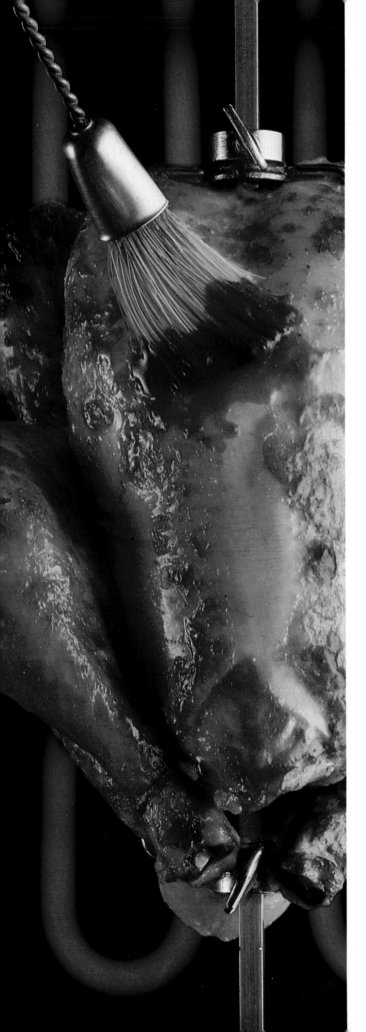

Glazed Whole Chicken

3 to 3½-pound broiler-fryer chicken
1 recipe Raspberry Glaze, page 100

Remove giblets and neck from chicken. Rinse and drain chicken. With string, tie wings and legs close to body of chicken.

Skewer chicken on spit. Secure with meat holders. Cook on "Hi", 60 to 75 minutes, or until meat thermometer inserted in thickest part (between breast and thigh) registers 185°F. Brush frequently with glaze after first 30 minutes. Remove spit and strings. Let chicken stand 15 minutes for easier carving. Serve chicken with any remaining glaze.

Variation: Follow the recipe above, substituting Apricot Glaze, page 100, for Raspberry Glaze.

4 servings

Marinated Whole Chicken

3 to 3½-pound broiler-fryer chicken
1 recipe Polynesian Marinade, page 97

Remove giblets and neck from chicken. Rinse and drain chicken. Place chicken in dish or large plastic food storage bag. Pour marinade over chicken. Cover dish or close bag. Refrigerate at least 3 hours, turning chicken occasionally. Reserve marinade for basting.

With string, tie wings and legs close to body of chicken. Skewer chicken on spit. Secure with meat holders. Cook on "Hi", 60 to 75 minutes, or until meat thermometer inserted in thickest part (between breast and thigh) registers 185°F. Brush occasionally with reserved marinade after first 30 minutes. Remove spit and strings. Let chicken stand 15 minutes for easier carving.

Variation: Follow the recipe above, substituting Lemony Herb Marinade, page 97 for Polynesian Marinade.

4 servings

Glazed Whole Chicken

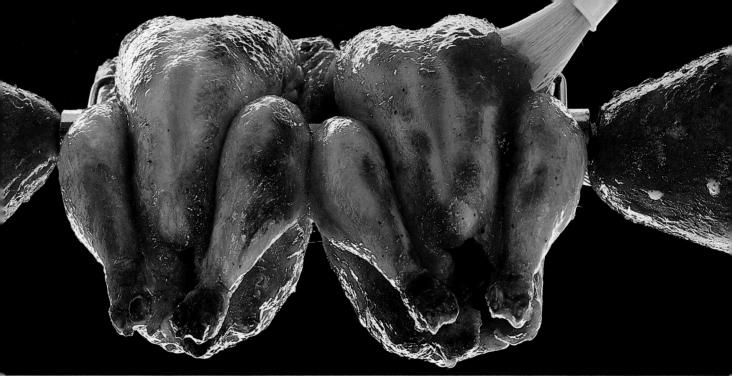

Glazed Cornish Hens with Pears

2 Cornish hens (16 to 24 ounces each), thawed if frozen
2 firm pears
1 cup whole cranberry sauce

Remove giblets and necks from hens. Rinse and drain hens. With string, tie wings and legs close to bodies of hens.

Carefully skewer one pear on spit. Skewer hens on center of spit. Secure with meat holders. Skewer remaining pear on split. Push pears close to hens. Cook on "Hi", 60 to 70 minutes, or until meat thermometer inserted in thigh registers 180° to 185°F. Brush with cranberry sauce every 15 minutes. Remove spit and strings. Cut pears in half. Remove cores. Spoon any remaining warmed cranberry sauce in pear centers.

2 servings

Rotissed Apples

2 large firm apples (3-inch diameter), cored
1 recipe Spiced Caramel Sauce, page 101

Skewer apples on spit through cored centers. Secure with meat holders in center of spit. Cook on "Hi", 30 to 35 minutes, or until fork tender. Remove spit. Cut apples in wedges. Serve apple wedges with caramel sauce.

2 to 4 servings

Duck with Hoisin Glaze

Glaze:
⅓ cup Hoisin sauce*
⅓ cup honey
2 teaspoons soy sauce
½ teaspoon 5-spice powder*
¼ teaspoon ground ginger
⅛ teaspoon garlic powder

4 to 5-pound duckling
1 small orange, cut into wedges
1 small onion, cut in half

For glaze: In small dish combine all ingredients. Set aside.

Remove giblets and neck from duckling. Rinse and drain duckling. Stuff cavity of duckling with orange wedges and onion. With fork, pierce skin of duckling in several places. Tie wings close to body of duckling with string.

Skewer duckling on spit. Secure with meat holders. Cook on "Hi", 1½ to 1¾ hours, or until meat thermometer inserted in thickest part (between breast and thigh) registers 185°F. Brush occasionally with glaze after first 60 minutes. (Check grease container before cooking. Empty if necessary.) Remove spit and strings. Let duckling stand 15 minutes for easier carving. Serve with any remaining glaze.

*Available in Oriental section of supermarkets.

4 servings

Shish Kebab

Shish Kebab

Your shish kebab attachment lets you add a festive touch to any meal. Plain or fancy, the results are always delectable. Spear a favorite combination of foods for an easy all-in-one meal for the family.

Or host a kebab party. Prepare an assortment of colorful foods and sauces beforehand so you can relax and enjoy the festivities when friends arrive. Let guests thread their own skewers from your selection of meats, vegetables and fruits.

Our recipes combine a variety of different foods into unique kebabs. You'll find ideas for appetizers, main dishes, meal accompaniments and even desserts. Be creative and invent your own combinations. Favorite fruits make great snack or dessert kebabs. Create appetizer kebabs with a crispy loaf of bread and a block of cheese. Kebabs are also a great way to use leftover meats. Make them moist and flavorful with sauces or bastes. The possibilities are endless with this easy and practical way to cook.

Parboil or partially precook onions, potatoes, squash or other firm vegetables before skewering to reduce kebab cooking time. To parboil, add vegetables to boiling water, cover and boil for the time specified in the recipe, or until just tender. Rinse under running cold water and drain. Steaming and microwaving are other good ways to shorten cooking time.

Divide kebab ingredients equally into four groups before threading them on the skewers for individual kebab servings. This will help you distribute the pieces evenly among the 4 skewers.

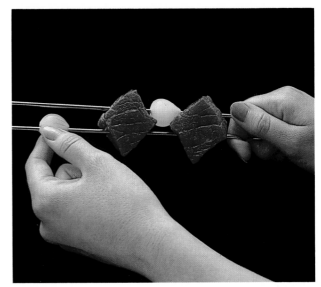

Thread food onto both prongs unless the recipe says to thread food on just one. Keep prongs parallel when skewering food. Thread a firm food, such as a meat cube or a firm vegetable or fruit, onto skewer first. This keeps the prongs from pulling apart, which causes food to split. If you have trouble threading the food, pierce with a wooden pick.

Leave a small space between most food pieces. Do not crowd the skewer. Spacing between pieces is necessary for food to cook evenly and completely.

Shield soft or quick-cooking foods by arranging them between two pieces of denser food. This helps to prevent them from overcooking or falling off the skewer.

Pictured on preceding page: Lobster Kebabs, recipe page 57

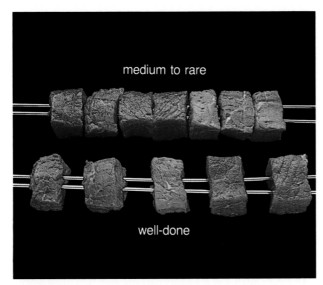

medium to rare

well-done

Arrange pieces of red meat close together for rare or medium-rare results. For well done meat (pork or chicken), leave space between pieces, or alternate meat with small chunks of fruit. This allows hot air to reach all sides of the meat.

Avoid overcooking skewered meat. It will be more tender and tasty if cooked rare or medium.

Turn on the grill element **after** accessory and food are in place. Preheating element is not necessary.

Baste kebabs with marinade (pages 97-101), fruit juice or seasoned butter or oil to keep food moist during cooking. Mushrooms, squash or other foods which dry out can be wrapped in partially-cooked bacon before skewering.

Shish Kebab Combinations

Cut meats into 1 to 1½-inch cubes unless skewering shrimp, bacon or chicken drummettes. Roast kebabs on "Hi" heat setting. Most kebabs cook in 30 minutes. Fresh vegetables and fruits take longer to cook than canned or parboiled vegetables and fruits. Combine longer-cooking meats like pork with fresh vegetables and fruits. For faster-cooking meats, use canned or parboiled foods.

Meat	Cut of Meat	Vegetables	Fruits
Beef	Tenderloin, Sirloin, Round or Chuck (tenderized)	Green Pepper, Onion, Squash, Cherry Tomatoes, Tomatoes	Crab Apples, Peaches, Pineapple Chunks
Pork	Bacon (to wrap foods which dry out), Boneless Shoulder, Loin or Tenderloin, Ham or Sausage (fully-cooked)	Water Chestnuts, Zucchini, Sweet Potato	Pineapple Chunks, Watermelon Pickles, Melon, Bananas, Apples
Lamb	Boneless Leg or Shoulder	(Any of above)	(Any of above)
Fish and Seafood	Lobster Tail, Salmon, Halibut, Shrimp (medium to jumbo)	Green Pepper, Mushrooms, Zucchini, Tomatoes	Lemons, Oranges
Chicken	Breast, Drummettes	Green Pepper, Squash, Mushrooms, Tomatoes	Bananas, Pineapple Chunks, Crab Apples, Peaches

Lemony Beef Kebabs

Gingered Ham Kebabs

Marinade:
¼ cup orange juice
¼ cup butter or margarine, melted
2 tablespoons packed brown sugar
10 whole cloves
2 teaspoons ground ginger
1 tablespoon grated orange peel

1 pound fully-cooked ham, cut into 1-inch
   cubes
1 jar (16 ounces) mini crab apples, drained
1 can (8 ounces) chunk pineapple, drained
   (12 chunks)

For marinade: In medium bowl or plastic food storage bag combine all ingredients. Add ham to marinade. Cover dish or close bag. Refrigerate at least 2 hours, turning ham occasionally. Reserve marinade for basting.

On each of four kebab skewers, alternately thread ham, crab apples and pineapple chunks.

Grill kebabs on "Hi", 15 to 20 minutes, or until heated. Brush frequently with reserved marinade.

Variation: Follow the recipe above, substituting whole cherry tomatoes and 1-inch pieces green pepper for crab apples and pineapple. To shield tomato from overcooking, sandwich between two pieces of green pepper.

4 servings

Lemony Beef Kebabs

1 pound boneless beef sirloin steak (1¼ inch
   thick), cut into 1¼-inch cubes
1 recipe Lemony Herb Marinade, page 97
8 fresh mushrooms (2-inch diameter),
   stems trimmed
1 lemon, cut lengthwise into eighths

Place beef cubes in deep dish or plastic food storage bag. Pour marinade over beef. Cover dish or close bag. Refrigerate at least 3 hours, turning beef occasionally. Reserve marinade for basting, if desired.

On each of four kebab skewers, alternately thread beef cubes and mushrooms. Start and end with lemon wedge.

Grill kebabs on "Hi", 15 to 25 minutes, or until steak is of desired doneness. Brush mushrooms occasionally with reserved marinade.

4 servings

Sausage Kebabs

2 small onions (about 2-inch diameter)
4 small white or red potatoes (about ¾ pound),
   cut in half
1 pound smoked Polish sausage, cut into
   1½-inch chunks
2 tablespoons butter or margarine, melted

Parboil onions for 4 minutes. Rinse under running cold water. Drain. Cut each onion lengthwise into 4 wedges. Parboil potatoes for 15 minutes, or until almost tender. Rinse under running cold water. Drain well.

On each of four kebab skewers, alternately thread sausage, potatoes and onions.

Grill kebabs on "Hi", 20 to 25 minutes, or until sausage is cooked. Brush onions and potatoes with butter occasionally.

4 servings

Ham and Sweet Potato Kebabs

1 pound fully-cooked ham (1 inch thick), cut into 1½ × 1½-inch chunks
1 can (18 ounces) sweet potatoes, cut into 1½ × 1½-inch chunks*
2 red cooking apples (3-inch diameter), cored and cut lengthwise into quarters
¼ cup peach preserves
2 tablespoons butter or margarine

On each of four kebab skewers, alternately thread ham, sweet potatoes and apples. Start and end with ham.

In small saucepan combine peach preserves and butter. Heat until butter melts. Set aside.

Grill kebabs on "Hi", 15 to 20 minutes, or until apples are tender and ham is heated through. Brush frequently with peach-butter mixture.

*Or 1 pound fresh sweet potatoes, parboiled 20 to 25 minutes, pared and cut as above.

4 servings

Sausage and Bread Appetizer Kebabs

¾ pound summer sausage (about 3-inch diameter)
½ cup butter or margarine, melted
¼ teaspoon dried basil leaves
¼ teaspoon seasoned salt
12 French bread slices (1 inch thick, about 2-inch diameter)
   Grated Parmesan cheese
8 midget dill pickles

Cut summer sausage into ¾-inch slices. Cut each slice into eight wedges. Set aside.

In small bowl combine butter, basil and seasoned salt. Brush both sides of bread slices with butter mixture. Sprinkle lightly with Parmesan cheese.

On each of four kebab skewers, alternately thread two sausage wedges, side-by-side (one on each prong), bread slices, and pickles (threaded crosswise on both prongs). Start and end with pickle.

Grill kebabs on "Hi", 10 to 15 minutes, or until sausage is hot.

6 to 8 servings

Ham and Sweet Potato Kebabs

Curried Chicken Kebabs

Lamb Kebabs

Marinade:
- ⅓ cup dry white wine
- 3 tablespoons olive oil
- ¾ teaspoon dried rosemary leaves, crushed
- 1 teaspoon lemon juice
- ¼ teaspoon salt
- ¼ teaspoon coarsely ground pepper
  Dash garlic powder

- 1 pound boneless lean lamb, cut into 1¼ to 1½-inch cubes
- 3 small zucchini, cut into 1-inch chunks
- 1 medium apple, cored and cut into eighths
  Butter or margarine, melted (optional)

For marinade: In medium bowl or plastic food storage bag combine all ingredients. Add lamb to marinade. Cover dish or close bag. Refrigerate at least 3 hours or overnight, turning lamb occasionally. Reserve marinade for basting, if desired.

Parboil zucchini 2 minutes. Rinse under running cold water. Drain.

On each of four kebab skewers, alternately thread lamb cubes, zucchini and apples.

Grill kebabs on "Hi", 25 to 30 minutes, or until lamb is desired doneness. Brush zucchini and apples with reserved marinade or melted butter during first 5 minutes of cooking.

4 servings

Curried Chicken Kebabs

Marinade:
- ⅔ cup honey
- ½ cup fresh lemon juice (about 3 to 4 lemons)
- 1 tablespoon grated lemon peel
- 1 teaspoon curry powder
- 1 teaspoon ground ginger

- 6 chicken breast halves, boned, skinned and cut into 1½-inch pieces
- 1 large green pepper, cut into 1-inch pieces
- 1 can (8 ounces) apricot halves, or 1 can (16 ounces) peach halves, cut in half

For marinade: In large bowl or plastic food storage bag combine all ingredients. Add chicken pieces to marinade. Cover dish or close bag. Refrigerate overnight, turning chicken occasionally.

On each of four kebab skewers, alternately thread several chicken pieces at a time, green pepper and apricots. Leave ¼-inch space between chicken pieces.

Grill kebabs on "Hi", 25 to 35 minutes, or until chicken is no longer pink.

4 servings

Chicken l'Orange Kebabs

1 cup Russian salad dressing
1 cup orange marmalade
1 envelope (1.375 ounces) regular onion soup
   mix
6 chicken breast halves, boned, skinned and
   cut into 1½-inch pieces
2 oranges, cut lengthwise into quarters, then
   each in half

In large bowl or plastic food storage bag combine Russian dressing, orange marmalade and soup mix. Add chicken pieces to marinade. Cover dish or close bag. Refrigerate overnight, turning chicken occasionally.

On each of four kebab skewers, alternately thread several chicken pieces at a time and oranges. Start and end with orange. Leave ¼-inch space between chicken pieces.

Grill kebabs on "Hi", 25 to 35 minutes or until chicken is no longer pink.

4 servings

Liver, Bacon and Onion Kebabs

1 jar (16 ounces) boiled whole onions, drained
8 slices bacon
1½ pounds chicken livers, rinsed and patted dry

On each of four kebab skewers, alternately thread onions and chicken livers with bacon accordian-style, with onions and chicken livers sandwiched between loops. Start and end with onions.

Grill kebabs on "Hi", 35 to 40 minutes, or until bacon is brown and liver is cooked.

4 servings

How to Assemble Liver Kebabs

Thread onions on one prong. Loop bacon around onions and livers.

Lobster Kebabs

1½ pounds raw lobster tail
2 white bread slices, trimmed of crust and
   quartered diagonally
3 tablespoons butter or margarine, melted
1 large green pepper, cut into 16 pieces
   (about 1-inch squares)
1 medium-size firm red tomato, cut
   lengthwise into eighths

Shrimp Sauce:
3 tablespoons butter or margarine
¼ cup all-purpose flour
1½ teaspoons dried parsley flakes (or 1
   tablespoon snipped fresh parsley)
1 teaspoon minced onion
½ teaspoon celery salt
⅛ teaspoon pepper
1 cup half-and-half
1 cup frozen cooked shrimp, thawed, and
   chopped
3 tablespoons dry sherry

Cut lobster meat away from shell. Cut into 1 to 1½-inch pieces. Set aside. Brush one side of each piece of bread with melted butter. Reserve remaining melted butter for basting.

On each of four kebab skewers, alternately thread green peppers, tomatoes, bread and several lobster pieces at a time. Leave ¼-inch space between lobster pieces.

Grill kebabs on "Hi", 20 to 30 minutes, or until lobster is opaque. Brush with reserved melted butter during first 5 minutes of cooking.

For shrimp sauce: In small saucepan melt butter. Stir in flour, parsley, onion, celery salt and pepper until smooth. Gradually blend in half-and-half. Heat on medium high, stirring constantly, until mixture thickens and just comes to boil. Reduce heat to setting "Lo". Stir in shrimp and sherry and heat through. Serve sauce with kebabs.

TIP: Lobster pieces will cook more evenly if placed in center of the skewer. To shield tomato pieces from overcooking, sandwich between two pieces of green pepper.

4 servings

Antipasto Kebabs

Seafood Kebabs

- 1 large salmon steak (1 inch thick), cut into 1-inch cubes
- ½ pound large scallops, cut into ½-inch thick slices
- 8 medium-size raw shrimp, shelled and deveined
- 1 lemon, cut lengthwise into eighths
- 1 recipe Garlic Dill Butter, page 97

On each of four kebab skewers, alternately thread salmon, scallops, shrimp and lemon. Start and end with lemon. Leave ¼-inch space between the seafood pieces.

Grill kebabs on "Hi", 10 to 20 minutes, or until scallops and shrimp are opaque and fish flakes easily. Brush frequently with Garlic Dill Butter.

4 servings

Antipasto Kebabs

- 1 medium zucchini (about 1 to 1½-inch diameter), cut into ¼-inch slices
- 1 jar (6 ounces) marinated artichoke hearts, drained, with marinade reserved
- 16 fresh mushrooms (1-inch diameter), stems trimmed
- 1 large green pepper, cut into 16 pieces (about 1-inch squares)
- 8 whole cherry tomatoes
- 8 jumbo pimiento-stuffed olives
- 8 extra large pitted ripe olives

On each of four kebab skewers, alternately thread all ingredients.

Grill kebabs on "Hi", 20 to 25 minutes, or until zucchini slices are fork tender. Brush frequently with reserved artichoke marinade.

TIP: To shield tomato from overcooking, sandwich between two pieces of green pepper.

6 to 8 servings

Mixed Vegetable Kebabs

1 acorn squash (about 1½ pounds), cut in half
3 medium zucchini (about 1¼-inch diameter),
   cut into 1-inch slices
1 large carrot, cut into ¾-inch pieces
4 small onions
2 tablespoons butter or margarine, melted

Parboil acorn squash for 10 minutes. Rinse under running cold water. Drain. Cut into 1½-inch pieces. Parboil zucchini for 2 minutes. Rinse under running cold water. Drain. Parboil carrots and onions together for 4 minutes. Rinse under running cold water. Drain.

On each of four kebab skewers, alternately thread vegetable pieces.

Grill kebabs on "Hi", 20 to 25 minutes, or until vegetables are fork tender. Brush occasionally with melted butter.

4 servings

Fruit and Cake Kebabs

¼ cup orange juice
2 tablespoons butter or margarine
1 teaspoon sugar
1 can (8 ounces) mandarin orange segments,
   drained (16 segments)
1 can (8 ounces) chunk pineapple, drained
   (16 chunks)
2 bananas, cut into 1½ to 2-inch pieces
2 pears, cored and cut into 4 chunks
16 maraschino cherries, drained
8 cubes angel food cake or pound cake
   (1½-inch cubes)
1 recipe Cherry Sauce, page 99, or
   Lemon Cream Sauce, page 99

In small saucepan combine orange juice, butter and sugar; heat until butter melts. Set aside.

On each of four kebab skewers, alternately thread fruit and cake cubes.

Grill kebabs on "Hi", 20 to 25 minutes, or until fruit is tender and cake is lightly toasted. Brush with orange juice mixture during first 5 minutes of cooking. Serve kebabs with Cherry Sauce or Lemon Cream Sauce.

TIP: Mandarin oranges, pineapple chunks and maraschino cherries should be threaded on one prong of skewer.

4 servings

Mixed Vegetable Kebabs

Bread and Cheese Kebabs

2 loaves (12 ounces each) French bread
   (about 2-inch diameter)
4 packages (6 ounces each) mozzarella
   cheese slices
1½ cups butter or margarine, melted
1 to 1½ teaspoons garlic powder

Cut French bread into ½-inch thick slices. Cut cheese into 2-inch squares. In small bowl combine butter and garlic powder. Brush both sides of bread slices with garlic butter.

On kebab skewers, alternately thread bread and cheese. Start and end with bread. Grill kebabs on "Hi", 5 to 10 minutes*, or until cheese melts.

TIP: Bread and cheese can be stacked in several layers and threaded on skewer together.

*Or reduce heat to setting "8" and grill kebabs 20 to 30 minutes.

8 to 10 servings

Wok

Wok

Your wok accessory is an exciting, versatile utensil that makes it easy to cook authentic Oriental dishes and many other popular foods. The wok is great for stir-frying, steaming, stewing, simmering, braising, deep-fat frying — even popping popcorn! Originally created by the Chinese to save on fuel, the wok has a large surface that heats very quickly.

Your wok fits directly onto its own heating element, which provides fast, high heat and prevents it from tipping during cooking. Substitute your wok for other utensils, such as a saucepan, deep-fat fryer, Dutch oven, sauté pan, or steamer. Included with the wok are a cover, steaming rack, tempura rack and bamboo rice paddles. Let our recipes introduce you to wok cooking. Then use the tips, charts and your own imagination to create other flavorful dishes with your wok.

Deep-Fat Frying Tips

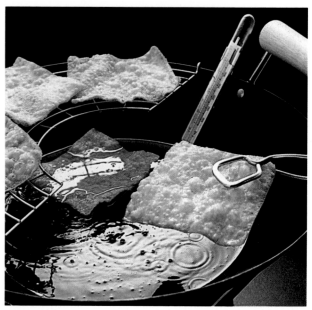

Use about 3 cups peanut or other vegetable oil for frying foods in wok. Before frying, attach a deep-fat thermometer. The tempura rack can be used to briefly drain foods before placing on paper towels. (Food will lose its crispness if left on the rack over hot oil for an extended time.)

The wok accessory includes: wok, cover, steaming rack, heating element, tempura rack, rice paddles.

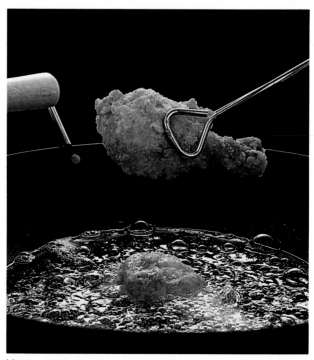

Use a slotted spoon, wire skimmer or long-handled tongs to add, turn and remove food from hot oil. To avoid spattering, do not drop food into hot oil. Fry only a few pieces of food at a time to help maintain proper oil temperature.

Pictured on preceding page: Shrimp and Vegetable Stir Fry, chart page 64

Steaming Tips

Steam foods such as seafood, poultry, vegetables, desserts and breads for moist, flavorful results. Steaming is a nutritious way to cook food, since no fat is used and more nutrients are retained. Reheating leftovers by steaming helps them stay moist and fresher-tasting.

Add 2 to 2½ cups water to wok. Then position the steaming rack so that the cut edges of the spokes are facing up. Rack should not touch the water. Cover wok. Heat on "Hi" until water boils. Place food directly on rack or in pan on rack, leaving space for steam to circulate around sides.

Drape foods such as desserts or breads with wax paper or foil to prevent condensation from falling on them. Then cover with the wok lid. Avoid lifting the lid too often while steaming, since this slows or stops the cooking process. Lift lid away from you to avoid getting burned by the steam. For long-term steaming, check water level occasionally to make sure wok has not boiled dry.

Steamed Vegetable Guide

In wok place 2 to 2½ cups water. Heat to boiling on "Hi", about 5 minutes. Place large vegetables directly on steaming rack or small vegetables on a plate on steaming rack. Cover and steam on setting "8", until vegetables are tender.

Vegetable	Steaming Time
1 pound broccoli flowerets, cut into 3-inch lengths	10 to 12 minutes
1 medium cauliflower, whole	25 to 30 minutes
4 to 5 ears corn, husk and silk removed	10 to 15 minutes
1 pound whole carrots, pared	25 to 30 minutes
Potatoes, white or sweet, whole, 2½-inch diameter	25 to 30 minutes
Acorn squash, cut in half, seeds removed	35 to 40 minutes
Summer squash or zucchini, whole, ends removed	20 to 25 minutes

Braising and Stewing Tips

Braise meat by first browning and then cooking slowly in a small amount of liquid in the covered wok. This is an excellent cooking method for less-tender cuts of meat. Add seasonings and vegetables for a complete one-dish meal.

Stir-Frying Tips

Heat oil in wok on "Hi", about 2 minutes, or until hot but not sizzling or smoking. A plastic condiment bottle can be used to ring the wok with vegetable oil. For one pound of cut-up vegetables or meat, use 1 to 2 tablespoons oil. Peanut oil is best for stir-frying because it can be heated to high temperatures without smoking, and its bland taste does not overpower the flavor of food.

Stir-Fry Combinations

Meat	Additional Ingredients	Cooking Sauce
Beef	Asparagus, Broccoli, Carrots, Bok Choy, Pea Pods, Mushrooms, Green Pepper, Zucchini, Sesame Seeds	1 or 3
Chicken & Shrimp	Almonds, Asparagus, Broccoli, Bok Choy, Carrots, Cashews, Lettuce, Sesame Seeds, Spinach, Pea Pods, Mushrooms, Green Onions, Red Peppers, Celery	1, 2, 3 or 4
Pork	Carrots, Pea Pods, Mushrooms, Green Pepper, Water Chestnuts, Pineapple Chunks, Mandarin Oranges, Cashews	3 or 4

Cooking Sauces

1) ½ c. water
   1 Tbsp. soy sauce
   2 tsp. cornstarch
   1 tsp. sugar
   ½ tsp. instant chicken or beef bouillon granules

2) ¼ c. water
   1 tsp. cornstarch
   ½ tsp. instant chicken bouillon granules
   ¼ tsp. sesame oil

3) 1½ Tbsp. sugar
   2 tsp. cornstarch
   ½ tsp. salt
   3 Tbsp. soy sauce
   2 Tbsp. white wine
   1 Tbsp. cider vinegar
   1½ tsp. sesame oil

4) ¼ c. sugar
   ¼ c. water
   ¼ c. catsup
   1 Tbsp. cornstarch
   ½ tsp. salt
   ½ tsp. sesame oil

Cut ingredients into small, uniform pieces. This helps food cook more quickly and evenly. Cutting foods on the diagonal helps tenderize them and exposes more food surface to the heat during cooking. Because of the speed of stir-frying, you should have all ingredients prepared before you start cooking.

Stir and toss foods constantly over high heat so that all pieces come in contact with the hot wok. Use the bamboo rice paddles or other nonmetallic utensils to protect the wok finish. First, stir-fry meat or other ingredients which take longer to cook. When almost done, remove them and add more oil if necessary. When oil is hot, add vegetables or other quick-cooking foods and stir-fry until tender-crisp. Return meat to wok and add sauce, if desired. Cook and stir until liquid boils. Serve at once.

Easy Wok Recipes

Popcorn. In wok on setting "10", heat ¼ cup vegetable oil and one test kernel of corn. When test kernel pops, oil is hot. Add ⅓ cup popcorn. Cover wok. Corn will pop in about 3 minutes. Remove corn immediately after popping to prevent burning. Salt while hot.

Steamed clams or oysters. Place 2 cups hot water in wok. Add steaming rack. Bring water to boil. Place clams or oysters in the shell (scrubbed) in pie plate on rack. Cover. Steam on setting "7" or "8", 5 to 10 minutes, or until shells begin to open.

Tempura

Batter:
1 egg, beaten
⅔ cup ice water
⅔ cup all-purpose flour
¼ cup cornstarch
½ teaspoon baking powder
¾ teaspoon salt
3 to 4 cups peanut or vegetable oil

In wok on "Hi", heat oil until deep-fat thermometer registers 350°F.

For batter: In small mixing bowl combine all ingredients just until flour is moistened. Dip food pieces in batter. Fry 4 to 6 pieces at a time (see Tempura Guide, below). Estimate yield at 4 to 6 servings per pound. Drain on paper toweling. Repeat with remaining food pieces. Keep warm.

About 1½ cups batter

Tempura Guide

Food	Cooking Time	Doneness Test
Jumbo raw shrimp, shelled and deveined	2 to 2½ minutes	golden
Scallops	2½ to 3½ minutes	golden
Green pepper, cut into ¼-inch rings	2 to 2½ minutes	light golden
Onion, cut into ¼-inch rings	2 minutes	light golden
Fresh mushrooms, floured	2½ to 3 minutes	light golden
Zucchini, ½-inch slices, floured	2½ to 3 minutes	light golden
Yellow squash, ½-inch slices, floured	2½ to 3 minutes	light golden
Cauliflower flowerets, parboiled 3 minutes	2 to 2½ minutes	golden
Broccoli flowerets, parboiled 3 minutes	2 to 2½ minutes	golden
Green onions, cut into 1½-inch pieces	1½ minutes	light golden
Fresh Pea Pods, separated lengthwise into halves	2 minutes	light golden

Shrimp-Filled Wontons

Shrimp-Filled Wontons

1 can (4½ ounces) shrimp, rinsed, drained
    and chopped
¼ cup minced green onion
1 tablespoon dry sherry
½ teaspoon cornstarch
½ teaspoon soy sauce
    Dash garlic powder
24 wonton skins
1 egg, beaten
3 cups oil or shortening for frying
    Sweet and Sour Sauce, page 101 or Hot
      Mustard Sauce, page 99

In small mixing bowl combine shrimp, green onion, sherry, cornstarch, soy sauce and garlic powder.

For each wonton: Place 1 heaping teaspoon shrimp filling in center of wonton skin. Brush 2 adjacent edges with small amount of beaten egg. Fold wonton in half to form triangle. Press edges to

seal. Fold opposite corners in, overlapping points. Seal with small amount of beaten egg.

In wok heat oil until deep-fat thermometer registers 375°F. Fry 6 to 8 wontons at a time, 1 to 2 minutes, or until crisp and golden brown. Drain (see Deep-Fat Frying Tips, page 62). Keep warm in 200°F oven. Repeat with remaining wontons. Serve with desired sauce.

24 wontons

Pork-Filled Wontons: Follow the recipe above, substituting pork filling for shrimp filling. Increase wonton skins to 36. Prepare filling as follows.

¼ pound ground pork
1 cup minced cabbage
2 tablespoons minced green onion
⅓ cup minced water chestnuts
1½ teaspoons soy sauce
¼ teaspoon salt
⅛ teaspoon pepper
    Dash garlic powder

In small skillet crumble pork. Cook on medium high heat, stirring occasionally, until pork is no longer pink. Stir in cabbage and green onion. Cook 2 minutes, or until vegetables are tender-crisp. Stir in water chestnuts, soy sauce, salt, pepper and garlic powder. Fill wonton skins and fry as directed.

36 wontons

Broccoli-Filled Wontons: Follow the recipe above, substituting broccoli filling for shrimp filling, and increasing the wonton skins to 48. Prepare filling as follows.

½ pound fresh broccoli, cut into stalks
2 tablespoons minced carrot
2 tablespoons grated Romano cheese
1 teaspoon minced dried onion
¼ teaspoon salt
⅛ teaspoon pepper

Trim tough ends from broccoli. Parboil broccoli 3 minutes. Drain and mince.

In small mixing bowl combine broccoli, carrot, Romano cheese, onion, salt and pepper. Fill wonton skins and fry as directed above.

48 wontons

TIP: Fried wontons may be frozen up to 2 weeks. To serve, unwrap and place frozen wontons on cookie sheet. Heat in 400°F **convection oven** 10 to 13 minutes (or heat in preheated 400°F **radiant bake** oven 10 to 13 minutes), or until hot.

Beef Brisket

3½ to 4-pound beef brisket
 4 cups water
 1 onion, sliced
 1 teaspoon instant beef bouillon granules
 6 whole peppercorns

In wok combine all ingredients. Heat to boiling. Simmer, covered, on setting "4" or "5", 3½ to 4 hours, or until beef is fork tender. Remove from liquid. Serve as desired or use for Barbecued Beef, below right.

8 to 10 servings

Beef and Peppers

Marinade:
2 tablespoons soy sauce
2 teaspoons cornstarch
1 tablespoon white wine
1 tablespoon peanut or vegetable oil

1 pound boneless beef sirloin or flank steak, cut across the grain into very thin slices
3 to 4 tablespoons peanut or vegetable oil, divided
2 green onions, sliced
1 clove garlic, minced
½ teaspoon minced fresh gingerroot
3 green or sweet red peppers, cut into ¼-inch thick strips
1 tablespoon prepared oyster sauce* (optional)

For marinade: In small mixing bowl blend all ingredients until smooth. Stir in meat slices. Refrigerate 30 minutes.

In wok on "Hi", heat 1 to 2 tablespoons oil 2 minutes. Add meat mixture. Stir-fry 1 to 2 minutes, until beef is no longer pink. Remove meat to platter.

In wok heat remaining 2 tablespoons oil 1 minute, or until hot. Add onions, garlic and gingerroot. Stir-fry 1 minute. Add green peppers. Stir-fry 4 to 5 minutes, or until tender-crisp. Stir in oyster sauce. Return meat to wok. Stir-fry until heated through.

Beef and Chinese Vegetables: Follow the recipe above, except omit green peppers. Parboil 1 cup fresh peapods 1 minute. Drain. Cook meat as directed. Stir-fry onion, garlic and gingerroot as directed. Add 2 cups sliced bok choy (with leaves). Stir-fry 2 to 3 minutes. Add 2 cups fresh bean sprouts and the peapods. Stir-fry 1 to 2 minutes, until vegetables are tender-crisp.

*Available in Oriental section of supermarket.

4 to 6 servings

Barbecued Beef

Barbecued Beef

2 tablespoons vegetable oil
1 medium onion, chopped
1 cup chopped celery
1 clove garlic, minced
2 cups water
1 can (6 ounces) tomato paste
¼ cup cider vinegar
3 tablespoons packed brown sugar
2 tablespoons Worcestershire sauce
2 teaspoons dried parsley flakes
1 teaspoon chili powder
1 teaspoon prepared mustard
½ teaspoon dried oregano leaves
½ teaspoon salt
¼ teaspoon cayenne
4 cups shredded cooked beef (about ½ recipe Beef Brisket, above left)

In wok on setting "8", heat vegetable oil 1 to 2 minutes, or until hot. Sauté onion, celery and garlic in oil until tender. Stir in water, tomato paste, vinegar, brown sugar, Worcestershire sauce, parsley, chili powder, mustard, oregano, salt and cayenne. Add beef. Heat to boiling.

Reduce heat to setting "4" or "5". Cook, covered, 50 to 60 minutes, or until sauce thickens. Serve in hamburger buns or hard rolls.

8 to 10 servings

Chicken and Dumplings

2½ to 3-pound broiler-fryer chicken
 1 can (13¾ ounces) chicken broth
 1 cup water
 1 medium onion, chopped
 1 cup chopped celery
 2 carrots, sliced
 2 tablespoons dried parsley flakes (or ¼ cup snipped fresh parsley)
 1 teaspoon salt
 ½ teaspoon dried marjoram leaves
 ¼ teaspoon dried basil leaves
 ¼ teaspoon pepper
 2 tablespoons all-purpose flour
 ¼ cup cold water

Dumplings:
1¼ cups buttermilk baking mix
 ½ cup milk
1½ teaspoons dried parsley flakes (or 1 tablespoon minced fresh parsley)
 ¼ teaspoon dried marjoram leaves

In wok place whole chicken, chicken broth, water, onion, celery, carrots, parsley, salt, marjoram, basil and pepper. Heat to boiling.

Reduce heat to setting "4" or "5". Simmer, covered, 1¼ to 1½ hours, or until very tender. Remove chicken from liquid. Discard skin and fat. Cut meat from bones. Chop into bite-size pieces. Return chicken to broth. In small bowl combine flour and cold water. Blend into broth. Heat to boiling, stirring occasionally.

For dumplings: In medium bowl combine all ingredients. Mix just until smooth. Drop dumplings by heaping tablespoons into boiling broth. Reduce heat to setting "5". Cover and cook 15 minutes.

4 to 6 servings

Chicken Kiev

 ½ cup unsalted butter, softened
 1 teaspoon freeze-dried chives
 ¼ to ½ teaspoon garlic salt
 ⅛ teaspoon pepper
 1 cup fine dry bread crumbs (unseasoned)
 ½ teaspoon salt
 ½ teaspoon poultry seasoning
 ⅛ teaspoon onion powder
 8 boneless chicken breast halves (about 2½ to 3 pounds), skin removed
 2 eggs, beaten
 3 cups vegetable oil or shortening for frying

In small bowl combine butter, chives, garlic salt and pepper. Divide mixture into 8 equal portions. Form each portion into 1½ × ¾-inch piece. Freeze butter pieces 15 minutes or until very firm.

In shallow dish combine bread crumbs, salt, poultry seasoning and onion powder. Set aside.

Pound chicken breasts to ¼-inch thickness. Place one frozen butter piece on short end of each chicken breast. Starting at short end, roll up chicken, tucking in edges to enclose butter. Secure with wooden picks. Repeat with remaining chicken breasts. Dip chicken in eggs. Roll in crumb mixture to coat evenly.

In wok heat oil until deep-fat thermometer registers 350°F. Fry 4 pieces chicken 5 to 6 minutes, or until deep golden brown. Drain (see Deep-Fat Frying Tips, page 62). Repeat with remaining chicken.

8 servings

Sesame Chicken and Vegetables

Marinade:
- 1 egg white
- 2 teaspoons soy sauce
- 1½ teaspoons cornstarch
- ¼ teaspoon sesame oil
  Dash garlic powder

- 4 boneless chicken breast halves (about 1 pound), skin removed, cut into thin strips

Cooking Sauce:
- ¼ cup water
- 1 teaspoon cornstarch
- ½ teaspoon instant chicken bouillon granules
- ¼ teaspoon sesame oil

- 5 tablespoons peanut or vegetable oil, divided
- 1 cup sliced fresh mushrooms
- 2 cups sliced bok choy (with leaves)
- 1 tablespoon sesame seed
- 1 package (6 ounces) frozen pea pods, thawed and drained
- 1 cup fresh bean sprouts

For marinade: In small mixing bowl blend all ingredients until smooth. Stir in chicken. Refrigerate at least 30 minutes.

For cooking sauce: In small bowl combine all ingredients. Set aside.

In wok on "Hi", heat 3 tablespoons oil 2 to 3 minutes, or until hot. Add chicken mixture. Stir-fry 2 to 3 minutes, or until chicken is no longer pink. Remove chicken to platter.

In wok heat 2 tablespoons oil 1 minute, or until hot. Add mushrooms and bok choy. Stir-fry 1 minute. Add sesame seed. Stir-fry 1 minute. Add pea pods and bean sprouts. Stir-fry 30 seconds. Add cooking sauce and chicken. Stir-fry until sauce thickens.

4 to 6 servings

Chow Mein Noodles

Cook desired amount of thin spaghetti or thin egg noodles according to package directions. Dry on several layers of paper toweling at least 2 hours.

In wok heat 3 cups oil until deep-fat thermometer registers 375°F. Fry small amount at a time, until golden brown. Drain on paper toweling. Repeat with remaining noodles. Serve with stir-fry dishes, soups, salads or casseroles, or sprinkle with salt or cinnamon-sugar and serve as a snack.

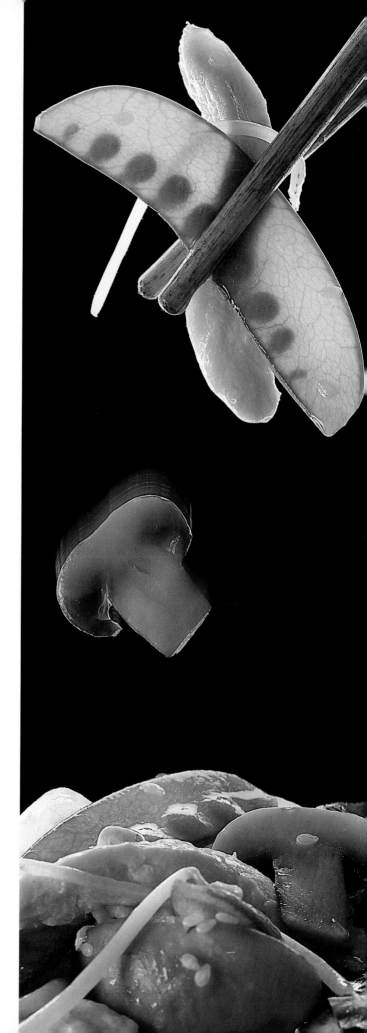

Sesame Chicken and Vegetables

Chicken and Cashews

Marinade:
1 egg white
2 teaspoons cornstarch
¼ teaspoon salt
¼ teaspoon sesame oil

4 boneless chicken breast halves (about 1
     pound), skin removed, cut into thin strips

Cooking Sauce:
½ cup water
1 tablespoon soy sauce
2 teaspoons cornstarch
1 teaspoon sugar
½ teaspoon instant chicken bouillon granules

3 to 4 tablespoons peanut or vegetable oil,
     divided
1 clove garlic, minced
8 to 10 green onions, cut into 1-inch pieces
1 cup sliced fresh mushrooms
1 cup salted cashews

For marinade: In small mixing bowl blend all ingredients until smooth. Stir in chicken strips. Refrigerate 30 minutes.

For cooking sauce: In small bowl combine all ingredients. Set aside.

In wok on "Hi", heat 2 tablespoons oil 2 minutes, or
until hot. Add chicken mixture. Stir-fry 2 to 3 minutes, or until chicken is no longer pink. Remove
chicken to platter.

In wok heat 1 to 2 tablespoons oil, about 1 minute,
or until hot. Add garlic, green onions and
mushrooms. Stir-fry 1 minute. Add chicken and
cooking sauce. Stir-fry until sauce thickens. Remove wok from heat. Stir in the cashews.

Shrimp and Cashews: Follow the recipe above,
substituting 1 pound medium-size raw shrimp,
shelled and deveined, for chicken.

4 to 6 servings

Kung Pao Chicken

2 tablespoons soy sauce
2 teaspoons cornstarch
6 boneless chicken breast halves (about
     1½ pounds), skin removed, cut into thin
     strips or ½-inch cubes

Cooking Sauce:
3 tablespoons soy sauce
2 tablespoons dry white wine
1½ tablespoons sugar
1 tablespoon cider vinegar
2 teaspoons cornstarch
1½ teaspoons sesame oil
½ teaspoon salt

3 to 4 tablespoons peanut or vegetable oil,
     divided
1 to 2½ teaspoons crushed red pepper
¾ cup salted peanuts (without skins)
1 teaspoon minced fresh gingerroot

In small mixing bowl blend soy sauce and cornstarch until smooth. Stir in the chicken. Refrigerate
30 minutes.

For cooking sauce: In small dish combine all ingredients. Set aside.

In wok on "Hi", heat 1 to 2 tablespoons oil and
crushed red pepper 1 to 2 minutes, or until hot.
Add peanuts. Stir-fry until pepper is almost black.
Remove pepper and peanuts from wok. Set aside.

In wok heat remaining 2 tablespoons oil about 1
minute, or until hot. Add gingerroot. Stir-fry 30
seconds. Add chicken mixture. Stir-fry about 3
minutes, or until chicken is no longer pink. Add
cooking sauce. Stir-fry mixture until sauce thickens. Remove wok from heat. Stir in reserved
peanuts and pepper.

4 to 6 servings

Mediterranean Lamb Meatballs

Meatballs:
¾ pound ground lamb
¼ pound lean ground beef
1 egg
⅓ cup milk
¼ cup fine dry bread crumbs (unseasoned)
½ teaspoon salt
¼ teaspoon pepper
¼ teaspoon bouquet garni

1 tablespoon olive oil
1 large onion, chopped
1 clove garlic, minced
1 cup chopped zucchini
1 can (16 ounces) whole tomatoes, chopped
1 can (6 ounces) tomato paste
1 can (4½ ounces) sliced mushrooms, drained
¼ cup lemon juice
1 tablespoon packed brown sugar
1 teaspoon dried oregano leaves
½ teaspoon ground cinnamon
½ teaspoon salt
¼ teaspoon pepper

In large bowl combine all meatball ingredients. Mix thoroughly. Form into 2-inch balls. In wok on setting "8", heat oil. Add half of meatballs and brown on all sides. Remove to platter. Repeat with remaining meatballs. Drain off all but 1 tablespoon drippings.

Sauté onion and garlic in drippings until tender. Blend in remaining ingredients. Add meatballs. Heat to boiling.

Reduce heat to setting "3" or "4". Simmer, covered, about 30 minutes. Uncover and simmer an additional 20 to 30 minutes, or until meatballs are firm and cooked through. Serve over rice, if desired.

Mediterranean Chicken: Follow recipe above, substituting 1 cut-up broiler-fryer chicken, 2½ to 3 pounds, for meatballs. Prepare chicken as follows.

In wok on setting "8", heat oil 2 minutes. Add 2 or 3 pieces of chicken and brown lightly. Remove to platter. Repeat with remaining pieces.

Sauté onion and garlic as directed. Blend in remaining ingredients and add chicken. Heat to boiling. Reduce heat to setting "3" or "4". Simmer, covered, about 30 minutes. Turn chicken. Simmer, uncovered, another 30 to 40 minutes, or until meat near bone is no longer pink and juices run clear.

4 to 6 servings

Pork Roast and Sauerkraut

Pork Roast and Sauerkraut

¼ cup all-purpose flour
1 teaspoon salt
¼ teaspoon pepper
3 to 3½-pound pork roast (loin or shoulder)
1 tablespoon vegetable oil
1 medium onion, thinly sliced
½ cup water
¼ teaspoon dried summer savory
1 jar (32 ounces) sauerkraut, rinsed and drained
2 medium apples, cored and chopped
1 tablespoon packed brown sugar
½ teaspoon caraway seed

In large food storage bag combine flour, salt and pepper. Add pork roast and coat with seasoned flour. In wok on setting "8", heat oil 1 to 2 minutes, or until hot. Add roast. Brown on all sides. Add onion, water and summer savory. Heat to boiling. Reduce heat to setting "3" or "4". Simmer, covered, about 2 hours. Add sauerkraut, apple, brown sugar and caraway seed. Increase heat to setting "5". Simmer, covered, 30 to 60 minutes, or until pork reaches internal temperature of 170°F.

6 to 8 servings

Crispy Pork Sandwiches

Crispy Pork Sandwiches

Mustard Sauce:
¼ cup mayonnaise
2 tablespoons dairy sour cream
1 teaspoon prepared mustard
¼ teaspoon salt
⅛ teaspoon ground thyme
⅛ teaspoon pepper

1 cup cornflake crumbs
1 teaspoon salt
¼ teaspoon ground sage
¼ teaspoon ground thyme
¼ teaspoon pepper
⅛ teaspoon ground allspice
1 egg
1 tablespoon milk
4 pork butterfly chops (½ inch thick, about
   1½ pounds), trimmed of excess fat
3 cups vegetable oil or shortening for frying
8 hamburger buns, split
   Lettuce leaves, tomato slices, onion slices
   (optional)

For mustard sauce: In small dish combine all ingredients. Refrigerate.

In shallow dish combine cornflake crumbs, salt, sage, thyme, pepper and allspice. Set aside. In shallow bowl blend egg and milk, set aside. Separate each chop down center into halves. Pound meat to ¼-inch thickness. Dip meat in egg mixture. Roll in crumb mixture to coat evenly.

In wok heat oil until deep-fat thermometer registers 350°F. Fry 2 or 3 pieces at a time about 2 to 3 minutes, or until deep golden brown. Drain (see Deep-Fat Frying Tips, page 62). Repeat with remaining pieces. Serve in buns topped with mustard sauce, lettuce, tomato and onion.

8 sandwiches

Sweet and Sour Pork

Marinade:
1 egg
1 tablespoon cornstarch
1 tablespoon soy sauce
1 tablespoon cold water
½ teaspoon salt

1 pound boneless lean pork, cut into 1-inch
   pieces

Cooking Sauce:
¼ cup sugar
¼ cup water or pineapple juice
¼ cup catsup
1 tablespoon cornstarch
½ teaspoon salt
½ teaspoon sesame oil

Batter:
¼ cup all-purpose flour
2 tablespoons cornstarch
½ teaspoon baking soda
¼ cup water

3 cups peanut or vegetable oil for frying
2 green or sweet red peppers, cut into
   1-inch pieces
1 cup fresh or canned pineapple chunks,
   drained

For marinade: In small mixing bowl blend all ingredients until smooth. Stir in pork. Refrigerate for 30 minutes.

For cooking sauce: In small bowl combine all ingredients. Set aside.

For batter: In small mixing bowl beat all ingredients. Remove meat from marinade with slotted spoon. Stir meat into batter to coat evenly.

In wok heat oil until deep-fat thermometer registers 350°F. Fry one third of meat at a time 3 to 4 minutes, or until golden brown. Drain on paper toweling. Repeat with remaining meat. Set aside.

Carefully pour off all but 2 tablespoons oil. Heat remaining oil 1 minute, or until hot. Add peppers. Stir-fry 2 to 3 minutes, until tender-crisp. Add pineapple chunks and cooking sauce. Stir-fry until sauce thickens. Stir in reserved pork.

TIP: If using fresh pineapple, add with peppers instead of with cooking sauce.

Sweet and Sour Chicken: Follow recipe above, substituting 1 pound boneless chicken breast, skin removed, cut into 1-inch pieces, for pork.

4 to 6 servings

Fish and Chips

Beer Batter:
1½ cups all-purpose flour
 1 teaspoon salt
 ½ teaspoon baking powder
 ½ teaspoon baking soda
 ¼ teaspoon lemon-pepper seasoning
 1 cup beer
 ⅓ cup evaporated milk
 1 egg, beaten
 1 tablespoon vegetable oil

 3 cups vegetable oil or shortening for frying
 1 to 1½ pounds fish fillets, ¼ to ½ inch thick,
     cut into serving pieces
 1 pound white potatoes, sliced into ¹⁄₁₆ to
     ⅛-inch slices for chips

For beer batter: In medium bowl combine all ingredients. Beat until smooth.

Pat fillets dry with paper toweling. Set aside.

In wok heat oil until deep-fat thermometer registers 375°F. Dip fish in batter. Shake excess batter into bowl. Fry 4 or 5 fish pieces at a time 3 to 4 minutes, until deep golden brown. Drain (see Deep-Fat Frying Tips, page 62). Repeat with remaining fish pieces. Keep warm in 200°F oven.

In wok fry half of potato chip slices in oil 6 to 8 minutes, until golden brown. Repeat with remaining chips. Drain as above.

4 to 6 servings

Steamed Fish

Steaming Liquid:
 1 cup water
 2 carrots, cut into 1-inch chunks
 1 small onion, coarsely chopped
 4 thin lemon slices
 1 teaspoon salt
 ¼ teaspoon dried basil leaves
 ¼ teaspoon dried dill weed
 ¼ teaspoon pepper

 1 to 2 pounds fish steaks or fillets,
     or small whole fish

For steaming liquid: In wok combine all ingredients. Place steaming rack in wok. Heat to boiling. Place fish on steaming rack. If pieces are too small, place in pie plate on steaming rack. Cover wok. Reduce heat to setting "7" or "8". Estimate cooking time at 10 minutes per inch thickness of fish. Steam until fish flakes easily.

Poached Fish: Follow recipe above, except add 1 cup dry white wine plus enough boiling water (about 5 cups) to cover fish completely. Proceed as directed above.

4 servings

Egg Drop Soup

Salmon Croquettes

  1 can (16 ounces) salmon, drained, cleaned
    and flaked*
  1 cup cooked rice
  1 egg, slightly beaten
  ½ cup fine dry bread crumbs (unseasoned)
  ¼ cup minced green onion
1½ teaspoons dried parsley flakes (or
    1 tablespoon snipped fresh parsley)
  1 teaspoon celery salt
  ½ teaspoon dried tarragon leaves
  ¼ teaspoon pepper
  3 tablespoons butter or margarine
  3 tablespoons all-purpose flour
  ¾ cup milk

Coating:
  ½ cup cornflake crumbs
  ½ teaspoon salt

  5 cups vegetable oil or shortening
    for frying
    Mushroom Sauce, page 100, or Garlic Dill
    Butter, page 97 (optional)

In medium bowl combine salmon, rice, egg, bread
crumbs, green onion, parsley, celery salt, tarragon
and pepper. Set aside.

In small saucepan melt butter. Stir in flour. Blend in
milk. Cook on medium high heat, stirring constantly, until thickened and bubbly.

Blend sauce into salmon mixture. Refrigerate at
least 2 hours. Shape into 8 cone-shaped croquettes, using about ½ cup mixture in each.

For coating: In small bowl combine all ingredients.
Roll croquettes evenly in mixture.

In wok heat 5 cups oil until deep-fat thermometer
registers 325°F. Fry 4 croquettes at a time 5 to 6
minutes, or until deep golden brown. Drain on paper toweling. Repeat with remaining croquettes.
Serve with Mushroom Sauce or Garlic Dill Butter.

Chicken Croquettes: Follow recipe above, except
substitute 2 cups chopped, cooked chicken and ½
teaspoon poultry seasoning for salmon and tarragon. Prepare, shape, and fry as directed.

*Or use 2 cups fresh or frozen salmon, cooked,
cleaned and flaked.

4 servings

Egg Drop Soup

  4 cups chicken broth*
  1 clove garlic, cut in half
  1 slice fresh gingerroot, about ⅛ inch thick
  ⅛ teaspoon pepper
  2 eggs, beaten
  2 green onions, sliced

In wok combine broth, garlic, gingerroot and pepper. Heat to boiling. Simmer, covered, on setting
"5" or "6", 5 minutes. Remove gingerroot and garlic. Discard.

Heat broth to boiling. Gradually add eggs in a slow
steady stream, stirring constantly, until eggs are
set. Remove from heat. Top with green onions.
Serve immediately.

*Or 4 cups water and ¼ cup instant chicken bouil-
lon granules.

Variation: Follow recipe above, except add ½ cup
minced cooked chicken or pork before serving.

4 to 6 servings

Fried Rice

1½ cups uncooked long-grain rice
   Water for rinsing rice
1½ cups cold water
 4 tablespoons peanut or vegetable oil, divided
 2 eggs, beaten
 ½ cup chopped celery
 1 cup fresh or canned bean sprouts, drained
1½ cups sliced fresh mushrooms
 1 cup chopped cooked chicken, turkey, pork
   or ham
 3 green onions, sliced
 2 tablespoons soy sauce
 2 tablespoons oyster sauce

Cover rice with water. Gently rub rice between fingers. Drain. Repeat until water is clear, about 6 or 7 times. In wok heat rice and 1½ cups cold water to boiling. Reduce heat to setting "2" or "3". Simmer, covered, 22 to 27 minutes, or until water is absorbed. Remove rice from wok. Set aside.

In wok on setting "8", heat 1 tablespoon oil 1 to 2 minutes. Add eggs. Stir-fry until eggs are set but still moist. Remove eggs from wok. Set aside.

In wok heat 2 tablespoons oil 1 to 2 minutes. Add rice. Stir-fry 1 to 2 minutes. Remove rice from wok. Set aside.

In wok heat 1 tablespoon oil about 1 minute, or until hot. Add celery. Stir-fry 1 minute. Add bean sprouts and mushrooms. Stir-fry 1 minute. Stir in meat, green onions, soy sauce and oyster sauce. Return rice and eggs to wok. Stir-fry 30 seconds.

6 to 8 servings

Rice Pilaf

 2 tablespoons butter or margarine
 1 cup coarsely chopped fresh mushrooms
 ⅓ cup chopped green pepper
 ¼ cup chopped onion
 2 cups water
 1 cup uncooked long-grain rice
 ¼ cup pine nuts (optional)
 1 tablespoon instant chicken bouillon granules
1½ teaspoons dried parsley flakes (or
   1 tablespoon snipped fresh parsley)
 ¼ teaspoon dried thyme leaves
 ⅛ teaspoon pepper

In wok on "Hi", melt butter. Add mushrooms, green pepper and onion. Sauté 3 minutes. Add remaining ingredients. Heat to boiling. Simmer on setting "3" or "4", covered, 22 to 27 minutes, or until tender.

4 to 6 servings

Fried Rice

Fried Potato Skins

Fried Apple Rings

Batter:
- 1 cup all-purpose flour
- 1 teaspoon baking powder
- 1 teaspoon pumpkin pie spice
- ¼ teaspoon salt
- ¾ cup plus 2 tablespoons water
- 1 egg

- 3 or 4 medium apples, pared, cored and cut into ½-inch thick rings
- ¾ cup confectioners' sugar, divided
- 3 cups vegetable oil or shortening for frying

For batter: In small mixing bowl combine flour, baking powder, pumpkin pie spice and salt. In small dish blend water and egg. Blend water mixture into flour mixture until smooth. Refrigerate at least 1 hour.

In wok heat oil or shortening until deep-fat thermometer registers 350°F.

Dredge apple rings in ½ cup confectioners' sugar to coat evenly. Then dip apple rings in batter. Deep-fry 2 or 3 apple rings at a time until golden brown. Turn once. Drain on paper toweling. Sprinkle with remaining ¼ cup confectioners' sugar. Repeat with remaining apple rings. Serve warm.

4 to 8 servings

Fried Potato Skins

- 6 medium-size white potatoes
- 1 egg, beaten
- ½ cup fine dry bread crumbs (seasoned)
- 4 cups vegetable oil or shortening for frying
- ¼ cup crisp cooked bacon bits
- 2 tablespoons thinly sliced green onion
- ¾ cup finely shredded Cheddar cheese
  Dairy sour cream (optional)

Pierce potatoes in several places. Bake in 375°F **convection oven** on rack 3, 50 to 55 minutes (or bake in preheated 375°F **radiant bake oven** 1 to 1¼ hours). Cut in half lengthwise. Scoop out potato, leaving ¼-inch shell.

Dip skin-side of each shell in egg. Dip or dredge in bread crumbs to coat evenly. In wok heat oil until deep-fat thermometer registers 375°F. Deep-fry half of potato skins 2 to 3 minutes, or until deep golden brown. Drain (see Deep-Fat Frying Tips, page 62). Repeat with remaining skins.

Sprinkle bacon, green onion and cheese inside skins. Place on grid of roasting pan. Broil skins at 550°F, 2 to 3 minutes, or until cheese is melted. Serve skins topped with sour cream.

Variation: Follow recipe above, except substitute Monterey Jack cheese for Cheddar cheese. Omit bacon and green onions. Add ¼ cup chopped olives or ¼ cup minced fully-cooked ham.

6 servings

Blushing Pears

- 4 to 6 ripe pears
- 2 tablespoons sugar (optional)
- 2 teaspoons cornstarch
- 1 package (10 ounces) frozen sweetened strawberries, thawed and pureed
- 2 to 3 tablespoons orange-flavored liqueur

In wok place pears in baking dish or pan on steaming rack over 2 cups boiling water. Cover. Steam on setting "5" or "6", 10 to 20 minutes, or until pears are tender. Hold pears under running cold water, rubbing gently to peel off the skin. Drain. Set aside.

In small saucepan blend sugar and cornstarch. Add strawberries. Stir until smooth. Bring to boil over medium high heat, stirring constantly. Boil and stir 1 minute. Stir in liqueur.

To serve, pour sauce over whole or halved and cored pears. Serve warm or cold.

4 to 6 servings

Fruit Pockets

Filling:
1 can (8 ounces) crushed pineapple, drained
1 package (3 ounces) cream cheese, softened
½ cup flaked coconut
¼ cup confectioners' sugar
2 tablespoons chopped maraschino cherries
2 tablespoons minced pecans
⅛ teaspoon ground nutmeg

1 package (17¼ ounces) frozen puff pastry
  sheets, defrosted
1 egg, beaten
3 cups vegetable oil or shortening for frying
  Confectioners' sugar (optional)

For filling: In medium bowl combine all ingredients.
Set aside.

Roll 1 puff pastry sheet very thin to a 12 × 16-inch
rectangle. Cut into 16 pieces, each measuring
4 × 3 inches. Place about one teaspoon filling off
center on each piece of dough. Brush edges of
dough with small amount of beaten egg. Fold over.
Press gently to remove air. Seal edges with fork.
Repeat with remaining pastry and filling.

In wok heat oil until deep-fat thermometer registers
350°F. Deep-fry 5 pockets at a time, about 5 minutes, or until puffy and light golden brown. Turn 2 or
3 times. Drain (see Deep-Fat Frying Tips, page 62).
Repeat with remaining pockets. Sprinkle confectioners' sugar over pockets.

Pumpkin Pockets: Follow the recipe above, except
substitute pumpkin filling for fruit filling. For pumpkin filling: In medium bowl combine 1 cup canned
pumpkin, 1 package (3 ounces) softened cream
cheese, ¼ cup packed brown sugar and 1 teaspoon pumpkin pie spice. Deep-fry pockets as
directed. Sprinkle with confectioners' sugar and ¼
teaspoon ground nutmeg, if desired.

32 pockets

Fruit Pockets

How to Fill Fruit Pockets

Roll pastry very thin. Cut into 16 pieces. Place
filling off center. Brush edges.

Fold pastry over top. Press gently to remove air.
Seal edges with fork.

Creamy Custard

3 eggs
¼ cup sugar
½ teaspoon vanilla
⅛ teaspoon salt
2 cups milk, scalded
Ground nutmeg

In medium mixing bowl beat eggs, sugar, vanilla and salt. Gradually beat in milk in a slow, steady stream. Pour mixture into 1-quart baking dish. Drape dish with wax paper (see Steaming Tips, page 63).

In wok place dish on steaming rack over 2 cups boiling water. Cover wok. Steam on setting "4" or "5", 12 to 16 minutes, or until knife inserted in center comes out clean. Sprinkle with nutmeg. Let stand 30 minutes. Serve warm or chilled.

TIP: Lift wax paper carefully to prevent condensation from falling onto surface of custard.

4 to 6 servings

Boston Brown Bread

1½ cups whole wheat flour
1 cup all-purpose flour
½ cup yellow cornmeal
2 teaspoons baking soda
1 teaspoon salt
2 cups buttermilk
½ cup dark molasses
1 cup raisins

Grease 10-cup fluted tube pan. Set aside.

In medium mixing bowl combine wheat flour, all-purpose flour, cornmeal, baking soda and salt. Add buttermilk and molasses. Stir just until flour is moistened. Stir in raisins. Spread batter in pan.

In wok place cake pan on steaming rack over 2 cups boiling water. Drape with wax paper (see Steaming Tips, page 63). Cover wok. Steam on setting "5" or "6", 40 to 45 minutes, or until knife inserted in center comes out clean.

Remove pan from wok. Cool 10 minutes. Loosen edges. Invert bread onto serving plate. Serve warm or cool.

TIP: Lift wax paper carefully to prevent condensation from falling onto bread.

1 loaf

Plum Pudding with Vanilla Sauce

Pudding:
4 cups soft bread cubes, crust removed
1 cup all-purpose flour
1 cup raisins
1 cup currants
1 cup chopped nuts (optional)
1 cup half-and-half
2 eggs
½ cup butter or margarine, melted
¼ cup packed dark brown sugar
¼ cup sherry
3 tablespoons molasses
1½ teaspoons pumpkin pie spice
1 teaspoon baking soda
½ teaspoon salt

Sauce:
¾ cup sugar
½ cup milk
1½ tablespoons all-purpose flour
1 teaspoon vanilla

Grease 10-cup fluted tube pan. Set aside.

For pudding: In large mixing bowl combine all ingredients. Beat on medium speed of electric mixer until blended.

Pour batter into pan. In wok place pan on steaming rack over 2 cups boiling water. Drape with wax paper (see Steaming Tips, page 63). Cover wok.

Steam on setting "5" or "6", 50 to 60 minutes, or until knife inserted in center comes out clean. Remove pan from wok. Cool 15 minutes. Loosen edges. Invert pudding on serving plate.

For sauce: In small saucepan combine sugar, milk and flour. Heat to boiling on medium high heat stirring constantly. Stir in vanilla. Serve warm sauce over pudding.

TIP: Lift wax paper carefully to prevent condensation from falling onto pudding.

8 to 10 servings

Steamed Spice Cake with Fudge Sauce

¾ cup butter or margarine
1 cup packed brown sugar
4 eggs
½ cup molasses
3 ounces semi-sweet chocolate, melted
3 cups all-purpose flour
2 teaspoons baking soda
2 teaspoons ground cinnamon
2 teaspoons ground allspice
½ teaspoon ground mace
½ teaspoon ground nutmeg
½ teaspoon salt
½ cup milk

Fudge Sauce:
1 ounce semi-sweet chocolate
2 teaspoons butter or margarine
⅓ cup half-and-half
¼ cup granulated sugar
¼ cup packed light brown sugar
1 tablespoon corn syrup
½ teaspoon vanilla

Grease 10-cup fluted tube pan. Set aside.

In large mixing bowl on medium speed of electric mixer, cream butter and sugar until light and fluffy. Blend in eggs one at a time. Add molasses. Mix in melted chocolate. Set aside.

In medium mixing bowl combine flour, baking soda, cinnamon, allspice, mace, nutmeg and salt. Blend half of flour mixture at a time into batter. Add milk. Beat on medium speed about 2 minutes.

Spread batter evenly in pan.

In wok place pan on steaming rack over 2½ cups boiling water. Drape with wax paper (see Steaming Tips, page 63). Cover wok. Steam on setting "6" or "7", 45 to 60 minutes, or until knife inserted in center of cake comes out clean.

Remove pan from wok. Cool 10 minutes. Loosen edges. Invert cake onto serving plate.

For fudge sauce: In small saucepan on low heat melt chocolate and butter. Stir in half-and-half. Cook on medium high heat, stirring constantly, until blended. Stir in sugars and corn syrup. Heat to boiling, stirring constantly. Boil, without stirring, 5 minutes. Remove from heat. Stir in vanilla. Serve warm or cool over cake.

TIP: Lift wax paper carefully to prevent condensation from falling onto cake.

1 cake

Steamed Spice Cake with Fudge Sauce

Cinnamon Crispies

½ cup granulated or confectioners' sugar
1½ to 2 teaspoons ground cinnamon
3 cups vegetable oil or shortening for frying
12 wonton skins (whole) or 3 egg roll skins, cut in fourths

In a small bowl, combine sugar and cinnamon. Set aside.

In wok heat oil until deep-fat thermometer registers 375°F. Fry 2 or 3 wonton pieces at a time, 30 to 90 seconds, or until golden brown. Turn once. Drain on paper toweling. Sprinkle with sugar mixture. Repeat with remaining wonton pieces.

Variation: Follow recipe above, except substitute 4 flour tortillas (10 to 12-inch diameter) for wonton skins. Cut each tortilla into fourths.

4 to 6 servings

French Fryer/Cooker

Your French fryer/cooker accessory expands your list of menu possibilities by adding two popular cooking methods—deep-fat frying and simmer cooking. You'll love the crispy texture of deep-fried foods, whether it's an appetizer like egg rolls, a main course like chimichangas or a dessert like Jenny cakes. Many of the recipes in the wok section can also be prepared in the French fryer/cooker. Simmer cooking blends flavors as spicy as chili, as elegant as beef burgundy or as surprising as paella. Follow the tips below for best results with your French fryer/cooker.

Use only quality vegetable oils or shortenings for deep-fat frying. Do not use butter, margarine or lard. These have low smoking points and give fried foods an unpleasant flavor.

Fill fryer with oil up to the line marked on the interior (3 quarts). Do not overfill. Use enough oil to cover the food and allow it to move freely in the fryer. When frying high-moisture foods such as French fries, use less oil (2½ quarts) to reduce bubbling and spattering.

Use the heat control to maintain a constant oil temperature during frying. Food will absorb fat if the temperature is too low. Food will overcook on the outside if the temperature is too high. To lessen the cooling effect of adding food to hot oil, cut food into small pieces and fry in small batches. Let oil return to proper temperature between batches.

Dry food on paper towels before frying or coating with batter to reduce spattering. Remove ice crystals from frozen foods, especially French fries.

Raise basket to drain position to allow excess oil to drip back into fryer. Drain foods promptly on paper towels.

Skim food particles from oil during frying. Strain oil after cooling. Cover and store in refrigerator.

Pictured on preceding page: Yogurt Cake Doughnuts, recipe page 87

Egg Rolls

- 1 pound unseasoned ground pork
- 1 teaspoon minced fresh gingerroot
- 1 clove garlic, minced
- 1 teaspoon salt
- ½ teaspoon 5-spice powder*
- ¼ teaspoon pepper
- ½ cup minced celery
- ½ cup minced green onion
- ¼ cup minced carrot
- 6 cups coarsely chopped cabbage (1 pound)
- 3 tablespoons soy sauce
- 2 cans (4½ ounces each) small deveined shrimp, rinsed and drained
- 1 can (14 to 16 ounces) bean sprouts, drained
- 1 can (8 ounces) water chestnuts, drained and minced
- 24 egg roll skins
- 1 egg, beaten
  Oil or shortening for frying
  Hot Mustard Sauce, page 99, or Sweet and Sour Sauce, page 101 (optional)

In fryer/cooker on "Hi", cook ground pork, gingerroot and garlic, stirring occasionally, until pork is browned. Drain off fat. Stir in salt, 5-spice powder, pepper, celery, green onion and carrot. Cook, stirring constantly, about 2 minutes, or until green onion is tender. Add cabbage. Cook, stirring constantly, 2 to 3 minutes, or until cabbage is tender-crisp. Stir in soy sauce. With slotted spoon, remove cabbage mixture to large mixing bowl. Add shrimp, bean sprouts and water chestnuts to cabbage mixture.

For each egg roll: Place one egg roll skin on flat surface, with one corner pointing toward you. Place ⅓ cup filling slightly below center of egg roll skin. Fold corner of skin pointing toward you over filling, tucking point under filling. Fold in and overlap the left and right corners. Brush top corner with beaten egg. Roll up. Press corner to seal.

In fryer/cooker heat oil until deep-fat thermometer registers 350°F. Fry 3 or 4 egg rolls at a time, 2 to 3 minutes, or until golden brown. Turn occasionally. Drain on paper toweling. Repeat with remaining egg rolls. Serve with desired sauce.

*Available in Oriental section of supermarket.

TIP: Fried egg rolls may be frozen up to 3 months. To serve, unwrap and place frozen egg rolls on baking sheet. Heat in 425°F **convection oven** about 15 minutes (or heat in preheated 425°F **radiant bake oven** about 20 minutes), or until hot.

24 egg rolls

Egg Rolls

How to Make Egg Rolls

Place ⅓ cup filling slightly below center. Fold corner over filling.

Overlap left and right corners. Brush top corner with egg. Roll up to seal.

Cheese-Stuffed Rice Balls

- 1 cup water
- 1 teaspoon instant chicken bouillon granules
- 1 tablespoon butter or margarine
- 1 tablespoon minced green onion
- ¼ to ½ teaspoon dried Italian seasoning
- ½ cup uncooked long-grain rice
- 1 egg, slightly beaten
- ¼ cup grated Parmesan cheese
- 18 to 20 ½-inch cubes mozzarella cheese (about 2 ounces)
- 1 egg
- 1 tablespoon water
- ¾ cup fine dry bread crumbs (seasoned)
  Oil or shortening for frying

In small saucepan combine water, bouillon granules, butter, onion and Italian seasoning. Heat to boiling. Add rice. Simmer on medium low heat, covered, 20 minutes, or until water is absorbed. Stir rice about 1 minute, or until sticky. Stir in 1 egg and Parmesan cheese. Place mixture in small bowl. Refrigerate 2½ to 3 hours, to chill thoroughly.

Mold 1 measuring-tablespoonful of rice mixture around each cheese cube. Beat 1 egg and water. Dip rice balls in egg mixture, turning to coat evenly. Then roll in bread crumbs, turning to coat evenly.

In fryer/cooker heat oil until deep-fat thermometer registers 350°F. Fry 6 rice balls at a time, 2 to 4 minutes, or until deep golden brown. Turn occasionally. Drain on paper toweling. Serve hot.

TIP: Fried rice balls may be refrigerated, covered, up to 2 days. To serve, uncover and place on cookie sheet. Heat in 400°F **convection oven** about 10 minutes (or heat in preheated 400°F **radiant bake oven** about 12 minutes), or until hot.

18 to 20 appetizers

Seafood Puffs

Seafood Mixture:
- 1 can (4½ ounces) small deveined shrimp, rinsed, drained and chopped
- 1 can (6 ounces) crab meat, rinsed, drained and flaked
- 1 cup shredded Monterey Jack cheese
- 1 package (3 ounces) cream cheese, softened
- 1 egg, slightly beaten
- 3 tablespoons fine dry bread crumbs (seasoned)
- 1 teaspoon freeze-dried chives
- ¼ teaspoon onion powder
- 3 to 4 drops hot pepper sauce

- ¼ cup all-purpose flour
- 1 egg
- 2 tablespoons milk
- 1¼ cups instant mashed potato flakes
  Oil or shortening for frying
  Lemon wedges or prepared seafood cocktail sauce

For seafood mixture: In medium mixing bowl combine all ingredients. Cover. Refrigerate mixture at least 2 hours.

For each puff: Form 1 tablespoon seafood mixture into 1 × 1½-inch rectangle. Roll each puff in flour to coat evenly. In small dish blend egg and milk. Dip each puff in egg mixture. Roll in potato flakes to coat evenly.

In fryer/cooker heat oil until deep-fat thermometer registers 350°F. Fry 6 puffs at a time, 1½ to 2 minutes, or until golden brown. Turn once. Drain on paper toweling. Repeat with remaining puffs. Serve with lemon wedges or prepared seafood cocktail sauce.

24 appetizers

Shredded Beef Chimichangas

2 tablespoons vegetable oil
4 cups shredded cooked beef (about ½ recipe Beef Brisket, page 67)
1 medium onion, chopped
¾ teaspoon garlic salt
½ teaspoon ground cumin
¼ teaspoon ground oregano
¼ teaspoon crushed red pepper
¼ cup prepared taco sauce
8 flour tortillas (8-inch diameter)*

Guacamole Topping:
1 ripe avocado, peeled
2 teaspoons lemon juice
¼ cup dairy sour cream
2 tablespoons mayonnaise
½ teaspoon salt
¼ teaspoon pepper
Dash garlic powder
2 tablespoons minced green onion
½ cup chopped fresh tomatoes

Oil or shortening for frying
Prepared salsa sauce (optional)

In wok or large skillet on medium high heat, heat vegetable oil 1 to 2 minutes, or until hot. Add beef, onion, garlic salt, cumin, oregano and pepper. Sauté mixture until onions are translucent. Stir in taco sauce. Heat 1 minute. Set aside.

For each chimichanga: Place about ½ cup beef mixture slightly below center of tortilla. Fold front over filling. Overlap left and right sides. Fold down top (see How to Make Egg Rolls, page 83). Secure with wooden pick.

For guacamole: In shallow dish mash avocado and lemon juice. Blend in sour cream, mayonnaise, salt, pepper and garlic powder, until smooth. Stir in green onion and tomatoes. Set aside.

In fryer/cooker heat oil until deep-fat thermometer registers 375°F. Fry 2 or 3 chimichangas at a time, 1½ to 2 minutes, or until golden brown. Turn once. Drain on paper toweling. Repeat with remaining chimichangas. Serve topped with guacamole topping and salsa sauce.

*Thin tortillas give best results.

4 to 8 servings

Shredded Beef Chimichangas

Carrot Fritters

1 pound carrots, diced
½ cup water
1 egg
1 tablespoon sugar
3 tablespoons all-purpose flour
1 teaspoon baking powder
¼ teaspoon salt
Dash pepper
Oil or shortening for frying

In medium saucepan place carrots in water. Heat to boiling. Reduce to medium low heat. Simmer, covered, 15 to 20 minutes, or until tender. Drain.

In medium mixing bowl, with electric mixer on medium speed, cream carrots, egg and sugar. Blend in the flour, baking powder, salt and pepper. Set aside.

In fryer/cooker heat oil until deep-fat thermometer registers 325°F. Drop half of carrot mixture by heaping tablespoonfuls into oil. Fry fritters 1 to 2 minutes, or until golden brown. Turn once. Drain on paper toweling. Repeat with remaining carrot mixture. Serve hot.

6 to 8 servings

Fried Chicken and Potato Wedges

1½ cups all-purpose flour
1 teaspoon salt
¼ teaspoon pepper
2½ to 3-pound broiler-fryer chicken, cut into 8 pieces
1½ cups buttermilk
Oil or shortening for frying
2 medium-size baking potatoes, each cut lengthwise into 8 wedges

In shallow dish combine flour, salt and pepper. Set aside. Dip chicken pieces in buttermilk. Roll in flour mixture to coat evenly.

In fryer/cooker heat oil until deep-fat thermometer registers 325°F. Fry 4 pieces at a time, 10 to 15 minutes, or until deep golden brown. Turn occasionally. Drain on paper toweling. Keep warm in 200°F oven. Repeat with remaining chicken.

Dip potato wedges in remaining buttermilk. Roll in remaining flour mixture to coat evenly. Fry potatoes about 10 minutes, or until golden brown. Serve potatoes with chicken.

TIP: Potatoes will float to surface when done.

4 to 6 servings

Jenny Cakes

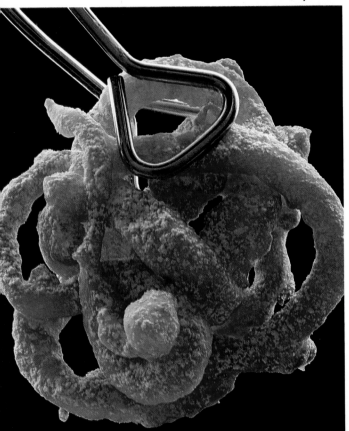

Pork Scotch Eggs

¾ pound pork sausage
¼ pound ground veal
½ teaspoon dried marjoram leaves
¼ teaspoon dried sage
8 hard-cooked eggs, shelled
1 egg
1 tablespoon milk
½ cup fine dry bread crumbs (seasoned)
Oil or shortening for frying

In medium mixing bowl combine sausage, veal, marjoram and sage. Divide mixture into 8 equal portions. Mold one portion of sausage mixture around each hard-cooked egg.

In small bowl blend egg and milk. Dip sausage-coated eggs in egg mixture. Roll in bread crumbs to coat evenly.

In fryer/cooker heat oil until deep-fat thermometer registers 350°F. Fry scotch eggs 4 to 7 minutes, or until deep golden brown. Turn occasionally. Drain on paper toweling. Serve warm.

4 to 8 servings

Jenny Cakes

3 eggs, beaten
2 cups milk
4 cups all-purpose flour
⅓ cup granulated sugar
½ teaspoon salt
1 tablespoon baking powder
Oil or shortening for frying
Confectioners' sugar

In medium mixing bowl beat eggs and milk. Gradually blend in flour, sugar, salt and baking powder, until very smooth. Pour into spouted pitcher.

In fryer/cooker heat oil until deep-fat thermometer registers 375°F. From pitcher slowly pour batter in a steady stream into oil to make a spiral pattern. Start in center and swirl outward. Fry 1 or 2 cakes at a time, 2 to 3 minutes, or until deep golden brown. Turn once. Drain on paper toweling. Immediately sprinkle with confectioners' sugar. Repeat with remaining batter. Serve warm.

TIP: Do not use wire fry basket in fryer/cooker.

About 20 cakes

Yogurt Cake Doughnuts

Doughnuts:
3½ cups all-purpose flour, divided
 1 cup sugar
2½ teaspoons baking powder
 1 teaspoon baking soda
 ¾ teaspoon salt
 ¼ teaspoon ground cinnamon
 ¼ teaspoon ground nutmeg
 ¼ teaspoon ground cardamom
 3 tablespoons butter or margarine, melted
 2 eggs
 1 cup plain yogurt

 Oil or shortening for frying

Coating:
 ¾ cup granulated or confectioners' sugar
 ¼ teaspoon ground nutmeg

For doughnuts: In large mixing bowl measure 2 cups flour and remaining ingredients. Blend on low speed of electric mixer, scraping bowl constantly. Beat 2 minutes on medium speed of electric mixer, scraping bowl occasionally. Gradually stir in remaining 1½ cups flour until a soft dough forms. Cover. Refrigerate at least 1 hour. (Chilled dough will be easier to handle.)

Divide dough in half. On generously floured surface, knead dough until smooth, about 3 to 5 minutes. Roll dough ⅜ to ½ inch thick. Cut dough with floured doughnut cutter. Reserve "holes". Repeat with remaining dough.

In fryer/cooker heat oil until deep-fat thermometer registers 350°F. With wide spatula slide doughnuts into hot oil. Fry about 6 doughnuts and 6 "holes" at a time, about 2 minutes, or until golden brown. Turn frequently. Drain on paper toweling.

For coating: In shallow dish or pie plate combine sugar and nutmeg. Roll warm doughnuts and "holes" in sugar mixture to coat evenly.

Fruit Doughnuts: Follow the recipe above, except first combine ½ cup chopped mixed dried fruits and 2 tablespoons warm brandy or apple juice. Stir fruit mixture into dough with the 1½ cups flour. Continue as directed.

About 20 doughnuts

Apple Fritters

Apple Fritters

1⅓ cups all-purpose flour
 ¼ cup granulated sugar
2½ teaspoons baking powder
 ¼ teaspoon ground cinnamon
 ¼ teaspoon salt
 ¾ cup milk
 2 eggs, beaten
1½ cups pared, chopped apple
 Oil or shortening for frying
 Confectioners' sugar

In medium mixing bowl combine flour, sugar, baking powder, cinnamon and salt. Stir in milk and eggs until flour is just moistened. Stir in apple.

In fryer/cooker heat oil until deep-fat thermometer registers 375°F.

Drop apple mixture by scant ¼-cupfuls into hot oil. Fry 3 or 4 fritters at a time, 4 to 5 minutes, or until deep golden brown. Turn occasionally. Drain on paper toweling. Sprinkle warm fritters with confectioners' sugar. Repeat with remaining apple mixture. Serve warm.

Pineapple-Banana Fritters: Follow the recipe above, except reduce milk to ⅔ cup. Omit apple. Stir in ¼ cup chopped walnuts, 1 can (8 ounces) crushed pineapple, *well* drained, and ¾ cup chopped bananas (about 2 small).

TIP: Do not use wire fry basket in fryer/cooker.

About 12 fritters

Maple-Glazed Long Johns

Maple-Glazed Long Johns

1 package (¼ ounce) active dry yeast
¼ cup warm water (110° to 115°F)
¼ cup butter or margarine
¾ cup buttermilk
1 egg
3 tablespoons sugar
¾ teaspoon salt
1 teaspoon vanilla
3 to 3½ cups all-purpose flour, divided
   Oil or shortening for frying

Glaze:
2 tablespoons butter or margarine, softened
2 tablespoons packed brown sugar
½ teaspoon maple flavoring
2 cups confectioners' sugar
4 to 5 tablespoons milk

½ cup chopped salted peanuts (optional)

In large mixing bowl dissolve yeast in warm water. Set aside.

In small saucepan melt butter. Add buttermilk. Heat, stirring constantly, until thermometer registers 110°F. Add butter mixture to yeast. Add egg, sugar, salt, vanilla and 1 cup flour. Beat mixture on medium speed 2 minutes. Stir in remaining 2 to 2½ cups flour until stiff dough forms. Cover. Let rise in a warm place (80° to 85°F) until dough has doubled in size, about 1 to 1¼ hours.

Turn dough onto lightly floured surface. Knead until dough is smooth, about 8 to 10 minutes. Roll dough to ½-inch thickness. Cut into 1½ × 4-inch pieces. Cover. Let rise in a warm place (80° to 85°F), until dough has doubled in size, about 1 hour.

In fryer/cooker heat oil until deep-fat thermometer registers 350°F. Fry 4 long johns at a time, 2½ to 3 minutes, or until deep golden brown. Turn after half the time. Drain on paper toweling. Repeat with remaining long johns. Cool.

For glaze: In medium mixing bowl cream butter, brown sugar and maple flavoring. Blend in confectioners' sugar. Stir in 1 tablespoon milk at a time, until smooth and of desired consistency.

Spread some of glaze on top of each long john. Sprinkle top of each with about 1½ teaspoons chopped peanuts.

About 15 long johns

Cheese Cake Squares

1 carton (15 ounces) ricotta cheese
4 egg yolks
⅔ cup confectioners' sugar
2 tablespoons cornstarch
1 teaspoon vanilla
1 teaspoon grated lemon peel
   Oil or shortening for frying
1 egg
1 tablespoon milk
⅓ to ½ cup graham cracker crumbs

Line 8 × 8-inch baking pan with foil, leaving a 2-inch overhang. In food processor or electric mixer, blend ricotta, egg yolks, confectioners' sugar, cornstarch, vanilla and lemon peel until smooth. Place in small saucepan. Cook on medium heat, stirring constantly, 10 to 15 minutes, until thickened.

Pour mixture into prepared pan. Spread evenly. Place plastic wrap directly on surface. Refrigerate and chill thoroughly. Carefully lift cheesecake out of pan, using foil overhang. Cut cheesecake into 1-inch squares.

In fryer/cooker heat oil until deep-fat thermometer registers 350°F. In small bowl blend egg and milk. Dip cheese cake squares in egg mixture. Roll in graham cracker crumbs to coat evenly. Fry one-third of squares at a time, 1 to 1½ minutes, or until golden brown. Turn occasionally. Drain on paper toweling. Repeat with remaining squares. Serve warm or cool.

64 squares

Beef Burgundy

In the following recipes we feature the French fryer/cooker as a simmer cooker.

Flemish Pot Roast

1 medium onion, sliced
2 stalks celery, cut into 3-inch pieces
1 cup beer
1 cup water
2 teaspoons instant beef bouillon granules
1½ teaspoons dried parsley flakes (or 1 tablespoon snipped fresh parsley)
½ teaspoon dried bouquet garni
10 whole peppercorns
4 whole cloves
1 bay leaf
3 to 3½-pound beef chuck roast*

Gravy:
  Reserved cooking liquid
6 tablespoons all-purpose flour
⅓ cup cold water
½ teaspoon bouquet sauce (optional)

In fryer/cooker combine onion, celery, beer, water, bouillon granules, parsley, bouquet garni, peppercorns, cloves and bay leaf. Heat to boiling.

Reduce heat to "3" or "4". Add roast. Simmer, covered, 2½ to 3½ hours, or until meat is fork tender. Remove meat from fryer/cooker. Reserve liquid. Keep meat warm.

For gravy: Strain reserved liquid. Skim off fat. Add enough water to liquid to measure 1¾ cups. Pour into small saucepan. Blend flour and ⅓ cup water until smooth. Gradually blend flour mixture into liquid. Cook on medium high heat, stirring constantly, until mixture thickens and just comes to boil. Stir in bouquet sauce. Serve gravy over meat.

*Frozen beef chuck roast may be substituted, if desired. Increase simmer time to 3½ to 4 hours.

4 to 6 servings

Beef Burgundy

¼ cup all-purpose flour
½ teaspoon salt
½ teaspoon dried bouquet garni
¼ teaspoon pepper
¼ teaspoon dried thyme leaves
1½ to 2-pound boneless beef round steak, cut into 1-inch cubes
4 slices bacon, cut-up
2 medium carrots, cut into julienne strips (¼ × 1½-inch)
2 small onions, each cut lengthwise into 6 wedges
2 cups Burgundy wine
1 cup water
½ teaspoon instant beef bouillon granules
1 tablespoon dried parsley flakes (or 2 tablespoons snipped fresh parsley)
8 ounces fresh mushrooms, sliced

In plastic food storage bag combine flour, salt, bouquet garni, pepper and thyme. Add meat to flour mixture. Shake bag to coat meat with flour.

In fryer/cooker on setting "10", fry bacon stirring constantly, until browned and crisp. With slotted spoon remove bacon from cooker. Drain on paper toweling. Set aside.

Add meat and any remaining flour to bacon drippings. Cook meat, stirring occasionally, until browned. Add carrots, onions, wine, water, bouillon granules, parsley and reserved bacon. Heat to boiling. Simmer on setting "3" or "4", covered, 2 to 2½ hours, or until meat is tender. Stir occasionally. Add mushrooms during last 10 minutes.

Serve over rice or noodles.

6 to 8 servings

Corned Beef Dinner

Corned Beef Dinner

3 to 4-pound corned beef brisket
½ cup chopped onion
¼ cup packed brown sugar (optional)
2 cloves garlic, minced
1 teaspoon dry mustard
2 bay leaves
  Dash ground cloves
6 medium potatoes, halved
6 carrots, halved
1 head cabbage (about 2 pounds), cut into 6
  wedges

In fryer/cooker place meat and contents of spice packet (if included in corned beef package). Add enough hot water to cover meat. Add onion, brown sugar, garlic, dry mustard, bay leaves and cloves. Heat on "Hi" to boiling.

Reduce heat to setting "3" or "4". Simmer, covered, 3½ to 4 hours, or until meat is fork tender. Add potatoes and carrots during last 30 minutes.

Remove meat from cooking liquid. Keep warm.

Gradually add cabbage wedges to potatoes and carrots. Remove excess liquid if necessary. Cook covered, on setting "7", 20 to 25 minutes, or until cabbage is tender.

To serve, cut meat across the grain into ¼-inch thick slices. Serve meat slices with vegetables.

6 to 8 servings

Beef Stew

½ cup all-purpose flour
1 teaspoon salt
½ teaspoon dried marjoram leaves
½ teaspoon dried basil leaves
½ teaspoon dried summer savory
¼ teaspoon pepper
2 pounds beef stew meat, cut into 1½-inch
  cubes
¼ cup vegetable oil
4 cups hot water
1 can (10½ ounces) beef consommé
¼ cup dry red wine
1 medium onion, chopped
1 bay leaf
2 medium tomatoes, peeled, seeded
  and coarsely chopped
2 carrots, cut diagonally into ¾-inch pieces
3 stalks celery, cut into ¾-inch slices
4 medium-size red potatoes, cut into quarters

In plastic food storage bag combine flour, salt, marjoram, basil, summer savory and pepper. Add meat. Shake bag to coat meat with flour.

In fryer/cooker heat oil on "Hi". Add meat and any remaining flour to oil. Brown meat. Stir in water, consommé, red wine, onion and bay leaf. Reduce heat to setting "3" or "4". Simmer, covered, 1 hour. Add remaining ingredients. Cover. Simmer 1¾ to 2 hours longer, or until meat is fork tender.

8 to 10 servings

Deviled Short Ribs

4 to 5 pounds beef short ribs, trimmed of
  excess fat
1 can (15 ounces) tomato sauce
1 can (6 ounces) frozen lemonade concentrate
1 medium onion, sliced into rings
¼ cup snipped fresh parsley (or
  2 tablespoons dried parsley flakes)
2 tablespoons packed brown sugar
2 teaspoons Worcestershire sauce
½ teaspoon dried thyme leaves
½ teaspoon celery salt
½ teaspoon crushed red pepper
1 bay leaf

In fryer/cooker combine all ingredients. Heat to boiling. Reduce heat to setting "3" or "4". Simmer, covered, 2½ to 3 hours, or until ribs are fork tender. Before serving, skim fat from sauce.

4 servings

Chili

- 2 to 3 pounds lean ground beef
- 4 cups chopped onion
- 12 large cloves garlic, minced
- 1 large green pepper, chopped
- 3 to 4 tablespoons chili powder
- 1 tablespoon plus 1½ teaspoons all-purpose flour
- 4 teaspoons salt
- 1 tablespoon sugar
- 1 tablespoon ground cumin
- 1 tablespoon ground coriander
- 1 tablespoon dried oregano leaves
- 1 to 2 teaspoons crushed red pepper
- 2 cans (16 ounces each) whole tomatoes, chopped
- 1 can (15 ounces) tomato sauce
- 1 can (8 ounces) tomato sauce
- 1 can (6 ounces) tomato paste
- 3 cans (16 ounces each) red kidney beans
- 1 square (1 ounce) unsweetened chocolate (optional)

In fryer/cooker on "Hi", cook ground beef, stirring occasionally, until browned. Add onion, garlic and green pepper. Cook until vegetables are tender. Add chili powder, flour, salt, sugar, cumin, coriander, oregano, pepper, whole tomatoes, tomato sauce and tomato paste.

Reduce heat to setting "3" or "4". Simmer, covered, 1 hour. Stir occasionally.

Stir in beans and chocolate. Simmer, covered, 20 to 30 minutes. Stir before serving.

TIP: Prepared chili may be frozen up to 2 months. To serve, thaw and heat thoroughly.

About 4 quarts

Thick Italian Tomato Sauce

- 1 cup chopped onion
- ¼ cup chopped green pepper
- 8 ounces fresh mushrooms, sliced
- 2 cloves garlic, minced
- 1 small carrot, minced
- ½ cup olive oil
- 2 cups water
- 2 cans (28 ounces each) whole tomatoes, chopped, liquid reserved
- 2 cans (6 ounces each) tomato paste
- ¼ cup snipped fresh parsley (or 2 tablespoons dried parsley flakes)
- 1 tablespoon dried basil leaves
- 2 teaspoons sugar
- 1½ teaspoons dried marjoram leaves
- 1 teaspoon salt
- ½ teaspoon dried thyme leaves
- ½ teaspoon dried oregano leaves
- ¼ teaspoon ground nutmeg
- ¼ teaspoon pepper
- 1 small bay leaf

In fryer/cooker sauté onion, green pepper, mushrooms, garlic and carrot in olive oil until tender. Add remaining ingredients. Heat on "Hi" to boiling.

Reduce heat to "3" or "4". Simmer, uncovered, 1½ to 2 hours, or until thick. Stir occasionally. Serve over pasta.

Meat Sauce: Follow the recipe above, except first cook 1½ pounds ground beef until browned. Drain off fat. Add onion, green pepper, mushrooms, garlic, carrot and olive oil. Continue as directed. Increase water to 4 cups.

TIP: Sauce may be frozen up to 2 months.

About 2 quarts

Paella

- 2 tablespoons olive oil
- 6 bone-in chicken breast halves (about 2½ to 3 pounds)
- 1 green pepper, chopped
- 1 medium onion, chopped
- 1 clove garlic, minced
- 2 cups uncooked long-grain rice
- 1 large tomato, peeled and chopped
- 1 cup cubed fully-cooked ham
- 3¾ cups water
- 1 tablespoon instant chicken bouillon granules
- ½ teaspoon salt
- ¼ teaspoon saffron or ½ teaspoon ground turmeric
- ⅛ teaspoon cayenne
- 1½ pounds medium-size raw shrimp, shelled and deveined
- 1 cup frozen green peas

In fryer/cooker on setting "10", heat oil until hot. Cook chicken breasts in oil until browned. Remove chicken from cooker. Set aside.

Sauté green pepper, onion and garlic in remaining oil on setting "8", until tender. Stir in rice, tomato, ham, water, bouillon granules, salt, saffron and cayenne. Place chicken, skin-side up, on top of mixture. Heat to boiling. Simmer on setting "3" or "4", covered, 10 minutes.

Arrange shrimp on and around chicken. Sprinkle peas over top. Simmer, covered, 15 to 20 minutes, or until shrimp are firm and opaque.

6 to 8 servings

Poached Whole Fish

Poaching Liquid:
- 8 cups water
- 2 cups dry white wine
- 1½ teaspoons dried parsley flakes (or 1 tablespoon snipped fresh parsley)
- 1½ teaspoons grated lime peel
- 8 whole peppercorns
- 2 bay leaves
- 1 carrot, cut into 2-inch pieces
- 1 stalk celery, cut into 2-inch pieces
- 1 small onion, sliced

- 1 whole pan-dressed trout, bass, whitefish or flounder (up to 12 inches long) or salmon piece

For poaching liquid: In fryer/cooker, combine all ingredients. Heat to boiling. Simmer on setting "4", covered, 15 minutes.

Place fish in wire fry basket. Lower basket into simmering liquid. Add more boiling water to cover fish if necessary. Simmer on setting "4" or "5", covered, until fish flakes easily.

To determine cooking time, measure thickness of fish. Cook fish 9 to 11 minutes per inch of thickness.

3 to 4 servings per pound

Paella

Seafood Gumbo

¾ cup butter or margarine, divided
2 boneless chicken breast halves (about ¾ pound), skinned, and cut into bite-size pieces
¾ cup all-purpose flour
1½ cups sliced celery
2 medium-size green peppers, chopped
1 large onion, chopped
¼ cup snipped fresh parsley
2 cloves garlic, minced
1 can (28 ounces) whole tomatoes, chopped and juice reserved
4 cups hot water
2 cans (10½ ounces each) chicken broth
1 can (6 ounces) tomato paste
½ pound fully-cooked Polish sausage or fully-cooked ham, chopped (optional)
2 tablespoons Worcestershire sauce
1 package (16 ounces) frozen sliced okra, thawed
2 teaspoons salt
1½ teaspoons sugar
1 teaspoon dried basil leaves
½ teaspoon dried thyme leaves
⅛ to ¼ teaspoon saffron (optional)
2 bay leaves
1 or 2 whole dried red chili peppers
2 pounds medium-size raw shrimp, shelled and deveined, cut in half crosswise*
2 pounds fully-cooked crab claws, cracked, meat removed*
1 pint shucked oysters, drained
Filé powder**

In fryer/cooker on setting "8", melt ¼ cup butter. Add chicken pieces. Sauté 6 to 9 minutes, or until

meat is no longer pink. Remove chicken from cooker. Refrigerate.

Add remaining ½ cup butter to drippings. Heat until melted. Stir in flour until smooth. Cook, stirring constantly, 10 to 12 minutes, or until flour is deep brown. Reduce heat to setting "4" or "5".

Add celery, green pepper, onion, parsley and garlic all at once to flour mixture. Immediately stir to blend. Cook vegetables 25 to 30 minutes, or until tender. Stir occasionally.

Stir in tomatoes, water, chicken broth, tomato paste, Polish sausage, Worcestershire sauce, okra, salt, sugar, basil, thyme, saffron, bay leaves and chili peppers. Heat on "Hi" to boiling. Reduce heat to setting "3" or "4". Simmer, uncovered, 2½ hours.

Add chicken, shrimp, crab meat, and oysters. Simmer, uncovered, 30 to 35 minutes, or until shrimp are opaque and oysters are firm.

Before serving, remove whole chilies and bay leaf. Serve over rice in bowls. Add filé powder to individual servings, as desired.

*Frozen shrimp and crab meat may be substituted, if desired.

**Available in gourmet section or seafood market.

TIP: If a thinner gumbo is desired, add water just before serving.

16 to 20 servings

Clam and Corn Chowder

granules, salt and pepper until smooth. Add pota-toes, carrots and reserved bacon. Gradually blend in reserved liquid from clams plus enough water to measure 2½ cups. Heat to boiling. Simmer on setting "5" or "6", covered, 15 to 20 minutes, or until potatoes are tender. Stir occasionally.

Add clams, corn and pimientos. Heat, stirring occasionally, 5 minutes longer.

Stir in milk and half-and-half. Heat chowder on setting "8", stirring occasionally, until thermometer registers 160°F.

About 2 quarts

Clam and Corn Chowder

    6 slices bacon, cut-up
    1 medium onion, chopped
    ½ cup chopped celery
    ¼ cup all-purpose flour
    2 tablespoons dried parsley flakes (or ¼ cup
       snipped fresh parsley)
    ½ teaspoon dried marjoram leaves
    1 teaspoon instant chicken bouillon granules
    ¼ teaspoon salt
    ¼ teaspoon pepper
    2 cups cubed (½-inch cubes) raw potatoes
       (about 1 pound)
    ½ cup chopped carrot
    3 cans (6½ ounces each) minced clams,
       drained, liquid reserved
       Water
    2 cups frozen whole kernel corn or 1 can
       (16 ounces) whole kernel corn, drained
    1 jar (2 ounces) diced pimientos, drained
 1½ cups milk
    1 cup half-and-half

In fryer/cooker on setting "10", fry bacon, stirring constantly, until browned and crisp. With slotted spoon, remove bacon from cooker. Set aside.

Sauté onion and celery in bacon drippings until tender. Stir in flour, parsley, marjoram, bouillon

Chicken Vegetable Soup

 2½ to 3-pound broiler-fryer chicken
    8 cups hot water, divided
    ½ cup dry white wine (optional)
    1 clove garlic, minced
 1½ teaspoons salt
    1 teaspoon dried basil leaves
    1 teaspoon dried chervil leaves
    ¼ teaspoon dried thyme leaves
    ¼ teaspoon pepper
    2 cups chopped cabbage
    1 cup chopped celery
    1 cup frozen cut green beans
    3 medium carrots, cut into ¼-inch slices
    2 medium zucchini (about ¼ pound each),
       cut lengthwise in half, then cut into
       ¼-inch slices
    1 medium onion, chopped
    ½ cup uncooked long-grain rice

Place chicken in fryer/cooker. Add 3 cups water, white wine, garlic, salt, basil, chervil, thyme and pepper. Heat on "Hi" to boiling.

Reduce heat to "4" or "5". Simmer, covered, 1¼ to 1½ hours, or until chicken is fork tender. Turn cook-er off. Remove chicken from liquid. Discard skin and fat. Cut meat from bones and chop into bite-size pieces.

Return chicken to broth. Stir in remaining 5 cups water, cabbage, celery, green beans, carrots, zuc-chini, onion and rice. Heat, covered, to boiling.

Reduce heat to "3" or "4". Simmer 20 to 30 minutes, or until vegetables are tender.

TIP: Prepared soup may be frozen up to 3 months. To serve, thaw and heat through.

About 2½ to 3 quarts

Cream of Vegetable Soup

1½ pounds broccoli
1½ pounds cauliflower
 2 cups water
 1 teaspoon instant chicken bouillon granules
 ½ teaspoon salt
 ⅔ cup butter or margarine
 ⅔ cup all-purpose flour
 ½ teaspoon dried sage
 6 drops hot pepper sauce
 7 cups milk
 2 cups shredded Cheddar cheese

Trim tough ends from broccoli. Discard. Cut into spears. Remove core from cauliflower. Separate into flowerets. Place spears and flowerets in fryer/cooker. Add water, bouillon granules and salt. Cover. Heat on "Hi" to boiling.

Reduce heat to "4" or "5". Simmer, stirring once, 20 to 25 minutes, or until vegetables are tender. Turn off heat. With slotted spoon, remove vegetables. Reserve liquid. Chop vegetables. Set aside.

In small saucepan melt butter. Blend in flour, sage and pepper sauce until smooth. Gradually blend flour mixture into liquid in cooker. Gradually blend in milk. Heat on setting "8", stirring occasionally, until mixture thickens and just comes to boil. Stir in cheese until melted. Add reserved vegetables. Heat until thermometer registers 160°F.

TIP: Ingredients can be cut in half for smaller quantity of soup.

About 2½ to 3 quarts

Christmas Spirit

 1 large orange, cut into thick slices
18 whole cloves
 4 quarts cranberry-apple juice
 ¼ cup packed brown sugar
 4 sticks cinnamon
 1 to 1½ cups light rum (optional)

Stud each orange slice with several cloves.

In fryer/cooker combine orange slices, cranberry-apple juice, brown sugar and cinnamon sticks. Heat, stirring constantly, until sugar dissolves. Do not boil. Steep on "Lo", covered, 30 minutes to blend flavors. Just before serving, stir in rum.

About 4 quarts

Winter Warmer Cocoa

Winter Warmer Cocoa

1¾ cups sugar
 1 cup cocoa
 ¼ teaspoon salt
10 cups milk, divided
 2 cups half-and-half
 ¾ cup creme de cacao
 ½ cup Kirsch
   Whipped cream (optional)

In fryer/cooker combine sugar, cocoa and salt. Gradually blend in 2 cups milk. Add remaining 8 cups milk and half-and-half. Heat on setting "9" or "10", stirring constantly, or until thermometer registers 150° to 160°F.

Reduce heat to "Lo". Stir in creme de cacao and Kirsch until blended. Ladle cocoa into cups. Top with whipped cream.

Spiced Cocoa: Follow recipe above, except add ½ teaspoon ground nutmeg to sugar mixture. After blending in 2 cups milk, add 3 or 4 cinnamon sticks. Heat as directed. Before serving remove cinnamon sticks.

About 3½ quarts

Marinades & Sauces

The right sauce or marinade can make a dish truly memorable. Marinades not only add flavor, but also tenderize meat. Allow about ½ cup marinade for each pound of meat. Marinate 4 to 6 hours or overnight, depending on how strong you want the flavor. Remember to cool any mixture before using as a marinade. Here are some tempting ideas. So go ahead — flavor up your meal!

Marinade Guide

Type	Ingredients and Procedure	For Use On
Curry 1 cup	1½ teaspoons curry powder, 1 teaspoon sugar, ¼ teaspoon ground nutmeg, ⅓ cup soy sauce, ¼ cup lemon juice, ¼ cup vegetable oil, 3 tablespoons water, 1 tablespoon honey, 1 clove garlic, minced. In small saucepan combine all ingredients. Heat to boiling, stirring constantly. Reduce heat. Cover. Simmer 5 minutes, stirring occasionally. Cool.	Beef Pork Chicken Lamb
Garlic Dill Butter ½ cup	1 large clove garlic (quartered), ½ cup butter, ¼ teaspoon lemon pepper seasoning, ¼ teaspoon dried dill weed. In small saucepan sauté garlic in butter until brown. Remove and discard garlic. Add remaining ingredients.	Fish Seafood
Lemony Herb About ¾ cup	½ cup vegetable oil, ¼ cup fresh lemon juice, ½ teaspoon dried oregano leaves, ¼ teaspoon ground cumin, ¼ teaspoon salt. In small mixing bowl combine all ingredients.	Chicken Lamb
Polynesian About 1 cup	¼ cup pineapple juice, ¼ cup soy sauce, ¼ cup vegetable oil, ¼ cup packed brown sugar, 2 tablespoons dry sherry, 1 teaspoon Worcestershire sauce, ½ teaspoon ground ginger. In small mixing bowl combine all ingredients.	Beef Pork Chicken
Red Wine About 1¼ cups	½ cup dry red wine, ½ cup water, 3 tablespoons coarsely chopped onion, 1 clove garlic (quartered), 3 tablespoons lime juice, 2 tablespoons packed brown sugar, ½ teaspoon salt. In small saucepan combine all ingredients. Heat to boiling, stirring constantly. Reduce heat. Cover. Simmer 5 minutes, stirring occasionally. Cool.	Beef
Variation	Follow the recipe above, substituting 1 can (10¾ ounces) beef consommé for wine and water.	
Teriyaki ¾ cup	¼ cup water, ¼ cup soy sauce, 2 tablespoons dry sherry, 1 tablespoon sesame oil (optional), 2 tablespoons packed brown sugar, ¼ cup chopped green onion, 1 clove garlic (quartered), ½ teaspoon minced fresh gingerroot. In small saucepan combine all ingredients. Heat to boiling, stirring constantly. Reduce heat. Cover. Simmer 5 minutes, stirring occasionally. Remove garlic. Cool.	Beef Chicken Pork Shrimp Fish
White Wine ¾ cup	½ cup dry white wine, ¼ cup olive oil, 1 teaspoon dried basil or oregano leaves, 1 teaspoon Worcestershire sauce, ½ teaspoon salt, ¼ teaspoon coarsely ground pepper, ⅛ teaspoon garlic powder. In small mixing bowl combine all ingredients.	Beef Veal Pork
Variation	Follow the recipe above, substituting 1 teaspoon dried rosemary for basil.	Lamb
Variation	Follow the recipe above, substituting 1 teaspoon dried tarragon leaves for basil.	Fish Shrimp Chicken

White Wine Marinade

Barbecue Sauce

Sauce Guide

Type	Ingredients and Procedure	For Use On
Barbecue About 1¾ cups	1 can (8 ounces) tomato sauce, ½ cup chopped onion, ⅓ cup packed brown sugar, ¼ cup catsup, ¼ cup vinegar, 1 tablespoon chili powder, 2 tablespoons prepared mustard, 1 clove minced garlic. In small saucepan combine all ingredients. Heat to boiling, stirring constantly. Reduce heat. Simmer, uncovered, 5 minutes, stirring occasionally.	Beef Pork Chicken
Bearnaise 1 cup	¼ cup vinegar, 1 tablespoon minced onion, 1 teaspoon dried tarragon leaves, ½ teaspoon dried parsley flakes, dash salt, ¾ cup butter or margarine, 4 beaten egg yolks. In small saucepan combine vinegar, onion, tarragon, parsley and salt. Cook, uncovered, on medium high heat until mixture is reduced by half. Set aside. In another small saucepan melt butter on medium high heat. Set aside. With wire whisk beat egg yolks into reduced vinegar mixture. Return to heat on medium low. Immediately pour melted butter into egg yolk mixture in a steady stream, beating with wire whisk while pouring. Cook, beating constantly, until mixture thickens. Serve hot.	Beef Eggs Fish

Type	Ingredients and Procedure	For Use On
Brandy Peach 2 cups	1 cup packed brown sugar, ⅓ cup orange juice, ¼ cup raisins, 3 tablespoons butter or margarine, 3 tablespoons brandy, 1 can (8¾ ounces) sliced, drained and chopped peaches.	Ham Ice cream Cake
	In small saucepan combine brown sugar, orange juice, raisins and butter. Heat to boiling, stirring constantly. Boil and stir 1 minute. Cool slightly. Stir in brandy and chopped peaches.	
Brown 1 cup	3 tablespoons butter or margarine, 3 tablespoons all-purpose flour, 1 cup beef broth.	Beef Pork
	In small saucepan melt butter. Stir in flour until smooth. Cook, stirring constantly until flour is deep brown. Gradually blend in beef broth. Heat to boiling, stirring constantly, until mixture thickens and just comes to boil.	
Butter Rum 1¼ cups	⅔ cup sugar, ⅓ cup dark corn syrup, ¼ cup butter or margarine, ⅓ cup half-and-half or whipping cream, ¾ teaspoon rum extract.	Ice cream Cake
	In medium saucepan combine sugar, corn syrup and butter. Cook on medium high heat, stirring constantly, until candy thermometer registers 234°F. Cover. Remove from heat. Cool 5 minutes. With wire whisk beat in half-and-half and rum extract until blended.	
Chocolate Rum	Follow the recipe above except after cooling sugar mixture, stir in 1 square (1 ounce) unsweetened chocolate until melted. Continue as directed.	
Butterscotch	Follow the recipe above, except omit rum extract.	
Cherry 2 cups	⅓ cup sugar, 1 tablespoon plus 2 teaspoons cornstarch, 1 can (16 ounces) dark sweet cherries (drained, with juice reserved), ½ cup port wine, 1 cinnamon stick.	Ice cream Plain cake
	In small saucepan combine sugar and cornstarch. Gradually blend in reserved cherry juice and wine. Add cinnamon stick. Heat, stirring constantly, until mixture thickens and boils. Stir in reserved cherries. Serve warm.	
Hot Mustard ¼ cup	¼ cup dry mustard, 1 tablespoon packed brown sugar (optional), 6 to 7 teaspoons water, vinegar or white wine.	Beef Pork Chicken Egg rolls Wontons
	In small bowl combine dry mustard and brown sugar. Gradually stir in water until mixture is of desired consistency. Let stand at room temperature at least 10 minutes.	
Lemon Cream About 1½ cups	½ cup chilled whipping cream, ¼ cup confectioners' sugar, 3 tablespoons dairy sour cream, 1 tablespoon lemon juice, ¾ teaspoon grated lemon peel, 2 tablespoons whipping cream.	Pound cake Angel food cake Grilled fruit
	In chilled deep bowl beat ½ cup whipping cream until stiff peaks form, gradually adding sugar. Set aside. In small bowl blend remaining ingredients. Fold into whipped cream.	
Mint 1¼ cups	⅔ cup cider vinegar, ⅓ cup water, ⅓ cup apple jelly, 1 tablespoon dried mint leaves.	Lamb
	In small saucepan combine all ingredients. Heat to boiling, stirring constantly. Reduce heat. Simmer, uncovered, 5 minutes, stirring occasionally.	
Variation	Follow the recipe above, substituting ⅓ cup sugar for apple jelly.	Lamb

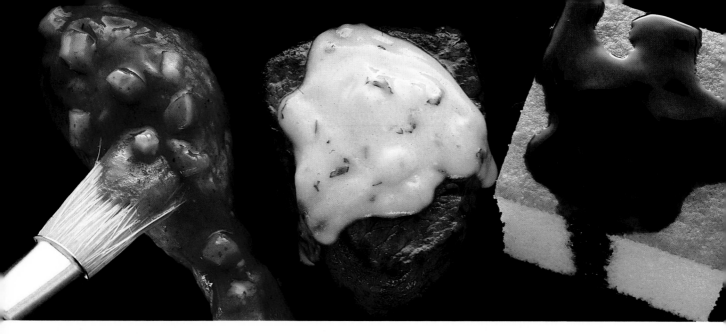

Sauce Guide (cont.)

Type	Ingredients and Procedure	For Use On
Mushroom About 2 cups	3 tablespoons butter or margarine, 1½ cups sliced fresh mushrooms, 2 tablespoons minced green onion, 3 tablespoons all-purpose flour, ¼ teaspoon white pepper, dash garlic powder, 1 cup milk, ¼ teaspoon Worcestershire sauce, ½ teaspoon instant beef bouillon granules, 1 tablespoon sherry (optional). In saucepan melt butter. Add mushrooms and onion. Sauté until just tender. Stir in flour, white pepper and garlic powder until smooth. Gradually blend in milk. Add Worcestershire sauce and bouillon granules. Heat to boiling, stirring constantly until mixture thickens and just comes to boil. Stir in sherry. Serve warm.	Chicken Fish Veal Beef
Orange Glaze About ⅔ cup	½ cup orange marmalade, 2 tablespoons packed brown sugar, ½ teaspoon dried mint leaves. In small saucepan combine all ingredients. Heat on medium high heat, stirring constantly, until sugar dissolves.	Fruit kebabs Chicken Lamb
Apricot Glaze	Follow the recipe above, substituting ½ cup apricot preserves for orange marmalade. Substitute 1 teaspoon lemon juice for mint leaves.	
Orange Raisin 1½ cups	1 cup water, ⅔ cup orange juice, 2 tablespoons cornstarch, ⅛ teaspoon ground allspice, ⅛ teaspoon salt, ½ cup orange marmalade, ⅔ cup raisins. In small saucepan blend water, orange juice, cornstarch, allspice and salt until smooth. Heat, stirring constantly until mixture thickens and boils. Stir in orange marmalade and raisins. Cook, stirring constantly, until marmalade melts and raisins soften.	Ham Pork Pound cake Ice cream
Raspberry Glaze About ¾ cup	1 tablespoon cornstarch, ¼ teaspoon salt, ⅛ teaspoon ground cinnamon, 4 tablespoons lemon juice (divided), ½ cup raspberry jelly, 2 tablespoons butter or margarine. In small bowl blend cornstarch, salt, cinnamon and 2 tablespoons lemon juice until smooth. Set aside. In small saucepan combine jelly, butter and 2 tablespoons lemon juice. Heat on medium high heat, stirring constantly, until jelly melts. Blend in cornstarch mixture. Heat, stirring constantly, until mixture thickens and boils. Use to glaze chicken during last portion of cooking time.	Chicken

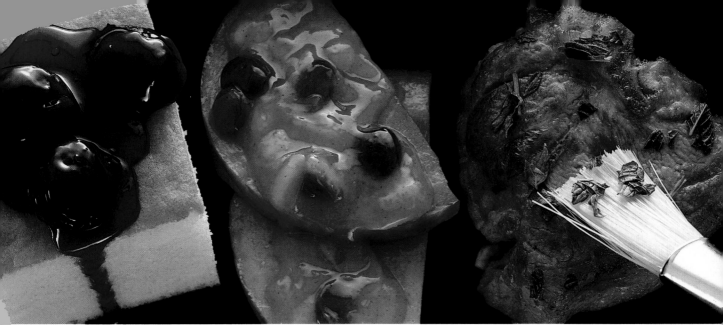

Barbecue Sauce, Bearnaise Sauce, Chocolate Rum Sauce, Cherry Sauce, Orange Raisin Sauce, Mint Sauce

Type	Ingredients and Procedure	For Use On
Smoky Southern Barbecue 1⅓ cups	¾ cup catsup, ¼ cup water, ¼ cup dark molasses, ¼ cup honey, 2 tablespoons cider vinegar, 2 tablespoons minced onion, 2 teaspoons all-purpose flour, ½ teaspoon dry mustard, ¼ teaspoon liquid smoke, dash celery salt. In small saucepan combine all ingredients. Heat to boiling, stirring constantly. Reduce heat to medium low. Simmer, uncovered, 10 minutes, stirring occasionally.	Beef Pork Chicken
Spiced Caramel 1 cup	2 teaspoons cornstarch, ⅓ cup cold water, ¼ cup butter or margarine (cut into pieces), ¼ cup packed brown sugar, 2 tablespoons honey, ¼ teaspoon ground ginger, ⅛ teaspoon ground nutmeg. In small saucepan blend cornstarch and water until smooth. Stir in remaining ingredients. Heat on medium high heat, stirring constantly, until mixture thickens and boils. Serve warm.	Rotissed apples Ice cream Pound cake
Sweet and Sour 1¼ cups	1 tablespoon plus 1 teaspoon cornstarch, ¼ cup cold water, ⅓ cup pineapple preserves, ⅓ cup packed brown sugar, ⅓ cup vinegar, 2 tablespoons prepared chili sauce, 1 tablespoon minced onion, ½ teaspoon salt. In small saucepan blend cornstarch and water until smooth. Stir in remaining ingredients. Heat, stirring constantly, until mixture thickens and boils.	Beef Pork Chicken Egg rolls
White About 1¼ cups	2 tablespoons butter or margarine, 2 tablespoons all-purpose flour, ¼ teaspoon salt, ⅛ teaspoon white pepper, ⅔ cup milk, ⅔ cup half-and-half. In small saucepan melt butter. Stir in flour, salt and pepper until smooth. Gradually blend in milk and half-and-half. Heat on medium high heat, stirring constantly, until mixture thickens and just comes to boil.	Vegetables Pasta
Cheese Sauce	Follow the recipe above, except add to thickened sauce 1 cup shredded Cheddar, Colby or Swiss cheese. Stir until cheese melts.	Pasta Vegetables Fish
Thick White Sauce	Follow the recipe above, except increase both flour and butter to 3 tablespoons each.	
Thin White Sauce	Follow the recipe above, except decrease both flour and butter to 1 tablespoon each.	

Combination Cooking

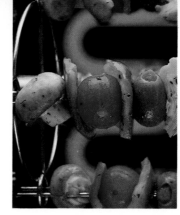

With all the accessories at your fingertips, it's easy to combine them for creative cooking. Use several different accessories in a sequence to create a single dish, or use them simultaneously to prepare an entire meal. Combine your range accessories and oven with other kitchen appliances for speed, convenience and versatility. Your blender, food processor, microwave oven and other appliances can work with your cooking system to save time and add special touches to your menus. The ideas on these pages will get you started with combination cooking. Use your imagination to adapt your own favorite recipes and create new ones using this versatile style of food preparation.

Combining Accessories to Prepare a Single Recipe

The accessories in your cooking system offer you unique and efficient ways to accomplish various steps in a recipe. Add the reheating ability of your microwave or radiant bake/convection oven, and you're all set to prepare foods in advance to be served later. Here are just a few examples of how accessories can be combined to create a single dish. Many of your own recipes can also be adapted for this kind of combination cooking.

Boil bagels in water in the wok or fryer/cooker. Bake in convection oven as directed on page 161.

Simmer corned beef in the wok or fryer/cooker as directed on page 90. Then rotiss or bake with your favorite glaze.

Grill extra hamburgers, steaks or chicken and freeze or refrigerate them. Reheat in the microwave oven for grilled flavor at another meal.

Steam foods like sausages or ribs in the wok or fryer/cooker to partially cook them before grilling. Finish on the grill for barbecued flavor and texture in less time.

Bake Sourdough English Muffins on the griddle as directed on page 36. Split, toast and top with your favorite cheese. Heat in the convection or radiant bake oven until cheese melts.

Start roasts or whole poultry in the microwave oven and finish them on the rotisserie to save time.

Bake potatoes in the convection or radiant bake oven. Use the wok or fryer/cooker to deep-fry the skins for Fried Potato Skins, page 76.

Prepare beef and vegetables for Steak and Vegetable Pie, page 119, in the wok. Assemble the pie and bake in the convection or radiant bake oven.

Combining Accessories to Prepare an Entire Meal

Whether you're entertaining or just preparing an everyday meal, you can put several parts of your cooking system to work at once to save time and steps. By using parts of an extra grill accessory, you can use even more accessories at the same time. This kind of combination cooking can be as simple as grilling appetizers while a roast cooks on the rotisserie. More elaborate menus may feature a dessert in the oven, soup in the wok, baked rolls rewarmed in the microwave and meat cooked on the grill. Here are some menus we've put together using recipes from this book. Add meal accompaniments such as salads and breads to complete the meals. You'll enjoy combining your own favorite recipes to make the most of the cooking methods at your fingertips.

Ladies Brunch
Oven	Sour Cream Brunch Bake, page 143
Griddle	Sourdough English Muffins, page 36 (prepare ahead)
Wok	Blushing Pears, page 76 (prepare ahead)

Holiday Dinner
Oven	Artichoke Squares, page 115 (prepare ahead)
Oven	Rich Cheese Puffs, page 113 (prepare ahead)
Oven	Roast Turkey, page 109
Cooktop	Broccoli, served with Cheese Sauce, chart on page 101
Kebab	Mixed Vegetable Kebabs, page 59
Wok	Plum Pudding with Vanilla Sauce, page 78 (prepare ahead)

Chinese Dinner
Fryer/Cooker or Wok and Oven	Egg Rolls, page 83 (prepare ahead and reheat)
Cooktop	Sweet and Sour Sauce, chart on page 101 (serve with Egg Rolls)
Rotisserie	Duck with Hoisin Glaze, page 49
Wok	Fried Rice, page 75

Company Dinner
Grill	Marinated Shrimp Appetizers, page 12
Grill	London Broil, page 15
Oven	Twice-Baked Potatoes, page 147
Oven	Onion and Artichoke au Gratin, page 147
Oven	Bread Sticks, page 160 (prepare ahead)
Kebab	Fruit and Cake Kebabs, page 59

Family Dinner
Griddle	Breaded Pork Chops, page 31
Oven	Sweet Potato Puff, page 149
Oven	Lemon-Dill Green Beans, page 146
Wok	Creamy Custard, page 78
Cooktop	Spiced Caramel Sauce, chart on page 101 (serve with custard)

Family Cookout Cooked-in
Kebabs	Antipasto Kebabs, page 58
Grill	Smoky Hamburgers, page 18
Grill	Toasted Hamburger Buns, page 25
Oven	Baked Beans, page 145 (prepare ahead)
Oven	Toffee Bars, page 176 (prepare ahead)

Rainy Day Lunch
Fryer/Cooker	Chicken Vegetable Soup, page 94
Griddle	Grilled Vegetarian Sandwiches, chart on page 38
Oven	Apple Crisp, page 175

Oven

Chances are, many of your favorite foods are dishes that come from the oven. Succulent roasts, delicate pastries, hearty casseroles and other delicious foods are oven specialties. In this section, we present a unique collection of recipes that has been specially developed for excellent results in either the **radiant bake** (conventional) or **convection oven.**

Most of the recipes in this section include both radiant bake and convection instructions. If your oven has both settings, we suggest using convection. The constantly recirculating air of the **convection oven** cooks foods more quickly and makes three-rack cooking possible. Meats stay more flavorful and juicy with less shrinkage. For recipes which list only radiant bake times, there is little advantage to convection cooking and the radiant bake setting is recommended.

Use the following techniques to help you get the best results from either the **convection** or **radiant bake oven.** The oven ideas at the end of this section offer more helpful tips. You'll find complete oven meals, recipes that use the oven in unusual ways — even directions for making dough art!

Use quality baking utensils, making sure the size is the same as that called for in the recipe. Shiny metal pans produce a light, golden crust. Enamel or glass pans will generally produce a crisp, brown crust.

Preheat oven only when necessary. A preheated oven is recommended for baked foods to help them rise and brown properly. Oven is preheated when the bake light cycles off. Foods like casseroles and roasts can be started in a cold oven. Low voltage may make preheating necessary for some of the convection recipes in this cookbook.

Arrange pans on opposite corners of the rack. When baking on two racks, stagger pans so that one does not shield another. Leave 1 to 1½ inches of space between pans and the sides of the oven walls. These techniques promote better heat circulation in the oven.

Adapt your own radiant bake recipes for use in the **convection oven.** For baked goods that require rising and browning, reduce the temperature by 25°F. Baking times should be about the same or slightly less. For other recipes, maintain the original temperature and reduce the time slightly.

Choose cookie sheets that do not have sides for convection baking. These allow circulating air to reach foods most effectively. A jelly roll pan or cookie sheet with sides can be inverted and used as a baking surface. Place on the oven rack according to the instructions in your use and care manual.

Pictured on preceding page: Braided Egg Loaf, recipe page 156

Bake frozen convenience foods according to package directions for oven temperature, foil covering and use of cookie sheets. Baking times will be similar. Preheating is not necessary.

Save time and energy by baking quantities of foods on multiple racks. The circulating heat of the **convection oven** is preferred for multiple-rack cooking. The **radiant bake oven** also provides good results for two-rack cooking, especially if pans can be staggered. Place racks in positions 1 and 3 for two-rack baking. (Positions 2 and 4 also provide satisfactory results.) For three-rack baking, use positions 1, 3 and 5 (except for pizza, which should be placed in positions 2, 3 and 4), or as specified in your recipe. (See additional directions below.)

Remove food on racks 1 and 5 first, allowing additional cooking time for browning foods on the middle rack. Thin foods like cookies will need 30 to 60 seconds longer. For biscuits, rolls or muffins, allow 1 to 3 minutes longer. Frozen pies and pizzas (which should be baked on a cookie sheet) will need about 2 to 4 minutes longer.

Choose convection or radiant baking, depending on the type of meat. Convection cooking is best for faster roasting of tender meat. Frozen meats (except poultry) can go right from the freezer to the **convection oven.** Use radiant baking for less-tender meats that require long, moist cooking, and for foods prepared in cooking bags, Dutch ovens or covered roasting pans.

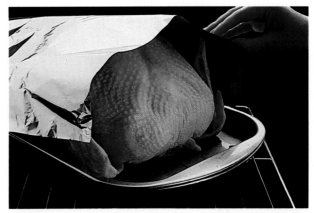

Prepare meats and poultry for convection roasting by placing on the slotted portion of the two-piece roasting pan included with the oven. Do not use a roasting pan with high sides. Do not cover roasts. Place roasts fat-side up so meat will self-baste. When large poultry reaches the desired degree of browning, shield the breast portion with a foil "tent". This prevents overbrowning.

Use a meat thermometer to test meats and poultry for doneness. Place thermometer in the thickest portion of the meat, making sure thermometer tip does not touch bone, fat or gristle. For poultry, insert thermometer in the thickest part of the inner thigh. Since meats continue to cook after they have been removed from the oven, remove roast from oven when it reaches an internal temperature about 5 degrees below the desired final temperature (see chart, page 109). For easier carving, let roast stand about 15 minutes after removing from oven.

Baking Guide

Item	Pan Size	Rack* Position	Convection Temp. (°F) Preheated***	Convection Time** (minutes)	Radiant Bake Temp. (°F) Preheated	Radiant Bake Time** (minutes)
Cake						
Yellow, 2 layers	9"	2 or 3	325°	30 to 35	350°	30 to 35
White, 2 layers	9"	2 or 3	325°	22 to 30	350°	25 to 30
Chocolate, 2 layers	9"	2 or 3	325°	30 to 35	350°	30 to 35
Bundt	tube	1 or 2	325°	40 to 45	350°	35 to 45
Angel Food	tube	1 or 2	350°	28 to 30	375°	30 to 40
Pound Cake	loaf	2	300°	40 to 50	325°	40 to 50
Snack Cake	8 × 8"	2	350°	25 to 30	375°	30 to 35
Cupcakes		3	325°	15 to 20	350°	15 to 20
Sheet Cake	15 × 10"	3	325°	20 to 25	350°	20 to 25
Pies						
Two-crust						
Fruit, fresh	9"	2	375° to 400°	35 to 45	400° to 425°	35 to 55
Fruit, frozen	9"	1	375° to 400°	45 to 55	400° to 425°	45 to 60
One-crust						
Custard, fresh	9"	3	325°	45 to 50	350°	35 to 40
Custard, frozen	9"	1	350°	50	375°	60 to 65
Pie Shell	9"	2	400° to 425°	10 to 15	425° to 450°	8 to 12
Cookies						
Chocolate Chip		3	325° to 350°	8 to 12	350° to 375°	8 to 12
Peanut Butter		3	325° to 350°	8 to 12	350° to 375°	8 to 12
Sugar		3	325° to 350°	8 to 12	350° to 375°	8 to 12
Brownies	8 × 8"	2	325°	30 to 40	350°	30 to 40
Breads, Yeast						
Loaf	loaf	1 or 2	350°	25 to 30	375°	30 to 40
Rolls		3	375°	10 to 15	375° to 400°	15 to 20
Breads, Quick						
Loaf, nut or fruit	loaf	2	325°	60 to 75	350°	60 to 75
Gingerbread	9 × 9"	2	325°	40	350°	40
Cornbread	8 × 8"	2	375° to 400°	15 to 30	400° to 450°	15 to 30
Cornbread Muffins		3	375°	10 to 15	400°	10 to 20
Biscuits		3	375° to 400°	10 to 20	400° to 425°	10 to 20
Muffins		3	375°	15 to 25	400°	15 to 25

*For Multiple Rack Baking, see page 107.

**Times given are based on specific brands of mixes or recipes tested. Actual times will depend on the ones you bake.

***The convection temperature is 25°F lower than recommended on package mix or recipe.

Roasting Guide (Thawed Meats Only)

Item	Weight (pounds)	Oven Temp. (°F)	Final Internal Temp.	Convection Roasting Time (minutes per pound)*	Radiant Bake Roasting Time (minutes per pound)*
Beef					
Rib Roast	4 to 8	325°	140° (rare) - 160° (well)	20 to 30	25 to 35
Rib Eye Roast	4 to 6	325°	140° (rare) - 160° (well)	20 to 30	25 to 35
Tenderloin Roast	2 to 3	400°	140° (rare)	15 to 20	20 to 25
Eye of Round Roast	4 to 5	325°	140° (rare) - 160° (well)	20 to 30	25 to 35
Top Sirloin Roast	3 to 6	325°	140° (rare) - 160° (well)	20 to 30	25 to 35
Round Tip Roast	4 to 6	325°	140° (rare) - 160° (well)	20 to 30	25 to 35
Pork					
Shoulder Blade Roast, boneless	4 to 6	325°	170°	30 to 40	35 to 45
Shoulder Blade Roast	4 to 6	325°	170°	25 to 35	30 to 40
Loin Blade or Sirloin Roast	3 to 4	325°	170°	30 to 40	35 to 45
Leg, fresh ham	10 to 16	325°	170°	20 to 30	25 to 35
Ham Half, fully-cooked	5 to 7	325°	140°	20 to 30	25 to 35
Ham, cured, uncooked	5 to 7	275°	160°	30 to 40	35 to 45
Arm Picnic Shoulder, fully cooked	5 to 8	325°	140°	20 to 25	25 to 30
Lamb					
Shoulder Roast, boneless	3½ to 5	325°	160° (med.) - 170° (well)	30 to 40	35 to 45
Leg, whole	5 to 7	325°	160° (med.) - 170° (well)	25 to 35	30 to 40
Leg, shank half	3 to 4	325°	160° (med.) - 170° (well)	25 to 35	30 to 40
Leg, sirloin half	3 to 4	325°	160° (med.) - 170° (well)	30 to 40	35 to 45
Veal					
Rib Roast	3 to 5	325°	170°	35 to 40	40 to 45
Shoulder, boneless	4 to 6	325°	170°	35 to 40	40 to 45
Leg Half, boneless	3 to 5	325°	170°	35 to 40	40 to 50
Poultry					
Turkey, unstuffed	8 to 16	325°	180° to 185°	14 to 18	18 to 22
	16 to 24	325°	180° to 185°	10 to 14	14 to 18
Turkey, whole, boneless	4 to 6	350°	170° to 175°	25 to 35	35 to 45
Turkey, breast	3 to 8	325°	180°	25 to 35	30 to 40
Chicken, fryer	2½ to 3½	375°	185°	18 to 22	20 to 24
Chicken, roaster	4 to 6	375°	185°	15 to 20	20 to 25
Capon, unstuffed	5 to 8	375°	180° to 185°	15 to 20	20 to 25
Cornish Hen	1 to 1½	375°	180° to 185°	35 to 45	45 to 55
Duck	4 to 6	350°	185°	15 to 20	20 to 25

*Time per pound will vary according to the size, shape, quality and starting temperature of the meat (times above are based on refrigerator-cold meat). Electrical voltage in your area will also affect time.

Appetizers

Layered Terrine

8 slices bacon, divided
2 medium onions, minced
2 cloves garlic, minced
¼ cup butter or margarine
8 ounces chicken livers, puréed or minced
½ pound ground pork
½ pound ground veal
1½ teaspoons salt
½ teaspoon dried rosemary leaves, crushed
½ teaspoon dried thyme leaves
¼ teaspoon ground allspice
¼ teaspoon ground nutmeg
⅛ teaspoon pepper
3 eggs
1 cup whipping cream
¼ cup sherry
½ pound smoked ham, cut into ½-inch strips
2 bay leaves
¼ cup snipped fresh parsley (optional)

Line bottom of a 9 × 5-inch loaf pan with 4 slices of bacon.

In medium skillet, sauté onions and garlic in butter, until onion is soft and translucent. Transfer to medium mixing bowl. Stir in chicken livers, pork, veal, salt, rosemary, thyme, allspice, nutmeg and pepper. Blend in eggs, cream and sherry.

Place half of meat mixture over bacon in loaf pan. Top with ham strips. Cover with remaining meat mixture. Place bay leaves on loaf and cover with remaining bacon strips. Set loaf pan in baking dish containing 1 inch hot water.

Bake in preheated 350°F **radiant bake oven** 1 hour 30 minutes to 1 hour 45 minutes, until juices and fat are clear and meat thermometer registers 165°F.

Cool. Drain fat. Cover terrine loosely with foil. Put weight on top. Refrigerate overnight.

To serve, place bottom of dish in hot water about 1 minute. Loosen sides. Unmold. Remove bay leaves and garnish with parsley. Serve with crackers.

1 loaf

Appetizer Turnovers

Lamb Filling:
2 slices bacon, cooked crisp, crumbled, with 1 tablespoon bacon fat reserved
½ pound ground lamb
½ cup minced green pepper
½ cup minced tomato
1 small clove garlic, minced
½ teaspoon dried rosemary leaves, crushed
½ teaspoon salt
⅛ teaspoon pepper

Turnover Pastry:
2 cups all-purpose flour
½ teaspoon salt
¾ cup butter or margarine, cut into chunks
3 to 4 tablespoons cold water

1 egg, slightly beaten
1 tablespoon melted butter or margarine

For lamb filling: In large skillet sauté lamb, green pepper, tomato and garlic in reserved bacon fat, until lamb is firm. Drain excess fat. Stir in crumbled bacon, rosemary, salt and pepper. Set aside.

For pastry: In bowl combine flour and salt. Cut in butter to form small crumbs. Add water, 1 tablespoon at a time, tossing with fork until mixture forms a ball. Roll half of dough ⅛ inch thick and cut into 3-inch circles. Repeat with remaining dough.

Fill each circle with 1 teaspoon filling. Brush half of inside edge of pastry with slightly beaten egg. Fold over filling and seal edges with fork. Brush with butter. Place on 2 ungreased baking sheets.

Bake in 350°F **convection oven** on racks 2 and 4, 25 to 30 minutes (or bake in preheated 350°F **radiant bake oven** 25 to 30 minutes), or until edges are lightly browned.

Swiss Cheese Turnovers:
1½ cups grated Swiss cheese
¼ cup snipped fresh parsley
¼ cup minced walnuts
½ teaspoon dry mustard
Dash nutmeg

Follow the recipe above, except substitute Swiss cheese filling for lamb filling.

For Swiss cheese filling: In medium bowl combine all ingredients. Mix thoroughly.

About 3 dozen turnovers

Stuffed Mushrooms

1 pound whole fresh mushrooms

Seasoned Beef Filling:
¼ pound lean ground beef
1 slice bacon, minced
3 tablespoons chopped onion
¼ teaspoon Italian seasoning
1 tablespoon chili sauce
2 tablespoons fine dry bread crumbs
(unseasoned)
¼ teaspoon salt
⅛ teaspoon pepper
⅓ cup grated Monterey Jack cheese

Remove stems from mushroom caps. Set caps aside. Chop stems.

For seasoned beef filling: In skillet cook beef and bacon, stirring constantly, until beef is no longer pink. Add mushroom stems, onion and Italian seasoning. Sauté until stems and onions are tender. Remove from heat. Stir in chili sauce, bread crumbs, salt and pepper. Add cheese.

Stuff each cap with filling. Place mushrooms on ungreased baking sheet.

Bake in 425°F **convection oven** on rack 3, 12 to 15 minutes (or bake in preheated 425°F **radiant bake oven** 15 to 18 minutes), or until hot and lightly browned on top.

Florentine Mushrooms:
2 tablespoons chopped onion
⅛ teaspoon dried dill weed
2 tablespoons butter or margarine
1 tablespoon all-purpose flour
1 ounce cream cheese, softened
4 teaspoons Dijon-style mustard
1 tablespoon minced almonds
1½ teaspoons dried parsley flakes
¼ teaspoon salt
⅛ teaspoon pepper
1 package (10 ounces) frozen chopped
spinach, thawed and thoroughly drained

Follow the recipe above, except substitute Florentine filling for seasoned beef filling.

For Florentine filling: In skillet sauté mushroom stems, onion and dill in butter until vegetables are tender. Blend in flour. Remove from heat. Stir in remaining ingredients.

6 to 8 servings

Stuffed Mushrooms, Appetizer Turnovers

Layered Phyllo Appetizers

- 1 cup ricotta cheese
- 1 package (10 ounces) frozen chopped broccoli, thawed and drained
- ½ cup minced ripe olives, drained
- 9 or 10 pieces bacon, coarsely chopped
- ⅓ cup chopped onion
- 5 eggs, beaten
- 2 cups shredded Gruyere or Swiss cheese
- 1 medium tomato, peeled, seeded and chopped
- 1 tablespoon dried parsley flakes (or 2 tablespoons snipped fresh parsley)
- ¼ teaspoon dried thyme leaves
- ¾ to 1 cup butter or margarine, melted
- 14 sheets phyllo dough

In small bowl blend ricotta cheese, broccoli and olives. Set aside.

In large skillet sauté bacon and onion until bacon is lightly browned. Drain well. In medium bowl combine bacon and onion, eggs, cheese, tomato, parsley and thyme. Set aside.

Lightly brush 13 × 9-inch pan with butter. Layer 4 phyllo sheets in baking pan, lightly brushing each with butter. Sheets will be "wrinkled" when fitted into pan. Spread half of ricotta mixture evenly over phyllo. Top with 2 sheets phyllo, lightly brushing each with butter. Top with half of egg mixture. Repeat with 2 sheets phyllo, remaining ricotta mixture, 2 sheets of phyllo, remaining egg mixture and final 4 layers of phyllo. Brush each layer of phyllo lightly with butter.

Score 7 times diagonally in each direction to form diamond pattern.

Bake in preheated 325°F **convection oven** on rack 3, 30 to 35 minutes (or bake in preheated 350°F **radiant bake oven** 35 to 45 minutes), or until crisp and golden brown.

To serve, cut along scored lines.

48 appetizers

Cheesy Appetizer Nuggets

Dough:
- ¾ cup all-purpose flour
- ⅓ cup grated American cheese food*
- ½ cup grated Parmesan cheese
- ¼ teaspoon seasoned salt
- ¼ teaspoon paprika
- ⅛ teaspoon cayenne
- ⅓ cup butter or margarine, cut into chunks
- 3 to 4 tablespoons cold water

Filling Options:
- 2 jars (7 ounces each) marinated artichoke hearts, drained and cut into 2 or 3 sections (4 to 4½ dozen pieces)
- 1 jar (6 ounces) stuffed olives or pitted ripe olives, drained
- ½ pound fully cooked ham, cut into 4 to 4½ dozen ½-inch cubes
- ½ pound cauliflower, broken into ¾-inch flowerets, parboiled 3 minutes, drained
- 6 ounces whole almonds

For dough: In small bowl combine flour, American and Parmesan cheeses, seasoned salt, paprika and cayenne. Cut in butter to form small crumbs. Sprinkle cold water over crumbs, 1 tablespoon at a time, stirring with fork until dough is moistened and crumbly. Cover and refrigerate at least 30 minutes for easier handling.

Wrap 1 heaping teaspoon dough around choice of artichoke, olive, ham, cauliflowerets or almonds. Place on 2 ungreased baking sheets.

Bake in 350°F **convection oven** on racks 2 and 4, 8 to 10 minutes (or bake in preheated 375°F **radiant bake oven** 8 to 10 minutes), or until dough is dry and bottoms are golden brown. Cool slightly before serving.

*Packaged like grated Parmesan or Romano cheese, in round, cardboard container.

48 to 54 appetizers

Rich Cheese Puffs

    1 cup butter or margarine, softened
    6 ounces cream cheese, softened
    2 eggs
    ¼ teaspoon hot pepper sauce
    2 cups finely shredded Cheddar cheese
 1½ cups all-purpose flour
    1 teaspoon salt

In large bowl blend butter and cream cheese. Beat in eggs and hot sauce until light and fluffy. Blend in cheese. Stir in flour and salt. Chill 30 minutes.

On generously floured board roll half of dough to ¼-inch thickness. Cut with 1¾ to 2-inch cookie cutter. Repeat with remaining dough. Place puffs close together on 3 ungreased baking sheets.

Bake in 350°F **convection oven** on racks 2, 3 and 4, 12 to 18 minutes (or bake in preheated 375°F **radiant bake oven** on racks 2 and 4, 12 to 18 minutes, rearranging once during baking, repeating with remaining dough). Puffs are done when they just begin to brown slightly. Remove. Cool on rack.

65 puffs

Party Mix

    4 cups bite-size shredded wheat cereal
 1½ cups nuts (Brazil nuts, pecans, whole
          unblanched almonds or mixed)
    ½ cup shredded coconut
    ⅓ cup butter or margarine
    ¼ cup frozen orange or pineapple juice
          concentrate
    2 tablespoons honey
    ¾ teaspoon ground ginger
    1 cup raisins

In large mixing bowl combine cereal, nuts and coconut. Set aside.

In small saucepan combine butter, frozen concentrate, honey and ginger. Cook on medium high heat until butter melts, stirring constantly. Add raisins. Cook, stirring constantly, until raisins are soft, about 2 minutes.

Add raisins and orange mixture to cereal mixture. Toss to coat thoroughly. Spread on jelly roll pan.

Bake in 325°F **convection oven** on rack 1, 12 to 15 minutes (or bake in preheated 350°F **radiant bake oven** 12 to 15 minutes), until cereal is lightly browned. Stir once. Cool. Store in covered container.

6 to 7 cups

Rich Cheese Puffs, Party Mix

Oven Seafood Spread, Seasoned Crackers

Oven Seafood Spread

12 ounces cream cheese, softened
⅓ cup minced green pepper
⅓ cup chopped green onion
2 tablespoons lemon juice
½ teaspoon Worcestershire sauce
½ teaspoon salt
　 Dash garlic powder
1 can (6 ounces) snow crab meat, drained,
　 shell and cartilage removed
1 can (4¼ ounces) small shrimp, drained
　 and rinsed
1 can (6½ ounces) minced clams, drained
¼ cup slivered almonds

In medium bowl blend cream cheese, green pepper, onion, lemon juice, Worcestershire sauce, salt and garlic powder. Stir in crab, shrimp and clams.

Turn mixture into 1-quart ungreased casserole or oven-proof serving dish. Sprinkle with almonds.

Bake in 350°F **convection oven** on rack 3, about 30 minutes (or bake in preheated 350°F **radiant bake oven** about 30 minutes), or until bubbly around edges and center reaches 130° to 140°F.

Serve with assorted crackers or Seasoned Crackers (right), if desired.

About 4 cups

Seasoned Crackers

1 cup all-purpose flour
½ cup whole wheat flour
¼ cup grated Parmesan cheese
2 teaspoons sugar
1 teaspoon baking powder
½ teaspoon Italian seasoning
½ teaspoon garlic salt
¼ cup butter, cut into chunks
½ cup water
1 teaspoon instant chicken bouillon granules
　 Salt

In medium bowl combine flours, Parmesan cheese, sugar, baking powder, Italian seasoning and garlic salt. Cut in butter to form small crumbs. Dissolve bouillon granules in water. Stir into flour mixture.

Divide mixture in half. On floured board knead one-half lightly until smooth, about 2 minutes. Roll dough very thin (about 1⁄16 inch thick). Cut shapes with 2½-inch round cookie cutter. Repeat with remaining dough. Transfer to 3 ungreased baking sheets. Prick tops of crackers with fork, 2 or 3 times. Sprinkle with salt.

Bake in 300°F **convection oven** on racks 2, 3 and 4, 16 to 22 minutes (or bake half of recipe in preheated 300°F **radiant bake oven** on racks 2 and 4, 23 to 28 minutes, repeating with remaining half), or until crackers just begin to brown. Remove to cooling racks. Cool completely. Store in covered container.

65 to 75 crackers

Appetizer Tarts

12 cocktail buns, 2-inch diameter
⅓ cup melted butter or margarine

Mushroom-Prosciutto Filling:
  2 cups thinly sliced fresh mushrooms
  1 tablespoon chopped green onion
  2 tablespoons butter or margarine
  1 tablespoon all-purpose flour
  ¼ cup whipping cream or half-and-half
  4 ounces prosciutto ham, coarsely chopped
  2 tablespoons snipped fresh parsley
  1 tablespoon fresh lemon juice
  ⅛ teaspoon fennel seed

With a sharp knife slice off tops of buns. Hollow out inside of each bun. (Save tops and inside bread to make bread crumbs for other recipes.) Brush inside of buns with melted butter. Place on ungreased baking sheet.

Bake in preheated 425°F **convection oven** on rack 3, 3 to 5 minutes (or bake in preheated 425° **radiant bake oven** on rack 3, 4 to 6 minutes), or until crisp and light golden brown. Remove from oven. Leave oven on.

For mushroom filling: In small saucepan sauté mushrooms and green onion in butter on medium heat until tender. Stir in flour. Blend in cream. Stir in prosciutto, parsley, lemon juice and fennel seed. Cook, stirring constantly, until filling is thickened and bubbly.

Fill each bun with about 1 tablespoon of filling. Bake in 425°F **convection oven** on rack 3, 3 to 5 minutes (or bake in 425°F **radiant bake oven** on rack 3, 4 to 6 minutes), or until golden brown.

Serve hot.

Asparagus Tarts:
  2 tablespoons butter or margarine
  1 tablespoon all-purpose flour
  ¼ cup whipping cream or half-and-half
  1 package (10 ounces) frozen cut asparagus, thawed and drained
  1 tablespoon orange juice
  1 teaspoon grated orange peel
  ¼ teaspoon salt
  ¼ teaspoon dried summer savory leaves

Follow the recipe above, except substitute asparagus filling for mushroom-prosciutto filling.

For asparagus filling: In small saucepan melt butter. Stir in flour. Blend in cream. Add remaining ingredients. Cook on medium heat, stirring constantly, until thickened and bubbly.

12 tarts

Appetizer Tarts

Artichoke Squares

Crust:
  2 cups buttermilk baking mix
  ½ cup milk

Topping:
  1 medium onion, chopped
  2 tablespoons butter or margarine
  2 jars (6 ounces each) marinated artichoke hearts, drained and chopped
  ⅓ cup slivered almonds
  3 eggs, beaten
  ½ teaspoon salt
  ½ teaspoon dried basil leaves
  ⅛ teaspoon garlic powder
  ⅛ teaspoon pepper
  2 cups shredded Monterey Jack cheese
  ½ cup shredded Cheddar cheese

For crust: In small bowl combine baking mix and milk. Mix until dough is moist. Press dough into bottom of ungreased 10 × 15-inch jelly roll pan.

Bake in 300°F **convection oven** on rack 3, 10 minutes (or bake in preheated 325°F **radiant bake oven** 10 minutes). Remove from oven. Leave oven on.

For topping: In medium skillet sauté onion in butter until tender. Place in bowl. Add remaining ingredients and mix well. Spread on partially baked crust. Return to oven.

Bake in **convection oven** an additional 30 to 35 minutes (or bake in **radiant bake oven** an additional 30 to 35 minutes), or until crust is golden brown.

Cut into forty 2 × 2-inch squares.

40 squares

Beef

Beef Wellington

3½ to 4-pound beef tenderloin
8 ounces fresh mushrooms, chopped
¼ cup chopped green onion
2 tablespoons dried parsley flakes (or ¼ cup snipped fresh parsley)
1 clove garlic, minced
2 tablespoons butter or margarine
2 teaspoons all-purpose flour
½ teaspoon bouquet garni
¼ teaspoon pepper
½ teaspoon Worcestershire sauce
1 package (17¼ ounces) frozen rolled puff pastry sheets, defrosted
1 egg
1 tablespoon water

Trim fat and sinew from tenderloin. Fold thin ends under, so roast is of equal thickness. Tie with string in 4 or 5 places. Place on roasting pan.

Bake in 400°F **convection oven** on rack 3 (or bake in preheated 425°F **radiant bake oven**) 20 minutes (rare) to 30 minutes (well-done).

Let stand 25 minutes. Remove string. (**Convection oven** can be turned off during standing time.)

In medium skillet on medium high heat, sauté mushrooms, green onion, parsley and garlic in butter until tender. Stir in flour, bouquet garni, pepper and Worcestershire sauce. Heat, stirring constantly, until thickened and liquid is evaporated. Set aside.

On floured board roll one sheet of pastry to ⅛-inch thickness. Spread mushroom mixture down center to cover area about the same size as the roast. Place tenderloin on mushroom mixture.

Beat egg and water together. Brush edges of pastry with egg mixture. Fold pastry over tenderloin and press edges together to seal. Fold over ends and seal with small amount of egg mixture.

Place seam-side down on roasting pan. Roll remaining sheet of pastry ⅛ inch thick and cut decorative cut-outs for top of pastry-wrapped roast, if desired. Attach with egg mixture. Brush entire pastry with egg mixture.

Bake in 400°F **convection oven** 20 to 25 minutes (or bake in preheated 425°F **radiant bake oven** 25 to 30 minutes), or until pastry is golden brown.

Let stand 10 minutes before carving.

8 to 10 servings

Beef Wellington

How to Make Beef Wellington

Spread mushroom mixture down center of pastry. Place tenderloin on mixture.

Press edges of pastry to seal. Decorative cutouts may be attached with egg mixture.

Sauerbraten

3 to 3½-pound beef rump roast

Marinade:
¾ cup water
½ cup cider vinegar
½ cup red wine
1 large onion, sliced
2 teaspoons mixed pickling spices
2 tablespoons packed dark brown sugar
1½ teaspoons salt
¼ teaspoon whole peppercorns
2 bay leaves

Gravy:
2 tablespoons reserved fat
2 tablespoons all-purpose flour
Cooking juices plus enough water to equal 2 cups
½ cup finely crushed gingersnaps (about 10 cookies)
½ cup dairy sour cream, optional

Place roast in oven cooking bag or baking dish.

For marinade: In small saucepan combine all marinade ingredients. Heat to boiling. Reduce to medium heat and simmer, covered, about 5 minutes. Cool slightly. Pour over meat. Secure bag or cover dish and marinate 2 to 3 days in refrigerator, turning roast over each day.

Transfer roast and marinade to a large casserole or covered Dutch oven.

Bake in preheated 325°F **radiant bake oven** 2 to 2¾ hours or until fork tender. Remove meat to platter.

For gravy: Strain juices. Skim fat, reserving 2 tablespoons. In medium saucepan blend flour into reserved fat. Blend in juices. Heat to boiling, stirring constantly.

Stir in crushed gingersnaps. Return to boiling. Remove from heat. Blend in sour cream.

Cut meat in thin slices across grain and serve with gravy.

6 to 8 servings

Stuffed Flank Steak

1 pound flank steak
1 recipe White Wine Marinade, page 97

Filling:
¾ cup coarsely chopped cabbage
½ cup shredded carrot
2 tablespoons sliced green onion
⅓ cup minced celery
1½ teaspoons dried parsley flakes (or 1 tablespoon fresh snipped parsley)
2 tablespoons butter or margarine
2 tablespoons fine dry bread crumbs (seasoned)
¼ teaspoon salt

1 teaspoon olive oil
½ cup beef broth (or ½ cup water plus ½ teaspoon instant beef bouillon granules)

Pound flank steak with meat mallet to flatten. Place in plastic food storage bag or baking dish. Pour marinade over meat. Secure bag or cover dish. Refrigerate at least 2 hours or overnight, if desired. Turn occasionally.

For filling: In medium skillet on medium high heat, sauté cabbage, carrot, green onion, celery and parsley in butter until tender. Remove from heat. Stir in bread crumbs and salt.

Remove meat from marinade, reserving marinade for cooking.

Spread vegetable mixture on surface of flank steak, pressing down slightly. Roll jelly roll style starting with short end. Tie with string.

In medium skillet on medium high heat, brown rolled flank steak on all sides in olive oil. Place meat in 8 × 8-inch pan. Combine marinade and beef broth. Pour on roast. Cover tightly with aluminum foil.

Bake in preheated 325°F **radiant bake oven** about 1 hour 30 minutes, until fork tender.

Remove from juices. Let stand 5 minutes before slicing. Spoon juices over meat, if desired.

4 servings

Stuffed Flank Steak

Steak and Vegetable Pie

⅓ cup all-purpose flour
¾ teaspoon salt
½ teaspoon dried marjoram leaves
½ teaspoon dry mustard
⅛ teaspoon pepper
⅛ teaspoon ground allspice
1½ pounds top round steak, cut into ¾-inch
    cubes
3 tablespoons butter or margarine
2 cups diagonally sliced carrots, ½-inch
    slices
1 cup chopped onion
1 cup diced rutabaga
1 cup chopped zucchini
¾ cup sliced celery
1 cup fresh sliced mushrooms
1 tablespoon dried parsley flakes (or 2
    tablespoons fresh snipped parsley)
1 cup beef broth (or 1 cup water plus 1
    teaspoon instant beef bouillon granules)
3 tablespoons brandy
1 sheet of frozen puff pastry, defrosted*
1 egg yolk, beaten
1 tablespoon melted butter or margarine

In plastic food storage bag combine flour, salt, marjoram, mustard, pepper and allspice. Add meat. Shake to coat meat pieces.

In wok on setting "8" or Dutch oven on medium high heat, brown meat and any remaining loose flour mixture in butter. Stir in carrots, onion, rutabaga, zucchini, celery, mushrooms, parsley, beef broth and brandy. Heat to boiling.

Simmer, covered, on medium low heat, about 45 minutes. Uncover. Cook another 15 minutes, stirring occasionally. Place in 12 × 8-inch baking dish. Set aside.

On lightly floured board, roll puff pastry to 12 × 8 inches. Brush surface with beaten egg yolk. Place brushed-side down on hot meat mixture. Cut slits in top. Brush top with melted butter.

Bake in preheated 400°F **convection oven** on rack 3, 20 to 25 minutes (or bake in preheated 425°F **radiant bake oven** 25 to 30 minutes), or until top crust is crisp and brown.

*One package (17¼ ounces) of puff pastry contains 2 sheets.

6 to 8 servings

Lasagna

Tomato sauce:
1 pound ground beef
⅓ cup chopped onion
1 clove garlic, minced
1 can (28 ounces) whole tomatoes, undrained,
    cut-up
1 can (6 ounces) tomato paste
2 teaspoons sugar
1½ teaspoons dried oregano leaves
1½ teaspoons salt
1 teaspoon dried basil leaves
½ teaspoon dried marjoram leaves
¼ teaspoon pepper

Ricotta layer:
3 cups ricotta cheese
½ cup grated Parmesan cheese
1 tablespoon dried parsley flakes (or 2
    tablespoons fresh snipped parsley)
1 egg, slightly beaten

12 lasagna noodles, cooked according to
    package directions
2 cups shredded mozzarella cheese
3 tablespoons grated Parmesan cheese

For sauce: In wok or Dutch oven, cook ground beef, onion and garlic until meat is no longer pink. Drain off fat. Add remaining ingredients. Heat to boiling. Simmer, uncovered, on medium low heat, about 45 minutes, or until thickened. Stir occasionally.

For ricotta layer: In small bowl combine all ingredients. Set aside.

Lightly grease 13 × 9-inch pan. Place 4 noodles on bottom of pan. Top with one-third of the sauce. Add one-third of ricotta mixture, dropping tablespoons of ricotta mixture over sauce. Repeat with remaining ingredients two more times. Top with mozzarella cheese. Sprinkle with Parmesan.

Bake in 325°F **convection oven** on rack 3, 45 to 50 minutes (or bake in preheated 350°F **radiant bake oven** 45 to 50 minutes), or until hot and bubbly.

Let stand 10 minutes before serving.

6 to 8 servings

Beef Tamale Pie

1 pound lean ground beef
1 medium onion, chopped
1 medium-size green pepper, chopped
1 clove garlic, minced
2 tablespoons olive oil
1 can (16 ounces) whole tomatoes, undrained, cut-up
1 can (6 ounces) tomato paste
1 jar (3 ounces) capers, undrained
⅓ cup raisins
1 tablespoon packed brown sugar
1¼ teaspoons dried oregano leaves
½ teaspoon dried marjoram leaves
½ teaspoon salt
¼ teaspoon ground cumin

Cornbread Topping:
¾ cup yellow cornmeal
1 tablespoon all-purpose flour
1 teaspoon sugar
1 teaspoon baking powder
¼ teaspoon salt
   Dash cayenne
1 egg, beaten
⅓ cup milk
2 tablespoons melted butter or margarine

In wok on setting "8" or large skillet on medium high heat, cook ground beef, onion, green pepper and garlic in olive oil, until beef is no longer pink and vegetables are tender.

Add tomatoes, tomato paste, capers, raisins, brown sugar, oregano, marjoram, salt and cumin. Simmer, uncovered, on medium low heat 10 minutes to blend flavors.

For topping: In small bowl combine cornmeal, flour, sugar, baking powder, salt and cayenne. Blend in egg, milk and butter.

Pour beef mixture into medium casserole. Drop topping by spoonfuls on top of mixture to form 4 to 6 mounds.

Bake in 350°F **convection oven** on rack 3, 20 to 25 minutes (or bake in preheated 375°F **radiant bake oven** 20 to 25 minutes), until top is lightly browned and filling is bubbly.

4 to 6 servings

Beef Tamale Pie

Rolled Meatloaf

Rolled Meatloaf

1½ pounds lean ground beef
 2 eggs, beaten
 1 slice bread, torn into small pieces
¼ cup chopped onion
¼ cup chili sauce
½ teaspoon dried thyme leaves
½ teaspoon salt
 1 package (10 ounces) frozen chopped
    broccoli, thawed, well drained
¾ cup shredded Monterey Jack cheese

In medium bowl blend ground beef, eggs, bread, onion, chili sauce, thyme and salt. On foil or wax paper form meat mixture into 12 × 8-inch rectangle. Spread broccoli over meat, leaving 1 inch around edges. Sprinkle cheese over broccoli.

Roll jelly roll style starting with short end. Press seam and ends to seal. Place roll in ungreased 9 × 5-inch loaf pan.

Bake in 325°F **convection oven** on rack 3, 1 to 1¼ hours (or bake in preheated 350°F **radiant bake oven** 1 to 1¼ hours), or until loaf is brown and completely set.

Remove from pan. Let loaf stand 5 to 10 minutes before cutting.

4 to 6 servings

Gruyere-Stuffed Meatloaf

1½ pounds lean ground beef
 2 eggs, beaten
¼ cup milk
¼ cup chopped onion
¼ cup fine dry bread crumbs (seasoned)
½ teaspoon dried savory leaves
½ teaspoon salt
 2 cups sliced fresh mushrooms
 2 tablespoons butter or margarine
 2 teaspoons all-purpose flour
½ to ¾ cup shredded Gruyere cheese

In medium bowl blend ground beef, eggs, milk, onion, bread crumbs, savory and salt. In an ungreased 9 × 5-inch loaf pan press half of meat mixture into bottom and up 1 inch on sides. Set aside.

In small skillet on medium high heat sauté mushrooms in butter about 3 minutes, until just tender. Blend in flour. Remove from heat.

Spread mushrooms over meat in pan. Sprinkle cheese over mushrooms. Top with remaining meat, pressing edges to seal loaf.

Bake in 325°F **convection oven** on rack 3, 45 to 60 minutes (or bake in preheated 350°F **radiant bake oven** 45 to 60 minutes), or until brown and completely set.

Remove from pan. Let loaf stand 5 to 10 minutes before slicing.

Variation: Follow the recipe above, substituting shredded Swiss cheese for Gruyere. Continue as directed.

4 to 6 servings

Veal

Marinated Veal Roast

2 to 3-pound boneless shoulder or sirloin
   veal roast
1 recipe White Wine Marinade, page 97
1 large clove garlic, slivered
½ teaspoon dried marjoram leaves
¼ teaspoon dried rosemary leaves
2 slices bacon

Place roast in large plastic food storage bag or baking dish. Pour marinade over roast. Close bag or cover dish. Refrigerate at least 3 hours or overnight, turning veal occasionally.

Remove roast. Discard marinade. Cut slits in roast and insert garlic slivers. Rub marjoram and rosemary on roast. Lay bacon on top. Place roast on roasting pan.

Bake in 325°F **convection oven** on rack 3, 35 to 45 minutes per pound (or bake in preheated 325°F **radiant bake oven** 40 to 45 minutes per pound), or until meat thermometer registers 160° to 170°F.

Let stand 5 to 10 minutes before carving.

6 to 8 servings

Veal Parmesan

Tomato Sauce:
1 medium onion, thinly sliced
1 clove garlic, minced
1 tablespoon olive oil
1 can (7½ ounces) whole tomatoes,
   undrained, cut-up
1 can (6 ounces) tomato paste
½ teaspoon dried basil leaves
¼ teaspoon dried oregano leaves
¼ teaspoon dried marjoram leaves
¼ teaspoon sugar
⅛ teaspoon pepper

1½ pounds veal cutlets
2 cups sliced fresh mushrooms
¼ cup sliced pitted ripe olives
½ cup grated Parmesan cheese

For tomato sauce: Sauté onion and garlic in olive oil on medium high heat until tender. Add remaining ingredients. Simmer on medium low heat, 5 minutes, stirring occasionally.

Place veal cutlets in 13 × 9-inch pan. Top with mushrooms and olives. Spread tomato sauce over cutlets. Sprinkle with Parmesan cheese.

Bake in 375°F **convection oven** on rack 3, about 25 minutes (or bake in preheated 375°F **radiant bake oven** about 30 minutes), or until veal is tender.

Remove with spatula to serving platter.

4 to 6 servings

Veal Parmesan, Veal Chops in Brandy-Cream Sauce

Veal Chops in Brandy-Cream Sauce

Brandy-Cream Sauce:
- 2 tablespoons chopped green onion
- 2 tablespoons butter or margarine
- 1 tablespoon all-purpose flour
- ¼ teaspoon dried marjoram leaves
- ¼ teaspoon instant chicken bouillon granules
- ⅛ teaspoon pepper
- 1 cup whipping cream
- 1½ teaspoons dried parsley flakes (or 1 tablespoon snipped fresh parsley)
- 1 tablespoon brandy

- 4 veal chops
- 2 tablespoons butter or margarine

For sauce: In medium saucepan on medium high heat sauté green onion in butter until tender-crisp. Blend in flour, marjoram, bouillon granules and pepper. Stir in cream. Add parsley. Cook, stirring constantly, until bubbly and thickened. Remove from heat. Stir in brandy. Set aside.

In medium skillet brown chops on both sides in butter. Remove from heat. Place chops in 9 × 9-inch pan. Top each with 1 to 2 tablespoons sauce.

Bake in 425°F **convection oven** on rack 3, 15 to 20 minutes (or bake in preheated 425°F **radiant bake oven** 15 to 20 minutes), or until chops are desired doneness. Reheat sauce. Serve over chops.

4 servings

Stuffed Veal Rolls

- 6 veal cutlets, pounded to ⅛-inch thickness
- 6 thin slices boiled ham (about 1 ounce each)
- 3 teaspoons Dijon-style mustard, divided
- 2 tablespoons minced green onion, divided
- ¾ cup chopped fresh mushrooms, divided
- 6 thin slices Provolone cheese (½ ounce each)
- 6 tablespoons melted butter or margarine
- ¾ cup fine dry bread crumbs (seasoned)
- 1 recipe Mushroom Sauce, page 100 (optional)

Place ham slice on each veal scallop. Spread ½ teaspoon mustard on ham. Top with 1 teaspoon green onion and 2 tablespoons mushrooms. Place cheese slice on top to within ½ inch of edges.

Roll up jelly roll fashion. Secure with wooden picks. Roll in melted butter. Coat evenly with crumbs. Place on grid of roasting pan.

Bake in 325°F **convection oven** on rack 3, 20 to 25 minutes (or bake in preheated 325°F **radiant bake oven** 25 to 30 minutes), or until lightly browned and veal is done.

Serve with mushroom sauce.

4 to 6 servings

Stuffed Crown Roast of Pork

10 pound pork crown roast

Stuffing:
1½ pounds ground pork
 1 medium onion, chopped
⅔ cup sliced celery
¾ teaspoon minced gingerroot
 2 tablespoons butter or margarine
 1 cup chicken broth (or 1 cup water plus 1 tablespoon instant chicken bouillon granules)
 2 cups herb seasoned stuffing mix
½ teaspoon dried basil leaves
¼ teaspoon dried thyme leaves
¼ teaspoon dried sage
¼ teaspoon pepper
¾ cup chopped walnuts
½ cup raisins
 1 medium apple, cored and chopped

On roasting pan place roast rib-ends down.

Bake in 325°F **convection oven** on rack 1, about 2 hours (or bake in preheated 325°F **radiant bake oven** about 2 hours), or until meat thermometer registers 150°F.

For stuffing: In wok or large skillet on medium high heat, brown ground pork until no longer pink. Drain and set aside.

In wok or large skillet on medium high heat, sauté onions, celery and gingerroot in butter until vegetables are tender. Stir in remaining ingredients.

After roast reaches 150°F, turn rib-ends up. Fill center with stuffing. Continue to bake 30 minutes to 1 hour, or until meat thermometer registers 165° to 170°F.

Let stand 5 minutes before cutting. Place fringe caps on rib bones before serving, if desired.

10 to 12 servings

Stuffed Crown Roast of Pork

Stuffed Pork Chops

- ¾ cup uncooked wild rice
- 2 cups hot water
- 2 teaspoons instant chicken bouillon granules
- 4 center cut pork chops (1 inch thick, with pocket)
- 1 tablespoon vegetable oil
- ½ cup chopped onion
- ½ cup chopped celery
- 3 tablespoons butter or margarine
- 1 can (8 ounces) apricot halves, drained
- ⅓ cup salted sunflower nuts
- 2 tablespoons dry white wine
- ½ teaspoon bouquet garni
- ½ teaspoon salt

Rinse and drain rice. In medium saucepan combine rice, water and bouillon granules. Heat to boiling. Simmer, covered, on medium low heat, 40 to 50 minutes, or until rice is tender. Check rice one or two times to be sure it is not sticking. Add more hot water, if necessary. Drain and set aside.

In large skillet brown chops in vegetable oil. Remove to plate.

In medium skillet sauté onion and celery in butter until tender. Stir in rice. Reserve 4 apricot halves for garnish, if desired. Chop remaining apricot halves and add to vegetables. Stir in sunflower nuts, white wine, bouquet garni and salt. Fill each pocket with some of rice mixture.

In ungreased 9 × 9-inch baking dish place any remaining rice. Arrange pork chops over rice.

Bake, covered, in 350°F **convection oven** on rack 3, 30 minutes (or bake, covered, in preheated 350°F **radiant bake oven** 30 minutes). Uncover. Bake an additional 20 to 25 minutes in **convection oven** (or 30 to 35 minutes in **radiant bake oven**), or until meat is no longer pink.

4 servings

Oven-Glazed Ham

- 5 to 6-pound bone-in picnic ham, fresh or smoked
- 1 recipe Curry Marinade, page 97, Orange Glaze, page 100, or Brandy Peach Sauce, page 99

Place ham on roasting pan. Bake in 325°F **convection oven** on rack 1, 20 to 30 minutes per pound (or bake in preheated 325°F **radiant bake oven** 30 to 35 minutes per pound), or until meat thermometer registers 165°F.

Brush with desired glaze or sauce during last hour of cooking.

15 to 20 servings

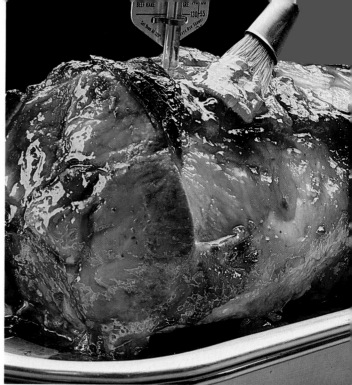

Guava-Glazed Pork Roast

Guava-Glazed Pork Roast

4 to 4½-pound bone-in pork loin roast

Marinade:
- ⅓ cup dry white wine
- ¼ cup water
- ¼ cup guava jelly
- 1 small onion, sliced
- 1 teaspoon dried chervil leaves
- ½ teaspoon salt
- ⅛ teaspoon pepper

Glaze:
- ½ cup guava jelly
- 1 tablespoon packed brown sugar

Place roast in large plastic food storage bag or baking dish. Set aside.

For marinade: In small saucepan combine all ingredients. Heat to boiling. Cool 5 minutes. Pour over roast. Secure bag or cover dish. Refrigerate at least 3 hours or overnight, turning occasionally. Remove roast and discard marinade. Place on roasting pan.

Bake in 325°F **convection oven** on rack 2, 30 to 40 minutes per pound (or bake in 325°F preheated **radiant bake oven** 35 to 45 minutes per pound), or until meat thermometer registers 165°F.

For glaze: In small saucepan melt jelly and brown sugar on medium heat. Brush on roast during last hour, when meat thermometer registers 150°F.

Let stand 10 minutes before carving.

6 to 8 servings

Sausage Pizza

Sausage Pizza

Dough:
- 1 teaspoon active dry yeast
- ½ cup warm water (110° to 115°F)
- 2 tablespoons olive oil
- 2 teaspoons sugar
- ½ teaspoon salt
- 1½ cups all-purpose flour

Sauce:
- ¼ cup chopped onion
- 1 tablespoon olive oil
- 1 can (8 ounces) tomato sauce
- 1 to 1½ teaspoons Italian seasoning
- ½ teaspoon sugar
- ¼ teaspoon salt
- ⅛ teaspoon pepper

Topping:
- 1 pound bulk Italian sausage, cooked and drained
- 1 cup sliced fresh mushrooms
- ¼ cup sliced pitted ripe olives
- 2 cups shredded mozzarella cheese

For dough: In medium bowl dissolve yeast in warm water. Stir in olive oil, sugar and salt. Stir in flour until dough forms. Knead on floured board until smooth and elastic, about 5 minutes. Place in greased bowl. Cover. Let rise in warm place until doubled in size, about 45 to 60 minutes.

For sauce: In small saucepan on medium high heat sauté onion in olive oil until tender. Add tomato sauce, Italian seasoning, sugar, salt and pepper. Heat to boiling. Reduce heat to medium low. Simmer, covered, 5 minutes. Remove pan from heat. Set aside.

Lightly grease 12-inch pizza pan. Pat dough into pan, spreading to fit.

Bake in 425°F **convection oven** on rack 3, 10 minutes (or bake in preheated 425°F **radiant bake oven** 10 minutes).

Spread sauce over hot crust. Spread topping ingredients over sauce.

Reduce heat to 400°F and bake in **convection oven** about another 20 minutes (or bake in 425°F **radiant bake oven** about another 25 minutes), or until the crust is brown.

4 to 6 servings

Ham Loaf with Horseradish Sauce

Loaf:
- 1 pound ground fully-cooked ham
- ½ pound ground pork
- 1 slice white bread, torn into small pieces
- ¼ cup chopped onion
- ¼ cup minced green pepper
- ¼ cup grated carrot
- 2 eggs, beaten
- 2 tablespoons prepared mustard
- ¼ teaspoon pepper

Sauce:
- ⅓ cup whipping cream
- 2 tablespoons prepared horseradish
- 2 teaspoons cider vinegar
- ¾ teaspoon dry mustard
- ⅛ teaspoon salt
  Dash pepper

For loaf: In medium mixing bowl combine all ingredients. Blend well. Form into loaf. Place in ungreased 8 × 4-inch loaf pan.

Bake in 350°F **convection oven** on rack 3, 50 to 60 minutes (or bake in preheated 350°F **radiant bake oven** 1 to 1½ hours), until set and meat thermometer registers 165°F.

Let stand 5 minutes, remove from pan.

For sauce: In small bowl whip cream until peaks form. Blend in remaining sauce ingredients. Refrigerate 10 minutes. Serve over ham loaf.

4 to 6 servings

Sausage Calzone

Dough:
- 1 package (¼ ounce) active dry yeast
- ¼ cup warm water (110° to 115°F)
- 4 cups all-purpose flour
- ½ teaspoon salt
- 1 tablespoon olive oil
- 1¼ cups water

Filling:
- 1 pound bulk Italian sausage
- 1 can (8 ounces) tomato sauce
- 1 cup chopped fresh mushrooms
- 1 large tomato, peeled, seeded and chopped
- ½ cup chopped green pepper
- ⅓ cup minced pitted ripe olives, drained
- 1 teaspoon dried oregano leaves
- ½ teaspoon salt
- ½ teaspoon sugar
- ¼ teaspoon dried basil leaves
- ¼ teaspoon dried crushed red pepper
- ⅛ teaspoon dried marjoram leaves

- 1½ cups shredded mozzarella cheese
- ¼ cup fresh grated Parmesan cheese
  Cornmeal
  Olive oil

For dough: In large bowl dissolve yeast in warm water. Stir in flour, salt and olive oil. Stir in water until dough forms. Knead on floured surface until smooth and elastic, about 5 minutes. Place in bowl greased with olive oil. Turn to coat. Cover. Let rise in a warm place until doubled in size, about 45 to 60 minutes.

For filling: Prepare filling while dough is rising. In large skillet on high heat, cook sausage until no longer pink. Drain well.

Stir in tomato sauce, mushrooms, tomato, green pepper, olives, oregano, salt, sugar, basil, red pepper and marjoram. Heat to boiling. Simmer, uncovered, on medium heat 15 minutes, until thickened, stirring occasionally. Set aside.

To assemble calzones: Punch down dough. Divide into 8 equal portions. Roll each on well-floured surface into 6 × 6-inch square.

Mix mozzarella and Parmesan cheeses into filling. Place about ⅓ cup of meat and cheese mixture on center of dough square. Moisten edges with water. Bring 4 corners together, pressing edges together to seal. Repeat for remaining calzones.

Sprinkle two baking sheets with cornmeal. Transfer calzones to baking sheets. Brush each calzone with olive oil. Make 4 slits in top of each.

Bake in 400°F **convection oven** on racks 2 and 4, 20 to 25 minutes (or bake in preheated 425°F **radiant bake oven** 20 to 25 minutes), or until brown.

8 servings

Sausage Calzone

Lamb

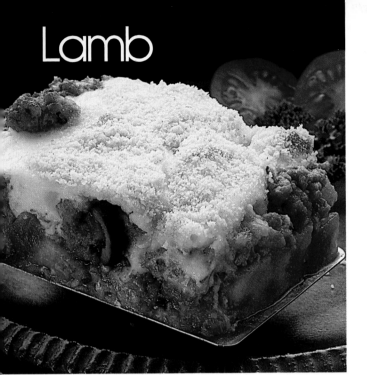

Moussaka

Moussaka

- 2 tablespoons fine dry bread crumbs (seasoned)
- 1 pound ground lamb
- ½ pound ground beef
- ½ cup chopped onion
- 1 clove garlic, minced
- 2 medium tomatoes, peeled, seeded and chopped
- 1 can (15 ounces) tomato sauce
- ½ cup sliced pitted ripe olives
- 1 teaspoon dried basil leaves
- 1 teaspoon salt
- 1 teaspoon sugar
- ½ teaspoon dried rosemary leaves
- ¼ teaspoon pepper
- 1 medium eggplant (about 1½ pounds)
- 3 tablespoons butter or margarine
- 3 tablespoons all-purpose flour
- ½ teaspoon salt
- ¼ teaspoon pepper
- 1½ cups half-and-half
- 2 eggs, beaten
- ½ cup shredded Swiss cheese
- ¼ cup fine dry bread crumbs (seasoned)
- ¼ cup grated Parmesan cheese

Grease bottom of 13 × 9-inch pan. Sprinkle with bread crumbs. Set aside.

In wok or large skillet combine ground lamb, ground beef, onion and garlic. Cook on medium high heat until meat is brown and onion is tender. Drain well.

Stir in tomatoes, tomato sauce, olives, basil, salt, sugar, rosemary and pepper. Heat until mixture

starts to bubble. Simmer on medium low heat 30 to 40 minutes, or until sauce is very thick, stirring occasionally.

Peel eggplant. Cut into ½-inch slices. In Dutch oven bring 2 quarts salted water to boil. Add eggplant. Bring to boil. Cover. Cook 2 to 4 minutes, or until eggplant is tender. Drain well on layers of paper toweling.

Layer eggplant in prepared pan. Top evenly with meat mixture. Set aside.

In small saucepan melt butter on medium high heat. Stir in flour, salt and pepper. Blend in half-and-half. Cook until thickened and bubbly, stirring constantly. Remove from heat.

Stir small amount of hot mixture into eggs. Blend eggs back into hot mixture. Stir in Swiss cheese. Return to heat. Cook, stirring constantly, until cheese melts. Pour over meat mixture.

In small bowl blend bread crumbs and Parmesan cheese. Sprinkle over top.

Bake in 350°F **convection oven** on rack 3, 20 to 30 minutes (or bake in preheated 350°F **radiant bake oven** 35 to 45 minutes), until bubbly.

Let stand 10 minutes before cutting.

6 to 8 servings

Leg of Lamb with Mint Sauce

- 5½ to 6½-pound leg of lamb, bone-in
- 1 large clove garlic, quartered
- 1 teaspoon dried mint leaves
- ½ teaspoon salt
- ¼ teaspoon pepper
- 1 recipe Mint Sauce, page 99

Cut 4 small slits in lamb. Insert garlic. Rub meat with mint, salt and pepper. Place on roasting pan.

Bake in 325°F **convection oven** on rack 2, 25 to 35 minutes per pound (or bake in preheated 325°F **radiant bake oven** 30 to 40 minutes per pound), until meat thermometer registers 160° to 170°F, or until desired doneness.

Brush roast with mint sauce during last 30 minutes of baking.

Let stand 10 minutes before carving. Serve with any remaining mint sauce.

10 to 12 servings

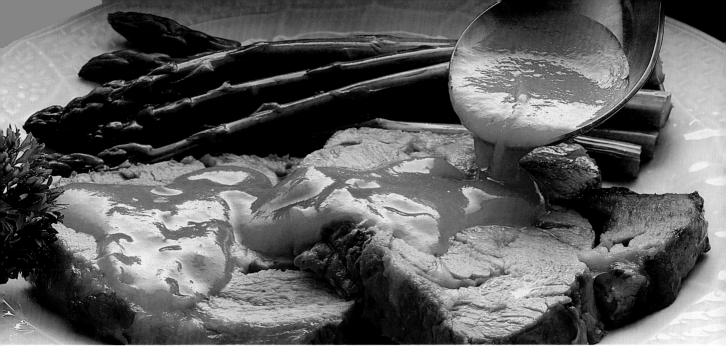

Glazed Lamb Roast

Glazed Lamb Roast

Marinade:
1 can (16 ounces) apricot halves packed
   in juice, apricots reserved
¼ cup vegetable oil
¼ cup white wine vinegar
1 tablespoon honey
¼ teaspoon salt
⅛ teaspoon ground nutmeg
   Dash pepper
   Dash ground allspice

4 to 5-pound boneless lamb shoulder roast

Glaze:
¼ cup packed brown sugar
1 tablespoon brandy
1 teaspoon grated orange rind
   Reserved apricots, puréed

For marinade: In small saucepan combine all ingredients. Bring to boil. Cool. In plastic food storage bag or dish pour marinade over roast. Close bag or cover dish. Refrigerate at least 4 hours or overnight. Remove roast from marinade. Place on roasting pan.

For glaze: In small saucepan combine all ingredients. Bring to boil, stirring constantly.

Bake in 325°F **convection oven** on rack 2, 30 to 40 minutes per pound (or bake in preheated 325°F **radiant bake oven** 35 to 45 minutes per pound), or until thermometer registers 160° to 170°F.

Brush with glaze during last 30 minutes.

Let stand 10 minutes before carving. Serve with any remaining glaze.

8 to 10 servings

Curried Lamb Bake

⅓ cup all-purpose flour
1 tablespoon curry powder
¼ teaspoon ground cardamom
1 teaspoon instant beef bouillon granules
1½ pounds boneless lamb stew meat
   (shoulder), trimmed well and cut into 1-inch
   cubes
¾ cup water
¼ cup dry white wine
2 tablespoons lemon juice
½ cup chopped onion
1 medium-size green pepper, cut into ¾-inch
   pieces
2 tablespoons butter or margarine
1 large apple, coarsely chopped
½ cup raisins
2 tablespoons cream of coconut* (optional)

In 2-quart casserole combine flour, curry, cardamom and bouillon granules. Add meat and toss to coat with flour mixture. Add water, wine and lemon juice. Mix well. Cover.

Bake in preheated 350°F **radiant bake oven** about 45 minutes. Remove from oven. Leave oven on.

In medium skillet sauté onion and green pepper in butter on medium high heat until tender-crisp. Stir in apple, raisins and cream of coconut. Add to lamb in casserole.

Re-cover casserole and return to **radiant bake oven**. Bake an additional 45 minutes to 1 hour, or until meat is very tender. Serve on rice.

*Available in mixed drink section of grocery store.

4 to 6 servings

Poultry

Veal-Stuffed Chicken

Veal-Stuffed Chicken

Stuffing:
- 1 slice bacon, cut-up
- ¼ pound ground veal
- 2 tablespoons chopped onion
- 2 tablespoons grated carrot
- 1 tablespoon butter or margarine
- ½ cup dry bread cubes (unseasoned)
- ¼ teaspoon dried summer savory leaves
- ⅛ teaspoon salt
- ⅛ teaspoon pepper

2½ to 3-pound broiler-fryer chicken

Coating:
- ¼ cup butter or margarine
- 2 teaspoons honey
- ⅛ teaspoon dried summer savory leaves

For stuffing: In small skillet cook bacon on medium high heat until brown. Crumble veal into skillet. Cook, stirring occasionally, until veal is no longer pink. Pour mixture into small mixing bowl.

In skillet sauté onion and carrot in butter until onion is tender-crisp. Add to mixture in bowl. Add remaining stuffing ingredients. Fill chicken loosely with stuffing.

For coating: In small bowl combine all ingredients. Spread over chicken. Place chicken on roasting pan.

Bake in 375°F **convection oven** on rack 2, 1 to 1¼ hours (or bake in preheated 375°F **radiant bake oven** 1¼ to 1½ hours), or until meat thermometer registers 185°F and juices run clear.

Let stand 5 to 10 minutes before carving.

4 servings

Herbed Chicken

2½ to 3-pound broiler-fryer chicken
  Olive oil
- 1 teaspoon dried marjoram leaves
- 1 teaspoon dried oregano leaves
- ¼ to ½ teaspoon garlic powder

Rub chicken with olive oil. Sprinkle with herbs and garlic powder. Place on roasting pan.

Bake in 375°F **convection oven** on rack 2, 1 to 1¼ hours (or bake in preheated 375°F **radiant bake oven** 1¼ to 1½ hours), or until meat thermometer registers 185°F and juices run clear.

Let stand 5 minutes before carving.

4 servings

Oven-Barbecued Chicken

- 1 recipe Barbecue Sauce, page 98
- 2 to 3-pound broiler-fryer chicken, cut-up

On roasting pan place chicken skin-side down. Brush with sauce.

Bake in 375°F **convection oven** on rack 3, about 30 minutes (or bake in preheated 375°F **radiant bake oven** about 30 minutes). Turn chicken pieces over. Brush again with sauce. Bake in **convection oven** an additional 20 to 30 minutes (or 30 to 45 minutes in **radiant bake oven**), or until juices run clear.

4 servings

Baked Chicken Dijon

- 4 boneless chicken breast halves (about 1½ pounds)
- ⅓ cup vegetable oil
- ¼ cup fresh lemon juice (juice of about 2 lemons)
- ½ teaspoon dried basil leaves
- ¼ teaspoon pepper

Dijon Sauce:
- 3 tablespoons white wine vinegar
- ¼ teaspoon dried tarragon leaves
- 6 tablespoons butter or margarine
- 3 tablespoons Dijon-style mustard
- 1½ tablespoons honey

In large plastic food storage bag or shallow dish place chicken breast halves. Combine oil, lemon juice, basil and pepper. Pour over chicken. Secure bag or cover dish. Marinate 30 minutes.

For Dijon sauce: In small saucepan combine vinegar and tarragon. Heat until very hot, but not boiling. Reduce heat to low. Blend in butter, 1 tablespoon at a time, until melted. Stir in mustard and honey. Remove from heat. Set aside.

Remove chicken from marinade. Discard marinade. In 8 × 8-inch baking dish place chicken skin-side up. Pour ¼ cup Dijon sauce over chicken.

Bake in 400°F **convection oven** on rack 3, 30 to 35 minutes (or bake in preheated 400°F **radiant bake oven** 35 to 45 minutes), or until chicken is no longer pink. Serve with remaining sauce.

4 servings

Parmesan Chicken

- 1 egg
- 1 tablespoon milk
- 4 boneless chicken breast halves, skin removed (about 1½ pounds)

Coating:
- ⅓ cup fine dry bread crumbs (seasoned)
- ¼ cup grated Parmesan cheese
- ½ teaspoon dried basil leaves
- ½ teaspoon dried thyme leaves
- ¼ teaspoon paprika
- ¼ teaspoon salt
  Dash pepper

In pie plate beat egg and milk together. Dip each chicken piece in egg to coat.

For coating: In shallow dish combine all ingredients. Dredge chicken in mixture to coat. Place on baking sheet.

Bake in 425°F **convection oven** on rack 3, 15 to 20 minutes (or bake in preheated 425°F **radiant bake oven** 20 to 25 minutes), or until crisp and juices run clear.

2 to 4 servings

Turkey Tetrazzini

Double Crust Chicken Pie

1 recipe Double Pie Crust, page 174
⅓ cup chopped onion
⅓ cup chopped celery
3 tablespoons butter or margarine
3 tablespoons all-purpose flour
1 tablespoon dried parsley flakes (or 2 tablespoons snipped fresh parsley)
1½ teaspoons instant chicken bouillon granules
½ teaspoon poultry seasoning
¼ teaspoon garlic salt
¼ teaspoon pepper
¾ cup milk or half-and-half
1½ cups chopped cooked chicken
1 cup thinly sliced carrot
1 cup diced potato
½ cup frozen peas
½ cup frozen corn
1 tablespoon milk

Prepare pastry as directed. Fit bottom crust into 9-inch pie pan. Leave ½-inch overhang around rim. Set aside.

In small saucepan on medium high heat sauté onion and celery in butter until tender. Stir in flour, parsley, bouillon granules, poultry seasoning, garlic salt and pepper. Blend in milk. Cook, stirring constantly, until bubbly and thickened. Add chicken, carrot, potato, peas and corn. Fill pastry shell with chicken mixture.

Roll out remaining pastry. Place over filling. Seal and flute edges. Cut several slits in pastry top. Brush milk over top before baking.

Bake in 350°F **convection oven** on rack 3, 55 to 60 minutes (or bake in preheated 375°F **radiant bake oven** 55 to 60 minutes), or until golden brown.

Let stand 10 minutes before serving.

4 to 6 servings

Turkey Tetrazzini

1½ cups sliced fresh mushrooms
¼ cup butter or margarine
¼ cup all-purpose flour
½ teaspoon salt
¼ teaspoon pepper
½ teaspoon instant chicken bouillon granules
1½ teaspoons dried parsley flakes (or 1 tablespoon snipped fresh parsley)
1½ cups half-and-half
¼ cup water
2 tablespoons sherry
2 cups chopped cooked turkey
2 cups cooked spaghetti or fettuccine
2 tablespoons melted butter
3 tablespoons fine dry bread crumbs (unseasoned)
⅓ cup grated Parmesan cheese
¼ teaspoon paprika (optional)

In medium saucepan on medium high heat sauté mushrooms in butter until tender. Stir in flour, salt, pepper, bouillon granules and parsley. Blend in half-and-half and water. Cook, stirring constantly, until mixture thickens and just comes to boil. Remove from heat. Stir in sherry. Add turkey.

In greased 9 × 9-inch pan layer spaghetti. Top with sauce mixture. In small bowl blend butter and bread crumbs. Stir in Parmesan and paprika. Sprinkle evenly over sauce mixture.

Bake in 375°F **convection oven** on rack 3, 20 to 25 minutes (or bake in preheated 375°F **radiant bake oven** 25 to 30 minutes), or until bubbly.

Variation: Follow the recipe above, substituting chicken for turkey.

4 to 6 servings

Duck with Cranberry-Orange Glaze

1 large orange
1 can (16 ounces) whole cranberry sauce, divided
1 small onion, cut into 8 pieces
4½ to 5-pound domestic duck

Glaze:
2 teaspoons reserved orange peel
2 tablespoons packed brown sugar
2 teaspoons cornstarch
¼ teaspoon salt
¼ teaspoon ground allspice
1 tablespoon orange-flavored liqueur
½ cup orange juice

Grate orange peel and reserve 2 teaspoons. Peel and section orange. In small bowl combine ½ cup cranberry sauce, orange sections and onion. Stuff duck cavity with cranberry mixture. Tie legs together. Score breast of duck with sharp knife. Place on roasting pan, breast-side up.

For glaze: In small saucepan combine orange peel, brown sugar, cornstarch, salt and allspice. Blend in orange liqueur, orange juice and reserved cranberry sauce. Heat on medium high heat, stirring constantly, until thickened and bubbly.

Bake in 350°F **convection oven** on rack 2, 15 to 20 minutes per pound (or bake in preheated 350°F **radiant bake oven** 20 to 25 minutes per pound), or until meat thermometer registers 185°F and juices run clear.

Brush with glaze during last 30 minutes of roasting. Let stand 5 minutes before carving.

2 to 4 servings

Orange-Rice Stuffing

¼ cup chopped celery
1 tablespoon butter or margarine
1 tablespoon chopped green onion
1 cup cooked rice
¼ cup chopped apple
2 tablespoons raisins
½ teaspoon grated orange rind
⅛ teaspoon dried marjoram leaves
⅛ teaspoon salt
  Dash pepper

In medium skillet sauté celery in butter until tender. Remove from heat. Stir in remaining ingredients.

TIP: Recipe will stuff one 2½ to 3-pound broiler-fryer or 2 Cornish hens.

About 1½ cups stuffing

Honey-Glazed Duck

4½ to 5-pound domestic duck
½ teaspoon dried thyme leaves
½ teaspoon salt
½ teaspoon dried rosemary leaves
2 tablespoons dried parsley flakes (or ¼ cup snipped fresh parsley)
1 medium onion, cut into 8 pieces
2 stalks celery, cut into ¾-inch pieces

Glaze:
¼ cup honey
1 tablespoon sherry
¼ teaspoon dried thyme leaves

Sprinkle inside of duck cavity with thyme, salt and rosemary. In small bowl combine parsley, onion, and celery. Stuff duck cavity with vegetable mixture. Tie legs together. Score breast of duck with sharp knife. Place on roasting pan, breast-side up.

For glaze: In small saucepan combine honey, sherry and thyme. Heat on medium heat until honey melts.

Bake in 350°F **convection oven** on rack 2, 15 to 20 minutes per pound (or bake in preheated 350°F **radiant bake oven** 20 to 25 minutes per pound), or until meat thermometer registers 185°F and juices run clear.

Brush with glaze during last 30 minutes of roasting.

Let stand 5 minutes before carving.

2 to 4 servings

Fennel-Mushroom Stuffing

1 cup coarsely chopped fresh mushrooms
¼ cup chopped onion
2 tablespoons butter or margarine
1 cup crushed herb seasoned stuffing mix
1½ teaspoons dried parsley flakes (or 1 tablespoon snipped fresh parsley)
⅛ teaspoon fennel seed
⅛ teaspoon salt
  Dash pepper
⅓ cup water

In medium skillet sauté mushrooms and onions in butter until tender. Add remaining ingredients. Mix well. Remove from heat.

TIP: Recipe will stuff one 2½ to 3-pound broiler-fryer or 2 Cornish hens.

About 1½ cups stuffing

Fish & Seafood

Creole-Stuffed Flounder

Creole-Stuffed Flounder

- 4 flounder or orange roughy fillets, ½ inch thick (about 1½ pounds)
- ½ cup chopped green pepper
- ¼ cup chopped green onion
- 2 tablespoons butter or margarine
- 1½ cups chopped small cooked shrimp, or 2 cans (4¼ ounces each) small deveined shrimp, rinsed and drained
- 1 jar (2 ounces) sliced pimiento, drained
- 3 teaspoons fresh lemon juice, divided
- ½ teaspoon salt
- ¼ teaspoon dried thyme leaves
- ¼ teaspoon sugar
- ⅛ teaspoon garlic powder
- ⅛ teaspoon cayenne
- 1 tablespoon butter or margarine, melted
  Paprika

Butter grid of roasting pan. Place 2 fillets on pan. Set aside.

In small skillet on medium high heat sauté green pepper and green onion in butter until tender. Remove from heat. Stir in shrimp, pimiento, 2 teaspoons lemon juice, salt, thyme, sugar, garlic powder and cayenne. Mound half of shrimp filling on each of 2 fillets to within ½ inch of edge.

Cut a slit lengthwise down center of remaining fillets to within 1 inch of ends. Place fillets on top of filling. (Filling should show through center slit.) In small dish combine melted butter and 1 teaspoon lemon juice. Brush top of fillets with butter mixture. Sprinkle with paprika.

Bake in 350°F **convection oven** on rack 3, 20 to 25 minutes (or bake in preheated 350°F **radiant bake oven** 25 to 30 minutes), or until fish flakes easily.

4 to 6 servings

Layered Salmon Loaf with Cucumber Sauce

Loaf:
- 1 can (15½ ounces) salmon, cleaned and flaked with ⅓ cup liquid reserved
- 1 cup buttery round cracker crumbs
- ⅓ cup half-and-half
- 2 eggs
- ¼ cup minced onion
- 1 teaspoon grated lemon peel
- ½ teaspoon salt
- ½ teaspoon dried tarragon leaves
- ⅛ teaspoon hot pepper sauce

- 1 package (10 ounces) frozen chopped spinach, thawed and thoroughly drained

Cucumber Sauce:
- ⅓ cup seeded and chopped cucumber
- 2 tablespoons butter or margarine
- 2 tablespoons all-purpose flour
- ½ teaspoon grated lemon peel
- ¼ teaspoon dried tarragon leaves
- ¼ teaspoon salt
- 1 cup half-and-half

Generously grease 8 × 4-inch loaf pan. Set aside.

For loaf: In medium mixing bowl combine all ingredients. Spread half of mixture in loaf pan. Top with spinach. Spread remaining mixture over spinach. Bake in 350°F **convection oven** on rack 3, 45 to 50 minutes (or bake in preheated 350°F **radiant bake oven** 55 to 60 minutes), or until firm.

For cucumber sauce: Sauté cucumber in butter on medium high heat until tender. Add flour, lemon peel, tarragon and salt. Stir until smooth. Gradually blend in half-and-half. Cook, stirring constantly, until mixture thickens and just comes to boil. Serve over salmon loaf.

4 to 6 servings

Stuffed Trout

Lemon-Wild Rice Stuffing:
⅓ cup sliced celery
2 tablespoons chopped green onion
2 tablespoons butter or margarine
1 cup cooked wild rice
½ cup coarsely chopped cashews
½ teaspoon grated lemon peel
¼ teaspoon dried summer savory leaves

4 small whole pan-dressed trout

For lemon-wild rice stuffing: In medium skillet sauté celery and green onion in butter until tender. Remove from heat. Stir in remaining ingredients.

Place fish on buttered grid of roasting pan. Fill each fish with one-fourth of stuffing.

Bake in 375°F **convection oven** on rack 2, 20 to 25 minutes (or bake in preheated 375°F **radiant bake oven** 20 to 25 minutes), or until fish flakes easily.

Orange-Zucchini Stuffed Trout:
1 medium zucchini, chopped
½ cup chopped onion
1 tablespoon butter or margarine
1 can (11 ounces) mandarin orange sections, drained
½ teaspoon dried oregano leaves
¼ teaspoon salt

Follow the recipe above, except substitute orange-zucchini stuffing for lemon-wild rice stuffing.

For orange-zucchini stuffing: In medium skillet sauté zucchini and onion in butter until onion is tender. Remove from heat. Stir in remaining ingredients.

4 servings

Fish Broiling Chart

Type	Cooking Time (min.)	
	1st Side	2nd Side
Whole (up to 2 inches thick and 10 to 14 inches in length)	5	4 to 8
Steaks 1 inch thick	5	2 to 4
Fillets ¼ inch	3 to 4	do not turn
½ to ¾ inch	3	1 to 4

Oven Fried Fish

1 pound fish fillets (¼ to ¾ inch thick), cut into serving-size pieces
1 egg
2 tablespoons milk

Coating:
⅔ cup fine dry bread crumbs (seasoned)
2 teaspoons grated orange or lime peel
½ teaspoon salt
⅛ teaspoon pepper

⅓ cup vegetable oil

Pat fillets dry with paper toweling. Set aside. In shallow bowl beat egg and milk. Set aside.

For coating: On wax paper or in shallow bowl combine all ingredients.

Dip fillets in egg mixture. Roll in bread crumb mixture to coat evenly. Set aside.

Put oil in 13 × 9-inch pan. Place in 450°F **convection oven** on rack 2 (or preheated 450°F **radiant bake oven**) 5 minutes. Remove from oven. Place fillets in hot oil. Turn to coat both sides with oil. Return to oven. Bake ¼-inch thick fillets 9 to 10 minutes, or until fish flakes easily. Bake ½-inch fillets 10 to 11 minutes. Bake ¾-inch fillets 11 to 12 minutes.

Variation: Follow recipe above, substituting ⅔ cup soda cracker crumbs, ¾ teaspoon poultry seasoning, ¼ teaspoon onion powder, ¼ teaspoon salt and ⅛ teaspoon pepper for coating mixture.

4 servings

Broiled Fish

1 pound fish fillets or 1 to 2 pounds whole fish or steaks
1 recipe Garlic Dill Butter, page 97

Preheat oven by setting dials on Broil and 550°F.

Butter grid of roasting pan. Place fillets skin-side up on pan. Brush with Garlic Dill Butter. Broil on rack 4 according to times in chart (left). Turn. Brush tops with butter. Continue to broil until fish flakes easily.

4 servings

Seafood Quiche

Pastry-Wrapped Fish Fillets

  8 ounces fresh mushrooms, sliced
⅓ cup chopped green onion
  2 tablespoons butter or margarine
½ cup snipped fresh parsley
¼ cup dry white wine
  1 tablespoon fresh lemon juice
¼ teaspoon dried marjoram leaves
¼ teaspoon salt
⅛ teaspoon pepper
  4 sole, haddock or flounder fillets (½ inch thick)
12 sheets phyllo dough, cut in half crosswise
  1 cup butter or margarine, melted

In medium skillet on medium high heat sauté mushrooms and green onion in butter until tender. Stir in parsley, wine, lemon juice, marjoram, salt and pepper. Reduce to medium heat. Simmer, uncovered, 10 to 15 minutes, or until liquid is absorbed. Stir occasionally. Set aside.

Pat fillets dry with paper toweling. Set aside.

For each fillet: Place one piece of phyllo on plastic wrap or dish towel. Brush surface with melted butter. Layer 5 pieces on top, brushing with butter between each layer. Spread one-fourth of mushroom filling on center of top layer. Place fillet on top of filling. Fold ends of phyllo over fillet. Brush with butter. Fold sides of phyllo in. Brush with butter to seal. Place seam-side down on jelly roll pan. Brush top with butter. Repeat with remaining fillets.

Bake in 375°F **convection oven** on rack 3, about 25 minutes (or bake in preheated 375°F **radiant bake oven** about 30 minutes), or until golden brown.

4 servings

Seafood Quiche

  1 recipe Single Pie Crust, page 174

Egg Mixture:
  4 eggs
½ teaspoon salt
½ teaspoon dry mustard
½ teaspoon Worcestershire sauce
1½ cups half-and-half

Shrimp and Crab Filling:
  1 cup shredded Swiss cheese
⅓ cup chopped green onion
  2 tablespoons dried parsley flakes (or ⅓ cup snipped fresh parsley)
  1 can (4¼ ounces) small deveined shrimp, rinsed and drained
  1 can (6 ounces) crab meat, drained, cleaned and flaked

Fit pastry into 10-inch pie plate or quiche dish. Bake as directed on page 174.

For egg mixture: In large mixing bowl beat all ingredients on low speed of electric mixer until blended. Set aside.

For shrimp and crab filling: Layer cheese, green onion, parsley, shrimp and crab meat on hot crust. Pour egg mixture over filling.

Bake in 325°F **convection oven** on rack 3, 35 to 40 minutes (or bake in 325°F **radiant bake oven** 45 to 50 minutes), or until knife inserted in center comes out clean.

Oyster Quiche:
  1 pint shucked oysters, thawed if frozen, chopped and drained with ½ cup oyster liquid reserved
  2 tablespoons butter or margarine
  1 cup shredded Cheddar cheese
⅓ cup chopped green onion
  2 tablespoons dried parsley flakes (or ⅓ cup snipped fresh parsley)

Follow the recipe above, except substitute ½ cup oyster liquid for ½ cup of half-and-half. Substitute oyster filling for shrimp and crab filling.

For oyster filling: In medium skillet sauté oysters in butter on medium heat 2 minutes. Drain. Set aside. Layer cheese, green onion, parsley and oysters on hot crust. Pour egg mixture over oysters.

6 to 8 servings

Lobster Thermidor

- 2 teaspoons salt
- 2 teaspoons lemon juice
- 4 raw lobster tails (6 to 8 ounces each), thawed if frozen
- ¼ cup chopped green onion
- 1 to 2 tablespoons dried parsley flakes (or ¼ cup chopped fresh parsley)
- ¼ cup butter or margarine
- 2 tablespoons all-purpose flour
- ½ teaspoon dry mustard
- ½ teaspoon salt
- ¼ teaspoon pepper
- 1 cup half-and-half
- 1 tablespoon dry sherry
- 2 teaspoons grated Parmesan cheese
- 2 teaspoons fine dry bread crumbs (unseasoned)

Fill wok or Dutch oven half full of water. Add salt and lemon juice. Bring to boil. Add lobster tails. Return to boil. Cook 3 to 6 minutes, or until meat is firm and opaque. Drain. Cool slightly.

With sharp knife or scissors, remove and discard undershell. Carefully remove meat. Reserve shells. Remove membrane from meat. Chop meat. Set aside. Wash and drain shells. Set aside.

In medium saucepan on medium high heat sauté green onion and parsley in butter. Stir in flour, dry mustard, salt and pepper. Blend in half-and-half. Cook, stirring constantly, until mixture thickens and just boils. Stir in sherry and reserved lobster meat.

Spoon lobster mixture evenly into reserved shells. Place on baking sheet. In small dish combine Parmesan and bread crumbs. Sprinkle on top of lobster mixture.

Bake in 375°F **convection oven** on rack 2, 15 to 20 minutes (or bake in preheated 375°F **radiant bake oven** 25 to 30 minutes), or until topping is browned.

4 servings

How to Remove Lobster Undershell

Cut undershell with sharp knife or scissors.

Lobster Thermidor

Pasta Eggs, & Cheese

Spinach-Stuffed Manicotti

Spinach-Stuffed Manicotti

Sauce:
- ¼ cup chopped onion
- 1 tablespoon olive oil
- 1 can (15 ounces) tomato sauce
- 1 can (8 ounces) whole tomatoes, undrained, cut-up
- ½ teaspoon dried basil leaves
- ½ teaspoon sugar
- ¼ teaspoon Italian seasoning
- ⅛ teaspoon salt
- ⅛ teaspoon pepper

- 1 package (8 ounces) manicotti shells (about 14 shells)

Filling:
- 1 container (15 to 16 ounces) ricotta cheese
- 1 package (10 ounces) frozen chopped spinach, thawed and thoroughly drained
- 1 cup shredded mozzarella cheese
- ¼ cup grated Parmesan cheese
- 2 tablespoons dried parsley flakes (or ¼ cup snipped fresh parsley)
- 2 eggs, beaten
- ½ teaspoon garlic salt
- ¼ teaspoon pepper
- ⅛ teaspoon ground nutmeg

- 1 cup shredded mozzarella cheese

Grease 13 × 9-inch baking pan. Set aside.

Prepare manicotti according to package directions. Rinse and drain. Set aside.

For sauce: In medium saucepan on medium high heat, sauté onion in olive oil until tender. Add remaining ingredients. Simmer 15 minutes to blend flavors and thicken sauce. Stir occasionally.

For filling: In medium mixing bowl combine filling ingredients. Carefully fill cooked manicotti shells with filling mixture. Arrange stuffed manicotti in bottom of pan. Pour tomato sauce over manicotti.

Top with mozzarella cheese.

Bake in 350°F **convection oven** on rack 2, about 30 minutes (or bake in preheated 350°F **radiant bake oven** about 35 minutes), or until hot and bubbly.

4 to 6 servings

How to Fill Manicotti Shells

Spoon filling into shell, pushing gently to fill.

Stuffed Shells Alfredo

  1 package (8 ounces) jumbo pasta
        shells (about 20 shells)

Filling:
  1 package (3 ounces) cream cheese,
        softened
1⅓ cups cottage cheese
 ¼ pound prosciutto ham or fully-cooked ham,
        diced
  2 tablespoons dried parsley flakes (or ¼
        cup snipped fresh parsley)
 ¼ cup chopped pitted ripe olives
  1 egg, slightly beaten
  3 tablespoons grated Romano or Parmesan
        cheese
  1 teaspoon dried basil leaves

Sauce:
  3 tablespoons butter or margarine
  2 tablespoons dried parsley flakes (or ¼
        cup snipped fresh parsley)
  3 tablespoons all-purpose flour
 ¼ teaspoon salt
 ⅛ teaspoon pepper
  1 cup milk
 ½ cup half-and-half
 ⅓ cup shredded Monterey Jack cheese

Prepare pasta shells according to package directions. Rinse. Set aside.

For filling: In medium mixing bowl combine all ingredients. Set aside.

For sauce: In medium saucepan melt butter. Stir in parsley, flour, salt and pepper. Blend in milk and half-and-half. Heat on medium high heat, stirring constantly, until mixture thickens and just comes to a boil. Add cheese. Stir until melted.

Pour half of sauce in bottom of 12 × 8-inch baking dish. Carefully fill cooked pasta shells with filling mixture. Arrange stuffed shells on top of sauce. Pour remaining sauce over shells.

Bake in 350°F **convection oven** on rack 3, about 20 minutes (or bake in preheated 350°F **radiant bake oven** about 25 minutes), or until hot and bubbly.

6 to 8 servings

Stuffed Shells Alfredo

Hungarian Noodle Ring

- 3 cups uncooked egg noodles
- ⅓ cup chopped green onion
- 2 tablespoons butter or margarine
- 2 tablespoons all-purpose flour
- ½ teaspoon salt
- ¼ teaspoon caraway seed
- ¼ teaspoon poppy seed
- ⅛ teaspoon paprika
- ⅛ teaspoon pepper
- ¾ cup milk
- 1 egg, beaten
- ⅓ cup dairy sour cream
  Fresh parsley (optional)

Butter 1-quart ring mold. Set aside.

Prepare noodles according to package directions. Rinse. Set aside.

In small saucepan sauté green onion in butter until tender. Remove from heat. Stir in flour, salt, caraway seed, poppy seed, paprika and pepper until smooth. Gradually blend in milk. Heat on medium high heat, stirring constantly, until mixture thickens and just comes to boil. Remove from heat. Slowly blend small amount of hot mixture into beaten egg. Blend back into hot mixture. Stir in sour cream.

In medium mixing bowl combine sauce and noodles. Pour mixture into ring mold.

Bake in 325°F **convection oven** on rack 3, 20 to 25 minutes (or bake in preheated 325°F **radiant bake oven** 25 to 30 minutes), or until firm and edges begin to bubble.

Loosen edges. Invert onto serving plate. Garnish with parsley.

4 to 6 servings

Macaroni and Cheese

- 1 package (5 ounces) corkscrew macaroni
- 1 package (10 ounces) frozen chopped broccoli, thawed and drained*
- 1 cup cubed fully-cooked ham, ½-inch cubes
- ¼ cup minced green pepper
- 2 tablespoons minced onion
- 3 tablespoons butter or margarine
- 3 tablespoons all-purpose flour
- ¾ teaspoon seasoned salt
- ½ teaspoon dry mustard
- ⅛ teaspoon pepper
- 1½ cups milk
- 1½ cups shredded Cheddar cheese
- 1 tablespoon dried parsley flakes (or 2 tablespoons snipped fresh parsley)

Prepare macaroni according to package directions. In 2-quart casserole place macaroni, broccoli and ham. Set aside.

In medium saucepan on medium high heat, sauté green pepper and onion in butter until tender. Stir in flour, salt, dry mustard and pepper. Blend in milk. Heat, stirring constantly, until mixture thickens and just comes to boil. Add shredded cheese. Stir until melted. Pour sauce over macaroni. Stir to mix. Sprinkle with parsley.

Bake in 350°F **convection oven** on rack 3, 15 to 20 minutes (or bake in preheated 350°F **radiant bake oven** 20 to 25 minutes), or until hot and bubbly.

Variation: Follow the recipe above, substituting Swiss cheese for Cheddar.

*Or 2 cups chopped fresh broccoli, parboiled 3 minutes, drained.

4 to 6 servings

Oven Frittata

1 cup sliced fresh mushrooms
½ cup chopped zucchini
⅓ cup chopped green pepper
¼ cup chopped onion
2 tablespoons olive oil
2 eggs, separated
¼ teaspoon cream of tartar
1 tablespoon milk
⅛ teaspoon dried summer savory leaves
⅛ teaspoon salt
  Dash pepper
  Dash garlic powder
1 tablespoon grated Romano or Parmesan
  cheese

Butter 9-inch pie plate. Set aside.

In medium skillet sauté mushrooms, zucchini, green pepper and onion in olive oil until tender. Spread in pie plate.

In medium mixing bowl beat egg whites and cream of tartar until stiff but not dry.

In small bowl combine egg yolks, milk, summer savory, salt, pepper and garlic powder. Fold mixture into egg whites. Spread evenly over mushroom mixture in pie plate. Sprinkle with cheese.

Bake in 350°F **convection oven** on rack 3, 10 to 15 minutes (or bake in preheated 350°F **radiant bake oven** 10 to 15 minutes), or until knife inserted in center comes out clean.

Loosen edges. Carefully remove to serving plate.

1 to 2 servings

Quiche Lorraine

1 recipe Single Pie Crust, page 174
10 slices bacon, cooked crisp and crumbled
1 cup shredded Swiss cheese
¼ cup chopped green onion
4 eggs, beaten
2 cups half-and-half
½ teaspoon salt
⅛ teaspoon pepper

Prepare pastry as directed, but do not bake.

Layer bacon, cheese and green onion on bottom of pie crust. In medium mixing bowl beat eggs, half-and-half, salt and pepper until blended. Pour egg mixture over green onion.

Bake in 325°F **convection oven** on rack 3, 45 to 50 minutes (or bake in preheated 325°F **radiant bake oven** 60 to 65 minutes), or until knife inserted in center comes out clean.

Ham and Green Chili Quiche: Follow the recipe above, substituting ¾ cup chopped fully-cooked ham and 1 can (4 ounces) diced green chilies, well drained, for bacon.

Zucchini-Mushroom Quiche: Follow the recipe above, except omit bacon. In medium skillet sauté 1½ cups chopped zucchini and 1 cup chopped mushrooms in 1 tablespoon butter until tender. Cool mixture slightly. Add to cheese and onion on bottom of pie crust.

4 to 6 servings

Herbed Cheese Soufflé

   Grated Parmesan cheese
 3 tablespoons butter or margarine
 3 tablespoons all-purpose flour
 ½ teaspoon salt
 ¼ teaspoon cayenne
 ¼ teaspoon dried dill weed
 1 cup milk
 ¾ cup shredded Cheddar cheese
 ½ cup shredded Swiss cheese
 4 eggs, separated
 ½ teaspoon cream of tartar

Grease 1½-quart soufflé dish. Sprinkle Parmesan cheese on bottom and sides to coat. Set aside.

In small saucepan melt butter. Stir in flour, salt, cayenne and dill weed. Blend in milk. Heat on medium high heat, stirring constantly, until mixture thickens and just comes to boil. Add cheeses. Stir until melted. Remove from heat.

Stir small amount of hot mixture into egg yolks. Blend egg yolks back into hot mixture. Beat egg whites and cream of tartar until stiff but not dry. Fold sauce gently into egg whites. Pour mixture into soufflé dish.

Bake in preheated 350°F **convection oven** on rack 3, 30 to 35 minutes (or bake in preheated 350°F **radiant bake oven** 40 to 45 minutes), or until set.

Serve immediately.

4 to 6 servings

Herbed Cheese Soufflé

How to Make Herbed Cheese Soufflé

Stir small amount of hot mixture into yolks. Blend yolks back into hot mixture.

Beat egg whites and cream of tartar until stiff but not dry.

Fold sauce gently into egg whites. Slowly pour mixture into soufflé dish.

Cheese Strata

- 12 slices white bread, crusts trimmed
- 2 cups shredded Cheddar cheese
- 4 eggs
- 1 tablespoon dried minced onion
- 1 teaspoon seasoned salt
- ½ teaspoon prepared mustard
- ½ teaspoon cayenne
- 2½ cups milk

Grease 12 × 8-inch baking dish. Arrange 6 slices bread on bottom of dish. Sprinkle with cheese. Top with remaining bread slices.

In medium mixing bowl beat eggs, onion, salt, mustard and cayenne. Blend in milk. Pour egg mixture evenly over bread. Cover dish. Refrigerate at least 2 hours, or overnight.

Bake in 325°F **convection oven**, uncovered, on rack 2, 40 to 45 minutes (or bake in preheated 325°F **radiant bake oven**, uncovered, 45 to 55 minutes), or until knife inserted in center comes out clean.

Variation: Follow recipe above, substituting 1 cup shredded Swiss cheese for 1 cup Cheddar cheese.

6 to 8 servings

Sour Cream Brunch Bake

- 1 container (15 to 16 ounces) ricotta cheese
- ⅔ cup confectioners' sugar, divided
- 1 egg, separated
- 9 eggs
- 1½ cups dairy sour cream
- ⅛ teaspoon salt
  Dairy sour cream
  Raspberry or apricot preserves

Grease and lightly flour 12 × 8-inch baking dish.

In small bowl combine ricotta, ⅓ cup confectioner's sugar and 1 egg yolk. Spread evenly in bottom of baking dish.

In medium mixing bowl combine eggs and remaining egg white, sour cream, remaining ⅓ cup confectioners' sugar and salt. Beat on medium speed of electric mixer 2 minutes.

Pour egg mixture over ricotta.

Bake in 325°F **convection oven** on rack 3, about 45 minutes (or bake in preheated 325°F **radiant bake oven** about 1 hour), or until puffy and set.

Serve pieces topped with sour cream and preserves.

6 to 8 servings

Vegetables & Fruits

Broccoli Lasagna

Sauce:
- 8 ounces fresh mushrooms, sliced
- ⅓ cup chopped onion
- 2 tablespoons olive oil
- 1 can (16 ounces) whole tomatoes, undrained, cut-up
- 1 can (6 ounces) tomato paste
- 1 tablespoon dried parsley flakes (or 2 tablespoons chopped fresh parsley)
- 1 teaspoon sugar
- ¾ teaspoon dried oregano leaves
- ½ teaspoon salt
- ⅛ teaspoon pepper

Filling:
- 3 cups coarsely chopped fresh broccoli (about ¾ pound)
- 1 carton (15 to 16 ounces) ricotta or creamed cottage cheese
- 2 eggs, slightly beaten
- ½ cup shredded mozzarella cheese
- 2 tablespoons grated Parmesan cheese
- ⅛ teaspoon pepper

- 6 lasagna noodles, cooked and drained according to package directions
- 1 cup shredded mozzarella cheese

Lightly grease 9 × 9-inch pan. Set aside.

For sauce: In wok or large saucepan on medium high heat, sauté mushrooms and onion in oil until tender. Add remaining ingredients. Heat to boiling. Reduce heat to medium low. Simmer 20 to 25 minutes, stirring occasionally, until thickened.

For filling: In medium saucepan place broccoli with enough water to cover. Heat to boiling. Reduce heat to medium and cook, covered, about 5 minutes, or until tender. Drain thoroughly. Set aside. In medium mixing bowl combine remaining filling ingredients. Add broccoli. Set aside.

Arrange 3 lasagna noodles in prepared pan. Spread half of broccoli mixture over noodles. Top with half of sauce mixture. Repeat with noodles, broccoli and sauce. Sprinkle mozzarella cheese over top.

Bake in 350°F **convection oven** on rack 3, 25 to 30 minutes (or bake in preheated 350°F **radiant bake oven** 25 to 30 minutes), or until hot and bubbly.

6 to 8 servings

Broccoli Lasagna

Broccoli Timbale

Paprika
3 cups fresh broccoli flowerets (1½ pounds)
½ cup grated Cheddar cheese
4 eggs, beaten
1 cup half-and-half
½ teaspoon salt
¼ teaspoon dry mustard
¼ teaspoon lemon pepper
¼ teaspoon onion powder
Dash cayenne

Grease 4-cup ring mold. Sprinkle evenly with paprika to coat. Set aside.

In medium saucepan place broccoli and enough water to cover. Heat to boiling. Reduce heat to medium and cook, covered, 3 minutes. Drain thoroughly. Place broccoli in prepared ring mold. Sprinkle cheese over broccoli. Set aside.

In small mixing bowl beat eggs, half-and-half, salt, mustard, lemon pepper, onion powder and cayenne until blended. Pour over cheese-topped broccoli.

Place ring mold in 10 × 10-inch baking dish. Pour hot water around ring mold to 1-inch depth.

Bake in 325°F **convection oven** on rack 2, 35 to 40 minutes (or bake in preheated 325°F **radiant bake oven** 35 to 40 minutes), or until knife inserted in center comes out clean. Loosen edges. Invert onto serving plate.

4 to 6 servings

Baked Beans

1 package (16 ounces) dried navy beans (about 2 cups)
2 cups water
8 to 10 slices (8 ounces) bacon, cut into 1-inch pieces
1 medium onion, chopped
¾ cup packed brown sugar
1 can (8 ounces) tomato sauce
1 can (6 ounces) tomato paste
⅓ cup dark molasses
1 tablespoon dried crushed celery flakes
1½ teaspoons salt
1 teaspoon dry mustard
½ to 1 teaspoon liquid smoke

Rinse and sort beans. Drain. Place beans and water in medium saucepan. Heat to boiling. Reduce heat to medium low. Simmer, covered, 30 minutes. Drain beans, reserving cooking water. If necessary, add enough water to reserved cooking water to equal 1½ cups. Place beans and water in 3-quart casserole. Set aside.

In medium skillet on medium high heat fry bacon until crisp. Remove and crumble bacon. Reserve 3 tablespoons drippings. Add bacon and reserved bacon drippings to beans. Stir in remaining ingredients. Cover.

Bake in 300°F **radiant bake oven** 6½ to 7½ hours, or until beans are tender. Stir every 2 to 3 hours.

TIP: Beans should not dry out during cooking. Add more water as needed.

10 to 12 servings

Hot Cabbage Salad

Savory Carrot Pudding

    4 cups sliced carrots
    1 bay leaf
 1½ teaspoons sugar
    ⅓ cup whipping cream or half-and-half
    3 eggs
    ½ teaspoon salt
    ¼ to ½ teaspoon dried thyme leaves
    ⅛ teaspoon ground cumin

Grease 1-quart casserole or soufflé dish. Set aside.

Place carrots in large saucepan. Cover carrots with water. Add bay leaf and sugar. Heat to boiling. Reduce heat. Simmer, covered, 15 to 25 minutes, or until very tender. Drain carrots. Remove and discard bay leaf.

In medium mixing bowl combine carrots and cream. Beat on medium speed of electric mixer until smooth. Beat in eggs, salt, thyme and cumin. Pour mixture into prepared casserole.

Bake in 350°F **convection oven** on rack 3, 40 to 45 minutes (or bake in preheated 350°F **radiant bake oven** 55 to 60 minutes), or until knife inserted in center comes out clean.

4 to 6 servings

Lemon-Dill Green Beans

    ½ cup chopped green onion
    3 tablespoons butter or margarine
    1 tablespoon all-purpose flour
    1 teaspoon grated lemon peel
    ½ teaspoon dried dill weed
    ½ teaspoon salt
    ¼ teaspoon pepper
    ⅔ cup dairy sour cream
    2 packages (10 ounces each) frozen
       French-style green beans, thawed and
       drained
    1 tablespoon cornflake crumbs

Grease 1-quart casserole. Set aside.

In medium saucepan on medium high heat, sauté green onion in butter until tender. Remove from heat. Stir in flour, lemon peel, dill, salt, pepper and sour cream. Stir in green beans. Pour mixture into prepared casserole. Sprinkle cornflake crumbs over top.

Bake in 350°F **convection oven** on rack 3, 20 to 25 minutes (or bake in preheated 350°F **radiant bake oven** 30 to 35 minutes), or until hot and bubbly.

4 to 6 servings

Hot Cabbage Salad

    2 to 2½-pound head cabbage
    3 strips bacon, chopped
    ⅔ cup chopped onion
    ⅓ cup grated carrot
    ½ cup salted peanuts
    2 tablespoons butter or margarine
    2 tablespoons all-purpose flour
    ½ teaspoon salt
    ¼ teaspoon pepper
    1 cup milk
    1 cup shredded Monterey Jack cheese
    ⅓ cup grated Parmesan cheese
    1 teaspoon vinegar

Quarter cabbage and remove core. Shred to make about 10 cups. Set aside. In wok or Dutch oven on medium heat cook bacon until browned. Remove bacon pieces from fat and drain on paper toweling. Set aside. Add cabbage, onion, carrot and peanuts to wok with reserved bacon fat. Cook and stir on medium heat until cabbage is tender. Remove from heat. Set aside.

In small saucepan on medium heat melt butter. Stir in flour, salt and pepper. Blend in milk. Cook, stirring constantly, until thickened and bubbly. Add cheeses. Stir to melt. Remove from heat. Stir in vinegar. Add sauce to cabbage mixture. Place mixture in 1½-quart casserole. Crumble reserved bacon over top.

Bake in 350°F **convection oven** on rack 3, about 20 minutes (or bake in preheated 350°F **radiant bake oven** about 25 minutes), or until hot and bubbly.

6 to 8 servings

Twice-Baked Potatoes

Onion and Artichoke au Gratin

- 1 extra large onion (about 1 pound), thinly sliced and separated into rings
- 1 clove garlic, minced
- 3 tablespoons olive oil, divided
- 1 can (14 ounces) whole artichoke hearts, drained and quartered
- 1 jar (2½ ounces) diced pimiento, drained
- 2 teaspoons lemon juice
- ½ teaspoon dried basil leaves
- ½ teaspoon salt
  Dash pepper
- ¼ cup grated Parmesan cheese
- 2 tablespoons fine dry bread crumbs (seasoned)

Grease 1-quart casserole. Set aside.

In large skillet sauté onion and garlic in 2 table-spoons olive oil until tender. Place in prepared casserole. Stir in artichokes, pimiento, lemon juice, basil, salt and pepper.

In small bowl combine Parmesan cheese and bread crumbs. Sprinkle over vegetables. Drizzle 1 tablespoon olive oil over top.

Bake in 375°F **convection oven** on rack 3, about 20 minutes (or bake in preheated 375°F **radiant bake oven** about 20 minutes), or until top is browned.

4 to 6 servings

Baked Potatoes

4 medium baking potatoes

Wash potatoes and pat dry. Prick skins with tines of fork. Bake in 375°F **convection oven** on rack 3, 50 to 55 minutes (or bake in preheated 375°F **radiant bake oven** 1 to 1¼ hours), or until tender.

4 servings

Twice-Baked Potatoes

- 4 medium baked potatoes (see recipe above)
- ⅓ cup butter or margarine
- ¼ cup milk or half-and-half
- 1 teaspoon freeze-dried chives
- 1 teaspoon dried parsley flakes
- ½ teaspoon salt
- ¼ teaspoon pepper
- 2 tablespoons crisp, cooked bacon, crumbled (optional)
  Paprika (optional)

Cut a thin strip from top of potato. Scoop out potato, leaving ¼-inch thick shell. In medium mixing bowl combine potato and butter. Blend with electric mix-er on low speed until butter melts. Add milk, chives, parsley flakes, salt, pepper and bacon bits. Beat on high speed until smooth. Spoon mixture into shells. Top with paprika. Place shells in baking dish or on baking sheet.

Bake in 375°F **convection oven** on rack 3, about 20 minutes (or bake in preheated 375°F **radiant bake oven** about 30 minutes), or until hot.

4 servings

Au Gratin Potatoes

Au Gratin Potatoes

3 tablespoons butter or margarine
3 tablespoons all-purpose flour
½ teaspoon salt
¼ teaspoon pepper
¾ cup milk
¾ cup half-and-half
4 medium-size white potatoes (about 1½
    pounds), thinly sliced
⅓ cup chopped onion
1 tablespoon dried parsley flakes (or 2
    tablespoons snipped fresh parsley)
1 cup grated Cheddar cheese

Grease 1½-quart casserole. Set aside.

In small saucepan melt butter. Stir in flour, salt and pepper. Blend in milk and half-and-half. Cook on medium high heat, stirring constantly, until heated through. Set aside.

Layer one-third of potato slices, half of onion, one-third of parsley, one-third of cheese and one-third of sauce in casserole. Repeat layers. Top with remaining potatoes, parsley, cheese and sauce.

Bake in 375°F **convection oven** on rack 3, 45 to 60 minutes (or bake in preheated 375°F **radiant bake oven** 1 to 1¼ hours), or until sauce is bubbly and potatoes are tender.

6 to 8 servings

Pilaf-Stuffed Tomatoes

4 large firm tomatoes
½ cup coarsely chopped fresh mushrooms
⅓ cup cracked wheat bulgur
⅓ cup chopped celery
2 tablespoons butter or margarine
1 tablespoon olive oil
1¾ cups water, divided
⅓ cup uncooked long-grain rice
1½ teaspoons instant chicken bouillon granules
½ teaspoon salt
½ teaspoon dried thyme leaves
1 bay leaf
⅓ cup chopped green onion
2 teaspoons grated Parmesan cheese
1 teaspoon fine dry bread crumbs
    (unseasoned)

Cut thin slice from top of each tomato. Scoop out centers. Place upside down on paper toweling to drain. Set aside.

In medium saucepan sauté mushrooms, bulgur and celery in butter and olive oil until celery is tender-crisp. Add 1¼ cups water, rice, bouillon granules, salt, thyme and bay leaf. Heat to boiling. Reduce heat to low. Simmer, covered, 15 to 20 minutes, or until rice is tender and water is absorbed. Remove from heat. Remove and discard bay leaf. Stir in green onion.

Fill each tomato with one-fourth of pilaf mixture. Place tomatoes in 8 × 8-inch baking dish. Pour ½ cup water around tomatoes.

In small bowl combine Parmesan cheese and bread crumbs. Sprinkle over tomatoes.

Bake in 350°F **convection oven** on rack 3, 15 to 20 minutes (or bake in preheated 350°F **radiant bake oven** 20 to 25 minutes), or until tops are light golden brown.

4 servings

How to Prepare Tomatoes

Cut thin slice from top. Scoop out center. Drain on paper toweling.

Sweet Potato Puff

1½ to 1¾ pounds yams or sweet potatoes,
    pared and cut in half (quarter larger
    potatoes)
3 eggs, separated
¼ teaspoon cream of tartar
¾ cup dairy sour cream
1 tablespoon honey
2 teaspoons grated orange peel
1 teaspoon ground cinnamon
½ teaspoon salt
¼ teaspoon ground allspice

Grease 1-quart casserole. Set aside.

In large saucepan place potatoes and enough water to cover. Heat to boiling. Simmer, covered, on medium low heat, 20 to 25 minutes, or until very tender. Drain.

In large mixing bowl beat egg whites and cream of tartar until stiff but not dry. Set aside.

In medium mixing bowl combine potatoes, sour cream, honey, orange peel, cinnamon, salt, allspice and egg yolks. Beat on medium speed of electric mixer until smooth. Fold into egg white mixture. Pour into casserole.

Bake in 350°F **convection oven** on rack 3, 45 to 50 minutes (or bake in preheated 350°F **radiant bake oven** 50 to 55 minutes), or until knife inserted in center comes out clean.

6 to 8 servings

Apple-Stuffed Squash

2 acorn squash (about 1½ pounds each)
¼ cup butter or margarine, divided
1 medium apple, chopped
¼ cup golden raisins
2 tablespoons white wine
2 tablespoons packed brown sugar
½ to 1 teaspoon curry powder
⅛ teaspoon ground cardamom
¼ cup shredded coconut

Grease 9 × 13-inch baking dish. Cut squash in half. Remove seeds. Place cut-side down in dish. Bake in 350°F **convection oven** on rack 2, 35 to 45 minutes (or bake in preheated 350°F **radiant bake oven** 45 to 50 minutes), or until tender.

In small saucepan melt 2 tablespoons butter. Sauté apple on medium high heat 4 to 5 minutes, or until tender-crisp. Stir in raisins, wine, sugar, curry and cardamom. Blend well and simmer on low heat 5 minutes.

Carefully scoop squash out of shells, leaving ⅛ to ¼-inch thick shell. Mash squash with remaining 2 tablespoons butter. Stir in apple mixture. Fill each shell with one-fourth of squash mixture. Sprinkle each with 1 tablespoon coconut. Place in 9 × 13-inch baking dish.

Bake in 350°F **convection oven** on rack 3, about 15 minutes (or bake in preheated 350°F **radiant bake oven** about 20 minutes), or until lightly browned.

4 servings

Apple-Stuffed Squash

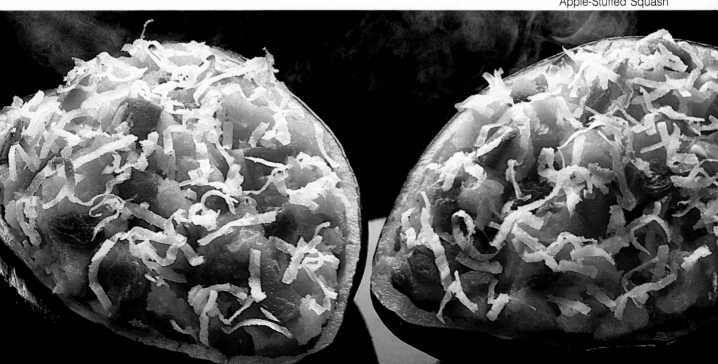

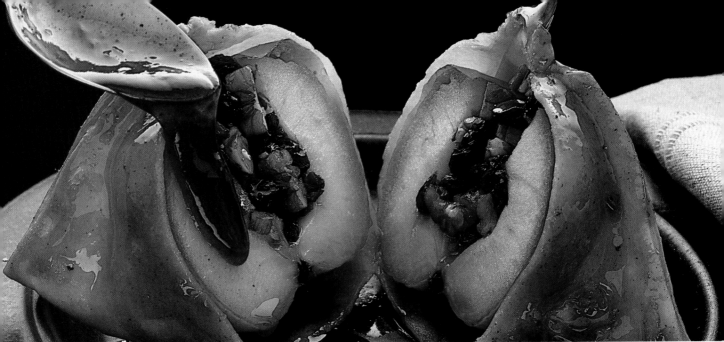

Apple Dumplings

Golden Vegetable Bake

 4 cups fresh cauliflower flowerets (about
   1½ pounds)
 1 package (10 ounces) frozen brussels
   sprouts, cooked according to package
   directions, drained
 ½ teaspoon celery salt
 ½ teaspoon sugar
 ¼ teaspoon dried rosemary leaves
 ¾ cup shredded Swiss or Gruyere cheese
 2 eggs, separated
 2 teaspoons milk or half-and-half
 ⅛ teaspoon salt
   Dash pepper
 2 tablespoons grated Parmesan cheese

Grease 1½-quart casserole. Set aside.

In medium saucepan place cauliflower and enough water to cover. Heat to boiling. Reduce heat to medium. Simmer, covered, 5 to 10 minutes, or until tender. Drain.

In casserole place cauliflower, brussels sprouts, celery salt, sugar and rosemary. Sprinkle Swiss cheese over top. Set aside.

Beat egg whites until stiff but not dry. Set aside. Beat egg yolks, milk, salt and pepper until thick and lemon colored. Gently fold egg yolk mixture and Parmesan cheese into egg whites. Spread over cheese-topped vegetables.

Bake in 350°F **convection oven** on rack 3, about 10 minutes (or bake in preheated 350°F **radiant bake oven** about 15 minutes), or until top is set and golden brown.

6 to 8 servings

Apple Dumplings

 1 recipe Single Pie Crust, page 174
 4 baking apples (6 to 8 ounces each)
 2 tablespoons raisins
 2 tablespoons chopped pecans

Sauce:
 ½ cup packed brown sugar
 ¼ cup honey
 ⅔ cup water
 ¼ teaspoon ground cinnamon
 ⅛ teaspoon ground nutmeg

Divide pastry in half. Roll one-half on floured surface into 14 × 7-inch rectangle. Cut in half to form two 7-inch squares. Repeat with remaining pastry.

Hollow out apples, leaving bottoms intact. In small dish combine raisins and pecans. Fill each apple with one-fourth of mixture. Place one apple on a pastry square. Bring opposite corners of pastry up over apple; press together. Press sides together to seal. Repeat with remaining pastry and apples.

Place dumplings in 8 × 8-inch baking dish or four 12-ounce ovenproof serving dishes.

For sauce: In small saucepan combine all ingredients. Heat to boiling. Pour over dumplings.

Bake in 400°F **convection oven** on rack 3, about 35 minutes (or bake in preheated 400°F **radiant bake oven** about 40 minutes), or until pastry is brown and apples are tender.

Cool slightly. Serve as side dish.

4 servings

Baked Pears with Wine Sauce

4 ripe pears (about 8 ounces each)

Sauce:
½ cup red currant jelly
⅓ cup sugar
¼ cup water
3 tablespoons port wine
1 cinnamon stick

Hollow out pears, leaving bottoms intact. Place pears in 8 × 8-inch baking dish or four 12-ounce ovenproof serving dishes.

For sauce: In small saucepan combine all ingredients. Heat to boiling. Remove and discard cinnamon stick. Pour sauce over pears.

Bake in 350°F **convection oven** on rack 3, about 45 minutes (or bake in preheated 350°F **radiant bake oven** about 50 minutes), or until fork tender.

Cool slightly. Serve as side dish.

4 servings

Baked Curried Fruit

Scandinavian Fruit Soup

1 cup dried apricots, cut-up
1 cup pitted prunes, cut-up
½ cup golden raisins
¼ cup dried currants
½ cup sugar
4⅔ cups hot water
¼ to ⅓ cup orange-flavored liqueur or orange juice
2 tablespoons quick-cooking tapioca
¼ teaspoon ground allspice
2 large oranges, peeled, sectioned and seeded
2 cinnamon sticks
Dash salt

In 3-quart casserole combine all ingredients. Cover. Bake in 325°F **radiant bake oven** 1½ to 2 hours, or until fruit is tender and liquid is thickened. Stir once.

Before serving, remove cinnamon sticks. Serve hot as side dish or first course. Top soup with sour cream, if desired.

6 to 8 servings

Baked Curried Fruit

1 small onion, sliced and separated into rings
½ cup chopped green pepper
1 tablespoon butter or margarine
⅓ cup dried apricots
⅓ cup raisins
1 can (8 ounces) pineapple chunks, drained, with 2 tablespoons juice reserved
1 medium apple, cored and chopped
⅓ cup dry white wine
3 tablespoons honey
1½ teaspoons curry powder
⅓ cup chopped cashews

In small skillet on medium high heat, sauté onion and green pepper in butter until tender. Place onion mixture in 1-quart casserole. Stir in apricots, raisins, pineapple and apple. In small bowl combine reserved pineapple juice, wine, honey and curry powder. Pour over fruit mixture.

Bake in 350°F **convection oven** on rack 3, 20 to 25 minutes (or bake in preheated 350°F **radiant bake oven** 35 to 40 minutes), or until sauce is hot and bubbly and apples are tender.

Sprinkle cashews over top of fruit. Serve as meal accompaniment.

4 to 6 servings

Breads

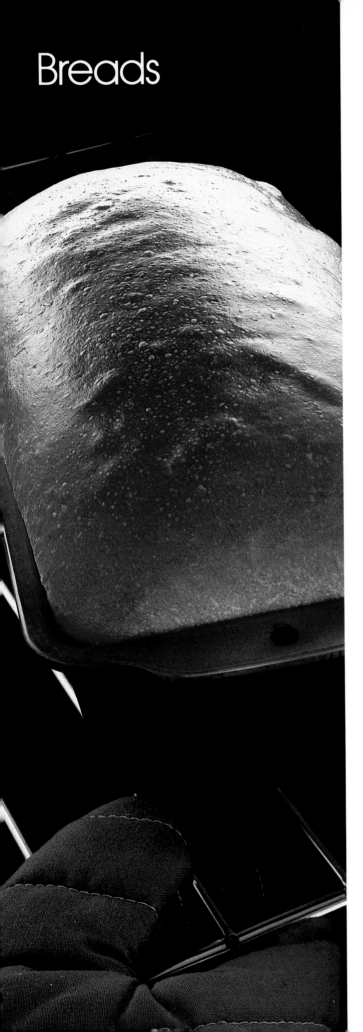

How to Make Bread

Knead dough on floured surface. Fold dough toward you. Rotate one quarter turn each time.

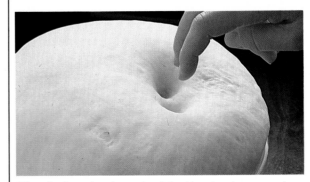

Check dough when doubled in size by pressing with fingers. Impressions should remain.

Roll out dough. Roll up, tucking in ends. Place seam-side down in pan.

Cool bread on rack. Turn loaf on its side to help preserve shape.

White Bread

Whole Wheat Bread

White Bread

  6 to 7 cups all-purpose flour, divided
  ¼ cup sugar
  2 packages (¼ ounce each) active dry yeast
  2 teaspoons salt
2¼ cups milk
  ¼ cup vegetable oil
  1 egg

In large mixing bowl combine 2 cups flour, sugar, yeast and salt. Set aside.

In small saucepan heat milk and oil until very warm (120° to 130°F). Add mixture and egg to dry ingredients. Blend on low speed of electric mixer until moistened. Beat 3 minutes on medium speed. Stir in remaining flour by hand to form stiff dough.

On floured surface knead until smooth and elastic, about 8 to 10 minutes. Place dough in greased bowl. Turn greased-side up. Cover. Let rise in warm place 45 to 60 minutes, or until light and doubled in size.

Generously grease two 9 × 5-inch or 8 × 4-inch loaf pans. Punch down dough; divide and shape into 2 loaves. Place in prepared pans. Cover. Let rise in warm place about 35 to 45 minutes, or until light and doubled in size.

Bake in preheated 350°F **convection oven** on rack 2, 20 to 25 minutes (or bake in preheated 375°F **radiant bake oven** 25 to 30 minutes), or until golden brown and loaves sound hollow when lightly tapped.

Remove from pans immediately. Cool on wire racks. Brush with melted butter, if desired.

Herb Bread: Follow recipe above, except add 1 tablespoon dried Italian seasoning, 1 tablespoon instant minced onion and ½ teaspoon garlic powder to first 2 cups flour. Continue as directed.

2 loaves

Whole Wheat Bread

  4 to 4½ cups all-purpose flour, divided
  2 packages (¼ ounce each) active dry yeast
  2 teaspoons salt
  2 cups water
  ¼ cup butter or margarine
  ¼ cup honey
  2 cups whole wheat flour

In large mixing bowl combine 2 cups all-purpose flour, yeast and salt. Set aside.

In small saucepan heat water, butter and honey until very warm (120° to 130°F). Add mixture to dry ingredients. Blend on low speed of electric mixer until moistened. Beat 3 minutes on medium speed. Stir in wheat flour and enough all-purpose flour to form stiff dough.

On floured surface knead dough until smooth and elastic, about 8 to 10 minutes. Place in greased bowl. Turn greased-side up. Cover. Let rise in warm place 45 to 60 minutes, or until light and doubled in size.

Generously grease two 9 × 5-inch or 8 × 4-inch loaf pans. Punch down dough; divide and shape into 2 loaves. Place in prepared pans. Cover. Let rise in warm place 45 to 60 minutes, or until light and doubled in size.

Bake in preheated 350°F **convection oven** on rack 2, 20 to 25 minutes (or bake in preheated 375°F **radiant bake oven** 25 to 30 minutes), or until deep golden brown and loaves sound hollow when lightly tapped.

Remove from pans immediately. Cool on wire racks. Brush tops with melted butter, if desired.

2 loaves

Sally Lunn Bread

Sally Lunn Bread

- 5 to 5½ cups all-purpose flour, divided
- ⅓ cup sugar
- 2 packages (¼ ounce each) active dry yeast
- 1 teaspoon salt
- 1 cup milk
- ½ cup water
- ½ cup butter or margarine
- 3 eggs

In large mixing bowl combine 2 cups flour, sugar, yeast and salt. Set aside.

In small saucepan heat milk, water and butter until very warm (120° to 130°F). Add mixture and eggs to dry ingredients. Blend on low speed of electric mixer until moistened. Beat 3 minutes on medium speed. Stir in enough of remaining flour by hand to make dough somewhat stiff (but too sticky to knead). Cover. Let rise in warm place 45 to 60 minutes, or until light and doubled in size.

Generously grease 12-cup fluted tube pan or 10-inch tube pan. Stir dough down; spoon into prepared pan. Spread evenly. Cover. Let dough rise in warm place 35 to 45 minutes, or until light and doubled in size.

Bake in preheated 350°F **convection oven** on rack 2, 25 to 30 minutes (or bake in preheated 375°F **radiant bake oven** 30 to 35 minutes), or until the loaf is deep golden brown and sounds hollow when lightly tapped.

Remove from pan immediately. Cool on wire rack. Cut into thin wedges.

1 large ring loaf

Pumpernickel Bread

- 2½ to 3 cups all-purpose flour, divided
- 3 packages (¼ ounce each) active dry yeast
- 1 tablespoon caraway seed
- 1 tablespoon salt
- 1½ cups water
- ½ cup dark molasses
- 2 tablespoons vegetable oil
- ¼ cup cocoa
- 2¾ cups rye flour
- Cornmeal

In large mixing bowl combine 2 cups all-purpose flour, yeast, caraway seed and salt. Set aside.

In small saucepan heat water, molasses, oil and cocoa until very warm (120° to 130°F). Add mixture to dry ingredients. Blend on low speed of electric mixer until moistened. Beat 3 minutes on medium speed. Stir in rye flour.

On floured surface knead dough about 8 to 10 minutes, adding ½ to 1 cup all-purpose flour until dough is smooth and elastic. (Dough will be slightly sticky.) Place in greased bowl; turn greased-side up. Cover. Let rise in warm place 1 to 1¼ hours, or until almost doubled in size.

Grease large cookie sheet. Sprinkle with cornmeal. Punch down dough. Shape into round loaf. Slash top with knife in crosshatch pattern. Place loaf on cookie sheet. Cover. Let rise in warm place 45 to 60 minutes, or until almost doubled in size.

Bake in preheated 350°F **convection oven** on rack 2, 25 to 30 minutes (or bake in preheated 375°F **radiant bake oven** for 30 to 35 minutes), or until crust is dark brown and loaf sounds hollow when lightly tapped.

Remove immediately. Cool on wire rack.

1 loaf

Individual Lemon Brioche

2½ to 3 cups all-purpose flour, divided
⅓ cup sugar
1 package (¼ ounce) active dry yeast
½ teaspoon salt
1 teaspoon grated fresh lemon peel
⅔ cup milk
¼ cup butter or margarine
2 eggs
   Butter or margarine, melted

In large mixing bowl combine 1 cup flour, sugar, yeast, salt and lemon peel. Set aside.

In small saucepan heat milk and butter until very warm (120° to 130°F). Add mixture and eggs to dry ingredients. Blend on low speed of electric mixer until moistened. Beat 3 minutes on medium speed. Stir in remaining flour to make soft dough.

On floured surface knead dough until very smooth and elastic, about 5 to 8 minutes. Place dough in greased bowl; turn greased-side up. Cover. Let rise in warm place 1 to 1¼ hours, or until light and doubled in size.

Grease 12 muffin cups. Punch down dough. Divide three-quarters of dough into 12 equal pieces. Form each piece into smooth ball. Shape remaining quarter of dough into 12 small balls. In each muffin cup place large ball of dough. Flatten slightly. Make **deep indentation** in each with finger or handle of wooden spoon. Set one small ball **firmly** into indentation. Brush with melted butter. Let rise, uncovered, in warm place 45 to 60 minutes, or until light and doubled in size.

Bake in preheated 325°F **convection oven** on rack 3, about 20 minutes (or bake in preheated 350°F **radiant bake oven** about 25 minutes), or until golden brown. Remove from pans immediately. Cool slightly on wire racks. Serve warm.

12 individual brioche

How to Form Brioche

Flatten dough slightly. Make deep indentation with finger. Set small ball firmly into indentation.

Individual Lemon Brioche

Cinnamon Raisin Loaves

1 recipe White Bread (unbaked), page 153
2 tablespoons butter or margarine, softened, divided
⅔ cup sugar
⅓ cup raisins
2½ teaspoons ground cinnamon
2 teaspoons grated fresh orange peel

Grease two 9 × 5-inch loaf pans. Set aside.

Divide White Bread dough in half. On floured surface roll each half to 16 × 8-inch rectangle. Spread each piece with 1 tablespoon butter, leaving ½ inch on one narrow end of each half for sealing.

In small bowl combine sugar, raisins, cinnamon and orange peel. Blend well. Sprinkle evenly over dough. Starting with 8-inch side, roll up toward side with ungreased edge. Pinch edges to seal. Place seam-side down in pans. Cover. Let rise in warm place about 45 to 60 minutes, or until light and doubled in size.

Bake in preheated 350°F **convection oven** on rack 2, 25 to 30 minutes (or bake in preheated 375°F **radiant bake oven** 30 to 35 minutes), or until golden brown and loaves sound hollow when lightly tapped.

Two 9 × 5-inch loaves

How to Braid Egg Loaf

Divide dough into three strips. Pinch together at one end.

Braid strips evenly. Pinch ends together. Turn under loaf.

Braided Egg Loaf

4½ to 5 cups all-purpose flour, divided
2 tablespoons sugar
1 package (¼ ounce) active dry yeast
1¼ teaspoons salt
1¼ cups milk
½ cup butter or margarine
2 eggs
1 egg yolk or 1 beaten egg
2 teaspoons sesame seed (optional)

In large mixing bowl combine 1½ cups flour, sugar, yeast and salt. Set aside.

In small saucepan heat milk and butter until very warm (120° to 130°F). Add mixture and 2 eggs to dry ingredients. Blend on low speed of electric mixer until moistened. Beat on medium speed for 2 minutes. Stir in remaining flour by hand to form stiff dough. (Dough will be somewhat sticky.)

On floured surface knead dough until smooth and elastic, about 8 to 10 minutes. Place dough in greased bowl; turn greased-side up. Cover. Let rise in warm place 1 to 1¼ hours, or until light and doubled in size.

Punch down dough; divide into 3 equal portions. Shape each portion into strip about 18 inches long. Grease large cookie sheet. Place strips side-by-side on cookie sheet, pinching together at one end to seal. Braid strips evenly. Pinch ends together to seal. Cover. Let rise in warm place 40 to 50 minutes, or until light and doubled in size. Brush with beaten egg or egg yolk. Sprinkle evenly with sesame seed.

Bake in preheated 350°F **convection oven** on rack 2, 20 to 25 minutes (or bake in preheated 375°F **radiant bake oven** for 25 to 30 minutes), or until deep golden brown and loaf sounds hollow when lightly tapped.

Remove from cookie sheet immediately. Cool on wire rack.

1 large 15-inch loaf

Herb Monkey Bread

3 to 3½ cups all-purpose flour, divided
2 tablespoons sugar
2 tablespoons grated Parmesan cheese
1 package (¼ ounce) active dry yeast
1 tablespoon dried parsley flakes
1 teaspoon salt
1 teaspoon dried thyme leaves
½ teaspoon dried basil leaves
½ teaspoon dried dill weed
½ teaspoon dried rosemary leaves
1 cup water
2 tablespoons butter or margarine
1 egg
⅓ cup butter or margarine

Grease 12-cup fluted tube pan or 2½-quart ring mold. Set aside.

In large mixing bowl blend 1½ cups flour, sugar, Parmesan cheese, yeast, parsley, salt, thyme, basil, dill weed and rosemary.

In small saucepan heat water and 2 tablespoons butter until very warm (120°F to 130°F). Add mixture and egg to dry ingredients. Blend on low speed of electric mixer until moistened. Beat on medium speed for 3 minutes. Stir in remaining flour by hand.

Knead dough on floured surface until smooth, about 3 to 5 minutes. Roll dough into 15 × 12-inch rectangle. Using pastry wheel or sharp knife cut dough into diamond-shaped pieces by cutting into 1½ to 2-inch strips diagonally across dough.

In shallow pan melt ⅓ cup butter. Dip each piece in melted butter and layer in prepared pan, overlapping pieces. Cover. Let rise in warm place 45 to 60 minutes, or until light and doubled in size.

Bake in preheated 375°F **convection oven** on rack 2, about 20 to 25 minutes (or bake in preheated 400°F **radiant bake oven** about 25 to 30 minutes), or until deep golden brown.

Cool 5 minutes. Remove from pan. Serve warm.

1 pull-apart ring loaf

Herb Monkey Bread

How to Make Herb Monkey Bread

Cut dough into diamond-shaped pieces with pastry wheel or sharp knife.

Dip pieces in melted butter. Overlap in pan. Let rise until doubled in size.

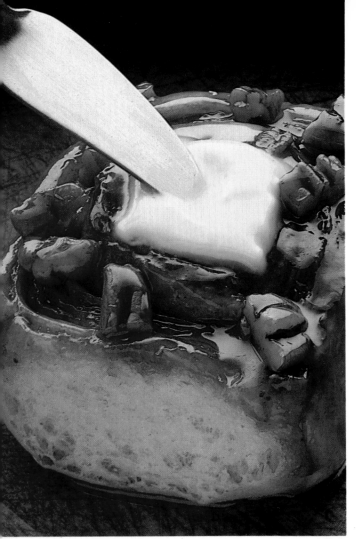
Caramel Rolls

Basic Sweet Dough

6 to 7 cups all-purpose flour, divided
½ cup sugar
2 packages (¼ ounce each) active dry yeast
2 teaspoons salt
½ cup butter or margarine
1 cup milk
1 cup water
1 egg

In large mixing bowl combine 2 cups flour, sugar, yeast and salt. Set aside.

In small saucepan heat butter, milk and water until very warm (120° to 130°F). Add mixture and egg to dry ingredients. Blend on low speed of electric mixer until moistened. Beat 3 minutes on medium speed. Stir in enough remaining flour by hand to form stiff dough. (Dough will be somewhat sticky.)

On floured surface knead dough until smooth and elastic, about 8 to 10 minutes. Place dough in greased bowl; turn greased-side up. Cover. Let rise in warm place 45 to 60 minutes, or until light and doubled in size. Punch down dough. Shape as directed in desired recipe.

Caramel Rolls

Caramel Topping:
1 cup packed brown sugar
1 cup chopped pecans
½ cup butter or margarine, melted
2 tablespoons light corn syrup

Rolls:
1 recipe Basic Sweet Dough (below left)
½ cup butter or margarine, melted, divided
1 cup packed brown sugar
4 teaspoons ground cinnamon

Grease two 13 × 9-inch pans. Set aside.

For caramel topping: In medium bowl combine all ingredients. Spread half of mixture in bottom of each pan. Set aside.

For rolls: Divide Basic Sweet Dough in half. On floured surface roll each half into 18 × 15-inch rectangle. Brush each piece with ¼ cup melted butter, leaving ½-inch on one 18-inch side for sealing.

Combine brown sugar and cinnamon. Divide in half. Sprinkle one-half evenly over one dough piece. Starting with 18-inch side, roll up toward side with ungreased edge. Pinch edges to seal. Cut into 15 slices. Repeat with remaining dough.

Place 15 slices cut-side down in each pan, directly on caramel topping. Cover. Let rise in warm place 45 to 60 minutes, or until light and doubled in size. Bake in preheated 350°F **convection oven** on racks 2 and 4, 15 to 20 minutes (or bake in preheated 375°F **radiant bake oven** 20 to 25 minutes, exchanging racks during baking), or until golden brown. Serve warm.

Cinnamon Rolls: Follow the recipe above, except omit caramel mixture. Form dough as directed. Place directly in greased pans. Let rise and bake as directed. Invert rolls onto serving platter.

Glaze:
⅔ cup confectioners' sugar
2 tablespoons butter or margarine, softened
¼ teaspoon vanilla
1 tablespoon plus 2 teaspoons milk or half-and-half

For glaze: In small bowl combine all ingredients. Stir until smooth. Drizzle rolls with glaze.

30 rolls

Refrigerated Potato Rolls

6½ to 7 cups all-purpose flour, divided
  ½ cup sugar
  1 package (¼ ounce) active dry yeast
1½ teaspoons salt
  1 cup milk
  ½ cup water
  ⅔ cup butter or margarine
  1 cup hot mashed potatoes
  2 eggs
  2 to 3 tablespoons butter or margarine, melted

In large mixing bowl combine 2 cups flour, sugar, yeast and salt. Set aside.

In medium saucepan heat milk, water and butter until very warm (120° to 130°F). Add mixture, mashed potatoes and eggs to dry ingredients. Blend on low speed of electric mixer until moistened. Beat 3 minutes on medium speed. Stir in remaining flour by hand to make soft dough.

On floured surface knead dough until smooth, about 3 to 5 minutes, adding flour if necessary. Dough will be soft and slightly sticky. Place in greased bowl. Cover. Let rise in warm place 45 to 60 minutes, or until doubled in size. Punch down dough. Brush with melted butter.

Place plastic wrap directly on dough. Cover top of bowl with plastic wrap or foil. Refrigerate up to 3 days. Punch down dough. Dough should be light and somewhat sticky. Shape dough into cloverleafs or bow knots (see below).

Bake in preheated 350°F **convection oven** on racks 1, 3 and 5, 10 to 13 minutes (or bake in two batches in preheated 375°F **radiant bake oven** on racks 2 and 4, 13 to 15 minutes, exchanging racks during baking), or until golden brown.

Cloverleaf Rolls: Grease 36 muffin cups. Divide dough into 36 parts; divide each part into 3 pieces. Shape into 1-inch balls. Place 3 balls in prepared muffin cup. Cover. Let rise in warm place 45 to 60 minutes, or until light and doubled in size.

Bow Knots: Grease 3 cookie sheets. Divide dough into 36 pieces. Roll each piece into pencil-shaped 10 to 11-inch roll. Tie in loose knots. Place on prepared cookie sheets. Cover. Let rise in warm place about 45 minutes, or until light and doubled in size.

TIP: Divide dough between cloverleafs and bow knots. Bake together.

36 rolls

Refrigerated Potato Rolls

How to Form Cloverleafs and Bow Knots

Shape dough into 1-inch balls. Place 3 balls in each of 36 muffin cups.

Roll dough into thin strands about 10 to 11 inches long. Tie each in loose knot.

Bran Rolls

½ cup water
½ cup butter or margarine
¼ cup honey
¾ cup 100% bran cereal
1½ teaspoons salt
1 package (¼ ounce) active dry yeast
½ cup warm water (105° to 115°F)
1 egg, beaten
1 cup whole wheat flour
2 to 3 cups all-purpose flour
Butter or margarine, melted

In small saucepan combine water, butter, honey, bran cereal and salt. Heat, stirring constantly, until butter melts. Remove to medium mixing bowl. Cool to 105° to 115°F.

Dissolve yeast in warm water. Add to bran mixture. Stir in egg, wheat flour and enough all-purpose flour to form stiff dough.

On well-floured surface knead dough until smooth and elastic, about 5 to 8 minutes. Place in greased bowl; turn greased-side up. Cover. Let rise in warm place about 1 hour, or until light and doubled in size.

Lightly grease two 9-inch round pans. Punch down dough. Cut into 24 equal pieces. Roll each piece into smooth ball. Place 12 balls in each pan. Brush with melted butter.

Bake in preheated 350°F **convection oven** on rack 3, 15 to 20 minutes (or bake in preheated 375°F **radiant bake oven** 20 to 25 minutes), or until golden brown. Remove from pans immediately. Serve warm.

24 rolls

Bread Sticks

1¼ cups very warm water (120° to 130°F)
3½ to 4 cups all-purpose flour, divided
1½ teaspoons salt
1 package (¼ ounce) active dry yeast
1 egg white, beaten with 1 tablespoon water
Coarse salt

In large mixing bowl combine very warm water, 1½ cups flour, salt and yeast. Beat on low speed of electric mixer until moistened. Beat for 3 minutes on medium speed. Stir in 1¾ cups remaining flour to form semi-stiff dough.

On floured surface knead in remaining ¼ to ¾ cup flour until smooth and elastic, about 8 to 10 minutes. Place dough in greased bowl; turn greased-side up. Cover. Let rise in warm place about 45 to 60 minutes, or until light and doubled in size.

Punch down dough. Divide dough into 18 equal pieces. Roll each piece about 10 inches long and ½ to ¾ inch in diameter. Grease two large cookie sheets. Place dough on cookie sheets. Brush with egg white-water mixture. Let rise in warm place, uncovered, 45 to 60 minutes. Brush again with egg white mixture. Sprinkle with coarse salt. Place 13 × 9-inch pan filled with 1½ inches hot water on rack 1 of oven.

Bake in preheated 400°F **convection oven** on racks 3 and 5, 15 to 18 minutes (or bake in preheated 425°F **radiant bake oven** 20 to 23 minutes, exchanging racks during baking), or until light golden brown.

Remove from pan immediately. Cool on wire racks.

18 bread sticks

Bread Sticks

Bagels

1½ cups very warm water (120° to 130°F)
2 packages (¼ ounce each) active dry yeast
4 to 4½ cups all-purpose flour, divided
3 tablespoons sugar, divided
1 teaspoon salt
6 cups water
1 egg yolk, beaten with 1 tablespoon water

In large mixing bowl combine very warm water, yeast, 1½ cups flour, 2 tablespoons sugar and salt. Beat on low speed of electric mixer until moistened. Beat on medium speed for 3 minutes. Stir in remaining flour to make stiff dough. On floured surface knead until smooth and elastic, about 8 to 10 minutes. Place in greased bowl; turn greased-side up. Cover. Let rest 20 minutes. Punch down.

Divide into 12 equal pieces. Shape into smooth balls. Punch hole in center of each ball. Pull gently to enlarge hole, working each bagel into uniform shape. Place on lightly floured board. Cover. Let rise 30 minutes.

In wok or large saucepan heat 6 cups water and remaining 1 tablespoon sugar to boiling. Reduce heat to gentle boil. Place 4 bagels at a time in water. Cook 1 minute on each side. Remove with slotted spoon or spatula to drain. Repeat with remaining bagels.

Grease two large baking sheets. Place 6 bagels on each sheet. Brush with egg yolk-water mixture.

Bake in preheated 350°F **convection oven** on racks 2 and 4, 20 to 25 minutes (or bake in preheated 375°F **radiant bake oven** 25 to 30 minutes), or until deep golden brown and crusty. Cool on wire rack.

12 bagels

Crisp Cracker Bread

1 cup plus 2 tablespoons all-purpose flour
1 teaspoon sugar
½ teaspoon baking powder
½ teaspoon salt
¼ cup water
2 tablespoons vegetable oil
Seasoned salt (optional)

In medium mixing bowl combine flour, sugar, baking powder and salt. Add water and oil. Stir until dough forms ball. (Add more water, if necessary.) Let dough rest 15 minutes.

Divide dough into 6 equal portions. Shape into balls. Roll each ball on lightly floured board or sheet of wax paper to form 6-inch circle. Prick thoroughly with fork. Sprinkle with seasoned salt. Repeat with remaining dough. Lightly grease three baking sheets. Place 2 rounds on each baking sheet.

Bake in preheated 450°F **convection oven** on racks 1, 3 and 5, 4 to 6 minutes (or bake in two batches in preheated 450°F **radiant bake oven** on racks 2 and 4, 7 to 9 minutes, exchanging racks during baking), or until golden brown and crisp.

6 crackers

Jam Muffins

Basic Muffins

    2 cups all-purpose flour
    ¼ cup sugar
    1 tablespoon baking powder
    ½ teaspoon salt
    1 egg, well beaten
    1 cup milk
    ¼ cup vegetable oil

Grease bottoms of 12 muffin cups. Set aside. In medium bowl combine flour, sugar, baking powder and salt. Stir in remaining ingredients just until dry ingredients are moistened. (Batter will be lumpy.) Spoon batter into prepared muffin cups, filling two-thirds full.

Bake in preheated 375°F **convection oven** on rack 3 (or 2 and 4 for 2 pans), 15 to 20 minutes (or bake in preheated 400°F **radiant bake oven** 20 to 25 minutes), or until golden brown.

Loosen edges. Remove from pan immediately. Serve warm.

Jam Muffins: Follow the recipe above, except divide batter in each cup into two layers. Place ½ teaspoon desired jam between layers before baking. Sprinkle with chopped nuts, if desired.

Cheese Muffins: Follow the recipe above, except add ½ cup shredded American or Cheddar cheese to dry ingredients.

Cinnamon and Sugar-Coated Muffins: Follow the recipe above, except after baking brush tops of hot muffins with 2 tablespoons melted butter or margarine. Dip tops into mixture of ¼ cup sugar and ¾ teaspoon cinnamon.

12 muffins

Flaky Biscuits

    2 cups all-purpose flour
    1 tablespoon baking powder
    ½ teaspoon salt
    ¼ cup vegetable shortening
    ¾ cup milk

In large bowl combine flour, baking powder and salt. Using pastry blender or fork, cut in shortening until mixture has consistency of coarse meal. Add milk. Stir with fork until soft dough forms. Turn dough onto floured surface. Sprinkle lightly with flour. Knead gently 10 to 12 times, until no longer sticky. Roll or press dough to ½-inch thickness. Cut with 2½-inch floured biscuit cutter. Place biscuits 1 inch apart on ungreased cookie sheet.

Bake in preheated 400°F **convection oven** on rack 3, about 12 minutes (or bake in preheated 425°F **radiant bake oven** about 13 minutes), or until golden brown. Remove from sheet. Serve warm.

Cheese Biscuits: Follow the recipe above, except add ¾ cup finely shredded Cheddar or American cheese to flour-shortening mixture before adding liquid. Grease cookie sheet to avoid sticking. Bake as directed.

Bacon Biscuits: Follow the recipe above, except add 5 strips cooked, drained and crumbled bacon to flour-shortening mixture before adding liquid. Bake as directed.

Ham Biscuits: Follow the recipe above, except add ½ cup finely diced, fully-cooked ham to the flour-shortening mixture before adding liquid. Bake as directed.

12 Flaky Biscuits or 14 to 16 biscuit variations

Popovers

- 2 eggs
- 1 cup milk
- 1 cup all-purpose flour
- ¼ teaspoon salt

Generously grease six 6-ounce custard cups or 8 muffin cups. Set aside.

In large mixing bowl beat eggs. Add remaining ingredients and beat on low speed of electric mixer just until smooth. Fill cups about three-fourths full with batter.

Bake in preheated 400°F **convection oven** on rack 2, 15 minutes, then reduce heat to 325°F and bake for 15 minutes longer (or bake in preheated 425°F **radiant bake oven** 15 minutes, then reduce heat to 350°F and bake 15 minutes longer), or until deep golden brown.

Remove from pan. Serve warm.

6 or 8 popovers

Cornbread

- 1 cup yellow cornmeal
- ¾ cup all-purpose flour
- 2 tablespoons sugar
- 1 tablespoon baking powder
- ½ teaspoon salt
- ⅛ to ¼ teaspoon cayenne
- 2 eggs, slightly beaten
- ¾ cup milk
- ⅓ cup vegetable oil

Grease 8 × 8-inch baking pan. Set aside.

In medium mixing bowl, stir together cornmeal, flour, sugar, baking powder, salt and cayenne. Add remaining ingredients. Stir until just moistened. Pour into pan.

Bake in preheated 350°F **convection oven** on rack 3, 20 to 25 minutes (or bake in preheated 375°F **radiant bake oven** 25 to 30 minutes), or until light golden brown.

One 8 × 8-inch pan

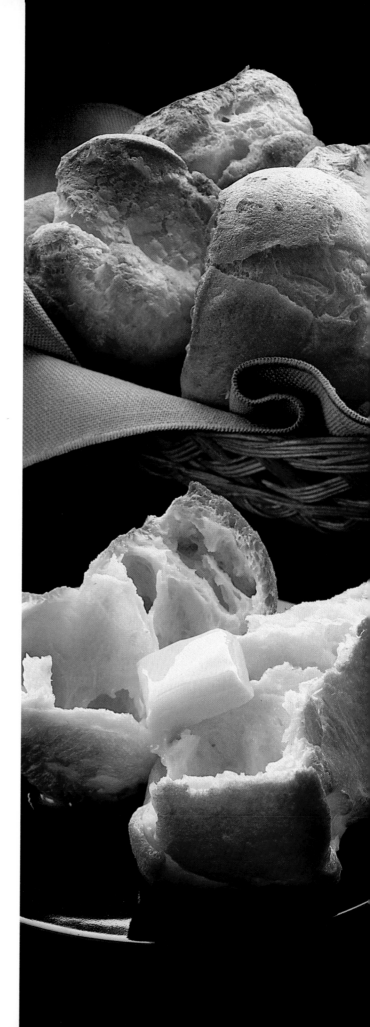

Popovers

Sour Cream-Blueberry Coffeecake

Sour Cream-Blueberry Coffeecake

Topping:
- ¼ cup all-purpose flour
- ¼ cup packed brown sugar
- ½ teaspoon ground cinnamon
- 2 tablespoons butter or margarine

- 1½ cups all-purpose flour
- ¾ cup sugar
- 1½ teaspoons baking powder
- ⅛ teaspoon salt
- ¾ cup dairy sour cream
- ⅓ cup milk
- 1 egg
- 1 teaspoon vanilla
- 1 cup fresh blueberries*

Grease and flour 9-inch round baking pan. Set aside. For topping: In small bowl blend all ingredients until crumbly. Set aside.

In medium mixing bowl combine flour, sugar, baking powder, salt, sour cream, milk, egg and vanilla. Blend on low speed of electric mixer. Beat on medium speed 2 minutes. Fold in blueberries. Pour into pan. Sprinkle with topping.

Bake in preheated 350°F **convection oven** on rack 2, about 35 minutes (or bake in preheated 350°F **radiant bake oven** about 40 minutes), or until wooden pick inserted in center comes out clean.

*Or 1 cup frozen blueberries (defrost and drain thoroughly before measuring).

6 to 8 servings

Banana Nut Bread

- 2 cups all-purpose flour
- ½ cup packed brown sugar
- ½ cup granulated sugar
- 1 teaspoon baking soda
- ¼ teaspoon salt
- ½ cup butter or margarine, softened
- ¼ cup sour milk*
- 2 eggs
- 1 cup mashed bananas (2 medium)
- 1 teaspoon vanilla
- ½ cup chopped walnuts

Grease bottom of 9 × 5-inch loaf pan. Set aside. Place all ingredients in large mixing bowl. Blend on low speed of electric mixer until moistened. Beat on medium speed 1 minute. Pour batter into pan.

Bake in preheated 325°F **convection oven** on rack 2, 50 to 55 minutes (or bake in preheated 350°F **radiant bake oven** 55 to 60 minutes), or until wooden pick inserted in center comes out clean.

Cool in pan 10 minutes. Loosen edges. Remove from pan. Place on wire rack. Cool completely.

*Or substitute 2 teaspoons vinegar plus enough milk to equal ¼ cup. (Let stand 5 minutes before adding to other ingredients.)

TIP: Recipe can be doubled.

One 9 × 5-inch loaf

Pumpkin Bread

2½ cups all-purpose flour
½ cup whole wheat flour
1 cup granulated sugar
1 cup packed brown sugar
2½ teaspoons pumpkin pie spice
2 teaspoons baking soda
1 teaspoon salt
⅔ cup vegetable oil
⅔ cup water
4 eggs
1 can (16 ounces) pumpkin
1½ cups raisins (optional)

Grease bottoms of two 9×5-inch loaf pans. Set aside. In medium mixing bowl combine all ingredients. Beat on low speed of electric mixer until moistened. Beat on medium speed 2 minutes. Stir in raisins. Divide batter evenly between pans.

Bake in preheated 325°F **convection oven** on rack 2, 45 to 50 minutes (or bake in preheated 350°F **radiant bake oven** 50 to 55 minutes), or until wooden pick inserted in center comes out clean.

Cool in pans 10 minutes. Loosen edges. Remove from pans. Place on wire racks. Cool completely.

Two 9×5-inch loaves

Zucchini Bread

2½ cups all-purpose flour
1⅔ cups sugar
2 to 3 teaspoons ground cinnamon
1 teaspoon baking soda
1 teaspoon baking powder
1 teaspoon salt
1 cup vegetable oil
3 eggs
2 cups shredded zucchini
1 teaspoon vanilla
½ cup chopped nuts

Grease bottoms of two 8×4-inch loaf pans. Set aside. In large mixing bowl place all ingredients. Beat 1 minute on medium speed of electric mixer. Divide batter evenly between pans.

Bake in preheated 325°F **convection oven** on rack 2, 40 to 45 minutes (or bake in preheated 350°F **radiant bake oven** 45 to 50 minutes), or until wooden pick inserted in center comes out clean.

Cool in pans 10 minutes. Loosen edges. Remove from pans. Place on wire racks. Cool completely.

Two 8×4-inch loaves

German Pancake

German Pancake

2 tablespoons butter or margarine
2 eggs
1 cup milk
1 cup all-purpose flour
¼ cup granulated sugar
¼ teaspoon salt
¼ teaspoon vanilla
2 cups sliced strawberries or peaches
Confectioners' sugar

Preheat **convection oven** or **radiant bake oven** to 425°F. Place butter in 9-inch round glass baking dish. Place in oven to melt butter.

In medium mixing bowl beat eggs on low speed of electric mixer. Add milk, flour, granulated sugar, salt and vanilla. Beat on low speed until smooth. Pour into hot pan.

Bake in preheated 425°F **convection oven** on rack 2, about 20 minutes (or bake in preheated 425°F **radiant bake oven** about 25 minutes), or until center is puffed and knife inserted in center comes out clean.

Fill with fruit. Sprinkle with confectioners' sugar. Serve immediately.

2 to 4 servings

Desserts

Grand Marnier Soufflé

Confectioners' sugar
1¼ cup butter or margarine
⅓ cup all-purpose flour
1 cup half-and-half
4 eggs, separated
¼ cup Grand Marnier or other orange-flavored liqueur
1 tablespoon grated fresh orange peel
1 tablespoon grated fresh lemon peel
¼ teaspoon salt
2 tablespoons sugar

Sauce: (optional)
2 tablespoons butter or margarine
¼ cup minced pecans
1 cup orange marmalade
2 tablespoons Grand Marnier or water

Grease 1½-quart soufflé dish. Coat with confectioners' sugar. Set aside.

In medium saucepan melt butter. Stir in flour. Blend in half-and-half. Cook on medium heat, stirring constantly, until thickened. Remove from heat. Add small amount thickened mixture to egg yolks. Blend yolks back into mixture, stirring constantly. Add Grand Marnier, orange and lemon peel and salt. Set aside.

In medium mixing bowl beat egg whites until foamy. Gradually beat in sugar. Beat until stiff but not dry. Fold egg yolk mixture into whites. Pour into prepared soufflé dish.

Bake in preheated 350°F **convection oven** on rack 2, 25 to 30 minutes (or bake in preheated 375°F **radiant bake oven** 30 to 35 minutes), or until knife inserted in center comes out clean. Serve immediately with warm sauce.

For sauce: In small saucepan melt butter on medium heat. Add nuts. Cook and stir about 1 minute. Add remaining ingredients. Cook and stir until hot.

6 to 8 servings

Cheese Strudel

½ cup raisins
2 tablespoons brandy, warmed
1½ cups ricotta cheese
1 package (8 ounces) cream cheese, softened
¾ cup sugar
2 egg yolks
2 tablespoons all-purpose flour
2 teaspoons grated fresh orange peel
1 teaspoon vanilla
1 cup butter or margarine, melted
15 sheets phyllo dough

Glaze:
1¼ cups confectioners' sugar
2 tablespoons orange juice
1 teaspoon grated fresh orange peel
3 tablespoons chopped nuts

In small mixing bowl soak raisins in warmed brandy for 30 minutes. Drain. Pat dry. Place in medium mixing bowl. Add ricotta cheese, cream cheese, sugar, egg yolks, flour, orange peel and vanilla. Beat on medium speed of electric mixer until smooth. Set aside.

Lightly brush 10 × 15-inch jelly roll pan with butter.

Place 1 sheet of phyllo dough on large dish towel. Lightly brush with butter. Repeat with 4 more sheets of phyllo to make 5 layers. Spread one-third of ricotta mixture (1 cup) lengthwise slightly off-center to within 2 inches of edges. Mixture will form 12 × 3-inch rectangle. Fold edge of phyllo over filling to center. Fold ends in. Fold opposite edge back toward filling, folding twice to form about 12 × 3-inch strudel. Place seam-side down on pan. Brush top with melted butter. Repeat procedure to form two more 12 × 3-inch strudels. Place on prepared pan.

Bake in preheated 350°F **convection oven** on rack 3, 20 to 25 minutes (or bake in preheated 375°F **radiant bake oven** 25 to 30 minutes), or until crisp and golden brown. Carefully lift with two spatulas to cooling rack. Glaze while warm.

For glaze: In a small bowl combine confectioners' sugar, orange juice and orange peel. Blend until smooth. Drizzle one-third over each strudel top. Sprinkle each with 1 tablespoon nuts.

3 strudels

Coffee Cream Eclairs

Filling:
½ cup sugar
2 tablespoons cornstarch
2 tablespoons all-purpose flour
1 teaspoon instant coffee granules
¼ teaspoon ground cinnamon
   Dash salt
2 cups half-and-half
3 egg yolks, slightly beaten

Shells:
1 cup all-purpose flour
2 teaspoons sugar
⅛ teaspoon salt
1 cup water
½ cup butter or margarine
4 eggs, room temperature

Glaze:
2 tablespoons butter or margarine
1 ounce (1 square) semi-sweet chocolate
1 tablespoon plus 1 teaspoon half-and-half
½ teaspoon vanilla
½ cup confectioners' sugar

For filling: In medium saucepan combine sugar, cornstarch, flour, coffee, cinnamon and salt. Slowly blend in half-and-half. Cook and stir on medium heat until thickened. Remove from heat. Stir small amount of hot mixture into egg yolks. Add yolks back to hot mixture, stirring constantly. Cook and stir on medium heat 1 more minute. Pour into small bowl. Cover by placing plastic wrap directly on surface of mixture. Refrigerate.

For shells: Grease large cookie sheet. Set aside. In small bowl combine flour, sugar and salt. Set aside. In medium saucepan heat water and butter on medium heat, stirring occasionally, until butter melts and mixture boils. Add flour mixture all at once. Stir vigorously about 1 minute, or until mix-ture forms a ball and leaves the sides of the pan. Remove from heat. Add eggs, one at a time, beat-ing with spoon after each addition until mixture is smooth. On prepared cookie sheet shape dough into twelve tubes and flatten into 2 × 3-inch rec-tangles, using a pastry bag or two spoons.

Bake shells in preheated 350°F **convection oven** on rack 3, 35 to 40 minutes (or bake in preheated 375°F **radiant bake oven** 40 to 45 minutes), or until golden brown. Remove from oven. Cut horizontally into two layers. Place cut-sides up on cookie sheet. Return to oven. Bake an additional 10 minutes. Turn oven off and allow shells to stand in oven 10 min-utes. Remove from oven. Cool shells on wire racks.

For glaze: In small saucepan on low heat melt butter and chocolate, stirring constantly. Add half-and-half and vanilla. Add confectioners' sugar. Stir until smooth.

Spoon prepared filling into bottom halves of shells. Cover with top halves. Spread glaze evenly on top of eclairs. Refrigerate until ready to serve.

12 eclairs

How to Shape Eclair Shells

Use pastry bag to shape dough into twelve tubes. Flatten into 2 × 3-inch rectangles.

Chocolate Chip Cheesecake

Chocolate Chip Cheesecake

1¼ cups chocolate wafer crumbs
¼ cup ground almonds
¼ cup butter or margarine, melted
2 containers (15 to 16 ounces each) ricotta cheese
12 ounces cream cheese, softened
⅓ cup almond liqueur
1 tablespoon creme de cocoa liqueur
2 cups confectioners' sugar
⅔ cup all-purpose flour
6 eggs
2 tablespoons grated semi-sweet chocolate

In small mixing bowl, combine crumbs, ground almonds and butter. Press evenly into bottom of 10-inch springform pan.

Bake in preheated 375°F **convection oven** on rack 3, 8 minutes (or bake in preheated 375°F **radiant bake oven** 10 minutes). Set aside.

In large mixing bowl combine ricotta, cream cheese, almond liqueur and creme de cocoa. Beat on medium speed until smooth. Blend in confectioners' sugar, flour, eggs and chocolate. Pour into prepared crust.

Bake in preheated 325°F **convection oven** 1 to 1¼ hours (or bake in preheated 325°F **radiant bake oven** 1¼ to 1½ hours), or until knife inserted in center comes out clean. Run spatula around edges. Cool to room temperature. Refrigerate overnight. Remove sides from pan.

Variation: Follow the recipe above, substituting ⅓ cup milk and 1 teaspoon almond extract for almond and creme de cocoa liqueurs.

One 10-inch round cheesecake

Walnut Rum Torte

⅔ cup granulated sugar
½ cup butter or margarine, softened
1 cup all-purpose flour
2 teaspoons baking powder
⅓ cup milk
2 eggs
1 cup minced walnuts, divided
2 tablespoons dark rum (optional)
½ cup apricot preserves, divided
½ cup pineapple preserves, divided
1 cup whipping cream
2 tablespoons confectioners' sugar

Grease and flour 9 × 9-inch baking pan. Set aside.

In medium mixing bowl place sugar, butter, flour, baking powder, milk and eggs. Beat on low speed of electric mixer until moistened. Beat on high speed 1 minute, scraping bowl frequently. Fold in ¾ cup minced nuts. Spread batter evenly in prepared pan.

Bake in preheated 325°F **convection oven** on rack 3, 25 to 30 minutes (or bake in preheated 350°F **radiant bake oven** 30 to 35 minutes), or until golden brown and top springs back when touched lightly. Cool 5 minutes. Loosen edges. Remove from pan. Cool on wire rack.

Sprinkle top of cake with rum. Wrap in foil and refrigerate until chilled. Cut in half to form 2 rectangles, then horizontally to form 4 layers.

To assemble torte: Spread 1 layer with ¼ cup apricot preserves. Top with another layer. Spread second layer with ¼ cup pineapple preserves. Repeat with remaining two layers and preserves.

Beat whipping cream and confectioners' sugar on high speed until stiff. Spread whipped cream on sides and top of torte. With pastry tube, pipe whipped cream around edges, if desired. Sprinkle with remaining nuts. Serve chilled.

6 to 8 servings

How to Cut Torte into Layers

Cut torte in half to form two rectangles. Cut each half horizontally to form four thin layers.

Baklava

1½ cups honey
1 cup lemonade
2 teaspoons grated fresh lemon peel
3 whole allspice
1 cinnamon stick
2 cups chopped pecans
2 cups shredded coconut
½ teaspoon ground cinnamon
¼ teaspoon ground allspice
1¼ cups butter or margarine, melted
20 sheets phyllo dough (about one 16-ounce package)

In medium saucepan combine honey, lemonade, lemon peel, whole allspice and cinnamon stick. Bring to boil. Reduce heat to medium low. Simmer, stirring occasionally, 15 minutes. Strain. Set aside.

Place pecans and coconut in food processor or blender. Grind well. Add ground cinnamon and allspice. Set aside.

Lightly brush 10 × 15-inch jelly roll pan with butter. Layer four phyllo sheets in pan, lightly brushing each with butter. (Sheets will be "wrinkled" when fitted into pan.) Sprinkle one-fourth of nut and coconut mixture over phyllo layer. Repeat phyllo and nut layers three more times. (Each phyllo layer has four sheets. Each sheet should be brushed with butter.) Top with remaining phyllo sheets. Brush each with butter.

Using sharp knife, score top, cutting diagonals 1½ inches apart to form diamond pattern.

Bake in preheated 325°F **convection oven** on rack 2, 30 to 35 minutes (or bake in preheated 350°F **radiant bake oven** 35 to 40 minutes), or until crisp golden brown on top. Remove from oven. Pour cooled syrup evenly over top. Cool before serving.

Variation: Follow recipe above, substituting orange juice and orange peel for prepared lemonade and lemon peel.

3½ to 4 dozen pieces

Baklava

Peppermint Meringues

½ cup granulated sugar
¼ cup confectioners' sugar
3 egg whites, room temperature
⅛ teaspoon cream of tartar
¼ cup crushed peppermint candy

Sift sugars together. Set aside. In medium mixing bowl beat egg whites and cream of tartar on medium speed of electric mixer until foamy. Beat on high speed, gradually adding sugar until stiff peaks form and sugars are dissolved.

Cover cookie sheet with parchment paper or plain brown paper. Drop mixture by heaping tablespoons to form sixteen 2-inch meringues. Use the back of a teaspoon to form a hollow in each. Fill each hollow with small amount of crushed peppermint candy.

Bake in preheated 225°F **convection oven** on rack 3, about 1 hour. Turn temperature selector to off. Leave oven fan on for 2½ to 3 hours, or until meringues are light and dry.

(Or bake in preheated 225°F **radiant bake oven** about 1 hour. Turn oven and temperature selector to off. Let stand overnight with door closed.)

Sixteen 2-inch meringues

Strawberry-Filled Chocolate Cake Roll

Cake:
- 6 eggs, separated
- ¼ cup granulated sugar
- ⅓ cup granulated sugar
- ⅓ cup cocoa
- ½ teaspoon baking powder
- ¼ teaspoon salt
- ½ teaspoon vanilla
- ½ cup all-purpose flour

- ⅓ cup confectioners' sugar
- 1 tablespoon cocoa

Filling:
- 3 ounces cream cheese, softened
- ⅓ cup confectioners' sugar
- ⅛ teaspoon vanilla
- Dash salt
- 3 tablespoons half-and-half or milk
- 1½ cups flaked coconut
- 1½ cups thinly sliced strawberries (about 1 pint)

Glaze:
- 3 tablespoons half-and-half or milk
- 2 ounces (2 squares) semi-sweet chocolate
- 1 tablespoon butter or margarine

Grease 10 × 15-inch jelly roll pan. Line bottom with wax paper. Grease wax paper. Set aside.

For cake: In medium mixing bowl beat egg whites with electric mixer until foamy. Gradually beat in ¼ cup sugar, until stiff but not dry. Set aside.

In medium mixing bowl beat egg yolks and ⅓ cup granulated sugar on medium speed of electric mixer until thick and lemon colored. Add ⅓ cup cocoa, baking powder, salt and vanilla. Beat on low speed until blended. Add flour. Beat on low speed just until smooth. (Mixture will be stiff.) Fold chocolate mixture into egg whites. Spread evenly into prepared pan.

Bake in preheated 325°F **convection oven** on rack 2, 10 to 12 minutes (or bake in preheated 350°F **radiant bake oven** 10 to 12 minutes), or until center springs back when touched lightly.

Mix confectioners' sugar and cocoa. Sprinkle over clean kitchen towel. Loosen edges of cake. Invert onto towel. Remove wax paper. Trim stiff edges. While cake is hot, carefully roll cake and towel from narrow end. Cool on rack 30 to 60 minutes.

For filling: In small mixing bowl blend cream cheese, confectioners' sugar, vanilla and salt. Blend in half-and-half. Stir in coconut. Unroll cooled cake. Spread mixture evenly over cake. Top with sliced strawberries. Roll up cake. Remove to serving platter.

For glaze: In small saucepan combine all ingredients. Cook on low heat, stirring constantly, until smooth. Pour over cake. Chill.

8 to 10 servings

How to Roll Cake

Sprinkle sugar and cocoa over clean kitchen towel. Roll cake and towel together.

Strawberry-Filled Chocolate Cake Roll

Angel Food Cake

Coconut Cake

1¼ cups sugar
⅔ cup butter or margarine, softened
3 eggs
1 teaspoon vanilla
½ cup milk
⅓ cup cream of coconut*
1¾ cups all-purpose flour
2 teaspoons baking powder
½ teaspoon salt

Frosting:
¼ cup butter or margarine, softened
3 tablespoons vegetable shortening
3½ cups confectioners' sugar
2 tablespoons cream of coconut
½ teaspoon vanilla
3 to 4 tablespoons half-and-half or milk

Grease and flour two 9-inch round cake pans. Set aside. In large mixing bowl cream sugar, butter, eggs and vanilla until light and fluffy. Add remaining ingredients. Beat on low speed of electric mixer until moistened. Beat on medium speed 2 minutes, scraping bowl occasionally. Pour into pans.

Bake in preheated 325°F **convection oven** on rack 3, 25 to 30 minutes (or in preheated 350°F **radiant bake oven** 30 to 35 minutes), or until center springs back when touched lightly. Cool 5 minutes. Loosen edges. Remove from pan. Cool on rack.

For frosting: In medium mixing bowl blend butter and shortening. Add confectioners' sugar, cream of coconut and vanilla. Beat on medium speed of electric mixer, gradually adding half-and-half, 1 tablespoon at a time, until smooth and creamy. Spread on cooled cake.

*Available in drink mix section of grocery store.

One 9-inch cake

Angel Food Cake

1⅓ cups confectioners' sugar
¾ cup all-purpose flour
¼ teaspoon salt
12 egg whites, room temperature
1¼ teaspoons cream of tartar
¾ cup granulated sugar
1½ teaspoons vanilla

In medium bowl combine confectioners' sugar, flour and salt. Set aside.

In large mixing bowl place egg whites and cream of tartar. With clean beaters beat on medium speed of electric mixer until foamy. Beat on high speed, gradually adding granulated sugar, until stiff peaks form and mixture is glossy. Add vanilla with last addition of sugar.

Sprinkle one-fourth of flour mixture over beaten egg whites. Fold in gently. Repeat until all flour mixture is folded in. Spread batter in ungreased 10-inch tube pan. Gently cut through batter with metal spatula or knife to eliminate large air bubbles.

Bake in preheated 350°F **convection oven** on rack 2, 30 to 35 minutes (or in preheated 375°F **radiant bake oven** 30 to 35 minutes), or until top springs back and cracks in center of cake feel dry.

Insert pan on heat resistant funnel or bottle. Cool several hours or overnight. Loosen edges and remove from pan.

Serve with Cherry Sauce, page 99, or fresh fruit and Lemon Cream Sauce, page 99.

One 10-inch tube cake

Carrot Cake

Fluffy Frosting

⅔ cup sugar
⅓ cup light corn syrup
2 tablespoons water
2 egg whites
¾ teaspoon vanilla

In small saucepan combine sugar, corn syrup and water. Cover. Heat to full boil. Insert candy thermometer. Boil, uncovered, on medium high heat until thermometer registers 242°F (firm ball stage).

In medium mixing bowl beat egg whites on high speed of electric mixer until stiff peaks form. While beating constantly on medium speed, pour hot syrup in slow, steady stream into egg whites. Add vanilla. Beat on high speed until stiff peaks form.

Maple Frosting: Follow the recipe above, substituting dark corn syrup for light corn syrup. Substitute maple flavor for vanilla.

About 3 cups (fills and frosts two 9-inch layers or one 13 × 9-inch pan)

Carrot Cake

2 cups all-purpose flour
¾ cup granulated sugar
½ cup packed brown sugar
1 teaspoon baking soda
¾ teaspoon baking powder
½ teaspoon salt
1½ teaspoons ground cinnamon
½ teaspoon ground allspice
½ teaspoon ground nutmeg
  Dash ground cloves
3 eggs
⅔ cup vegetable oil
½ cup milk
1½ teaspoons vanilla
1¾ cups shredded carrots
¾ cup chopped walnuts

1 recipe Cream Cheese Frosting (below)

Grease and flour 13 × 9-inch baking pan. Set aside. In large mixing bowl combine all ingredients except walnuts. Blend on low speed of electric mixer until moistened. Beat on high speed 1 minute, scraping bowl occasionally. Stir in nuts. Pour into prepared pan.

Bake in preheated 325°F **convection oven** on rack 3, 30 to 35 minutes (or bake in preheated 350°F **radiant bake oven** 35 to 40 minutes), or until top springs back when touched lightly. Cool 5 minutes. Loosen edges. Remove from pan. Cool on wire rack. Frost with Cream Cheese Frosting.

Spice Cake: Follow the recipe above, except omit carrots. Increase granulated sugar to 1 cup and increase milk to 1 cup.

One 13 × 9-inch cake

Cream Cheese Frosting

2½ cups confectioners' sugar
3 ounces cream cheese, softened
2 tablespoons butter or margarine, softened
2 to 3 tablespoons half-and-half or milk
½ teaspoon vanilla

In medium mixing bowl combine confectioners' sugar, cream cheese, butter, 2 tablespoons half-and-half and vanilla. Blend on low speed of electric mixer. Beat on high speed until smooth and creamy. Gradually beat in additional half-and-half (about 1 tablespoon), until frosting reaches desired consistency.

1¾ cups (frosts one 13 × 9-inch cake)

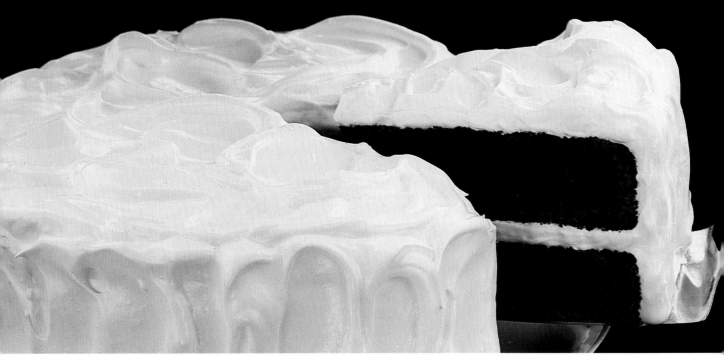

Devil's Food Cake

Devil's Food Cake

- 4 ounces (4 squares) unsweetened chocolate
- 1⅔ cups sugar
- ½ cup vegetable shortening
- 2 eggs
- 1 teaspoon vanilla
- 1¼ cups milk
- 1¾ cups all-purpose flour
- 1¾ teaspoons baking soda
- ¼ teaspoon salt

- 1 recipe Fluffy Frosting, page 172

Grease and flour two 9-inch round cake pans. Set aside. In small saucepan melt chocolate on low heat, stirring constantly. Pour into large mixing bowl. Add sugar, shortening, eggs and vanilla. Cream with electric mixer until light and fluffy.

Add remaining ingredients. Beat on low speed until moistened. Beat on medium speed for 2 minutes, scraping bowl occasionally. Pour batter into prepared pans.

Bake in preheated 325°F **convection oven** on rack 3, 25 to 30 minutes (or bake in preheated 350°F **radiant bake oven** 30 to 35 minutes), or until top springs back when touched lightly. Cool 5 minutes. Loosen edges. Remove from pans. Cool on wire rack. Frost with Fluffy Frosting.

13 × 9-inch cake: Follow the recipe above, except grease and flour 13 × 9-inch cake pan. Bake in preheated 325°F **convection oven** on rack 3, 30 to 35 minutes (or bake in preheated 350°F **radiant bake oven** 35 to 40 minutes).

Two 9-inch layers or one 13 × 9-inch cake

Pound Cake

- Granulated sugar
- 3 cups confectioners' sugar
- 1½ cups butter or margarine, softened
- 1 teaspoon vanilla
- 1 teaspoon lemon or rum extract
- 5 eggs
- 3 cups all-purpose flour
- 1 teaspoon baking powder
- ½ teaspoon salt
- ¾ cup half-and-half

Grease a 10-inch tube pan or fluted ring pan. Coat evenly with granulated sugar. Set aside.

In large mixing bowl cream confectioners' sugar and butter. Add vanilla and lemon. Beat in eggs one at a time until light and fluffy. In another bowl mix flour, baking powder and salt. Add half of dry mixture to egg and butter mixture. Beat until smooth. Mix in half-and-half. Add remaining dry mixture. Beat until smooth. Pour into prepared pan.

Bake in preheated 325°F **convection oven** on rack 2, 1 to 1¼ hours (or bake in preheated 350°F **radiant bake oven** 1¼ to 1½ hours), or until wooden pick inserted in center comes out clean. Cool 10 minutes. Loosen edges. Remove from pan. Cool on wire rack.

Cherry Chocolate Chip Pound Cake: Follow the recipe above, except substitute ½ cup maraschino cherry juice and ¼ cup water for half-and-half and lemon extract. Stir ½ cup chopped maraschino cherries and 1 ounce (1 square) grated semi-sweet chocolate into batter before pouring into prepared pan.

One 10-inch tube cake

Apple Pie

    1 recipe Double Pie Crust (below right)
6½ to 7½ cups cored, pared and sliced apples
    ¾ to 1 cup sugar
    ¼ cup all-purpose flour
    ½ teaspoon ground cinnamon
    ¼ teaspoon ground cardamom
    ⅛ teaspoon salt
    2 tablespoons butter or margarine, cut-up

Fit bottom crust into 9-inch pie pan. Set aside. In large mixing bowl, combine apples, sugar, flour, cinnamon, cardamom and salt. Place in prepared shell. Dot with butter pats.

Top with pastry. Trim, leaving 1-inch overhang. Roll edges under, catching bottom crust. Flute edges. Brush top crust lightly with milk and sprinkle with sugar, if desired. Cut slits in top.

Bake in 375°F **convection oven** on rack 3, 50 to 55 minutes (or bake in preheated 400°F **radiant bake oven** 55 to 60 minutes), or until crust is golden brown and filling bubbles through slits.

TIP: Shield pie crust edges with foil strips to prevent edges from browning too much during baking.

One 9-inch pie

Coconut Custard Pie

    1 recipe Single Pie Crust (right)
    ¾ cup sugar
    5 eggs, beaten
1¼ cups half-and-half
    1 cup milk
    1 teaspoon vanilla
    ⅛ teaspoon salt
1½ cups flaked coconut, divided

Prepare pastry as directed, but do not bake.

In medium mixing bowl blend sugar, eggs, half-and-half, milk, vanilla and salt. Stir in 1 cup coconut. Pour into pastry shell. Top with remaining ½ cup coconut.

Bake in preheated 400°F **convection oven** on rack 2, 10 minutes (or bake in preheated 400°F **radiant bake oven** 10 minutes).

Reduce temperature to 325°F. Continue baking in **convection oven** 15 to 20 minutes (or in **radiant bake oven** 25 to 30 minutes), or until knife inserted in center comes out clean. Cool slightly. Refrigerate before serving.

One 9-inch pie

Pear Pie

    1 recipe Double Pie Crust (below)
    6 cups cored, pared and sliced pears
    ½ cup sugar
    1 tablespoon grated fresh lemon peel
    ¼ teaspoon ground ginger
    2 tablespoons cornstarch

Fit bottom crust into 9-inch pie pan. Set aside.

In medium mixing bowl combine pears, sugar, lemon peel, ginger and cornstarch. Place in prepared shell. Top with pastry. Trim, leaving 1-inch overhang. Roll edges under, catching bottom crust. Flute edges. Brush top crust lightly with milk and sprinkle with sugar, if desired. Cut slits in top.

Bake in 375°F **convection oven** on rack 3, 50 to 55 minutes (or bake in preheated 400°F **radiant bake oven** 55 to 60 minutes), or until crust is golden brown and filling bubbles through slits.

TIP: Shield pie crust edges with foil strips to prevent edges from browning too much during baking.

One 9-inch pie

Single Pie Crust

1¼ cups all-purpose flour
    ½ teaspoon salt
    ¼ cup butter or margarine, cut-up
    2 tablespoons vegetable shortening
    3 to 4 tablespoons cold water

In medium mixing bowl combine flour and salt. Cut in butter and shortening until mixture is like coarse meal. Add water 1 tablespoon at a time, stirring with fork, until particles are moistened and stick together. Form pastry into a ball. On floured surface, roll to ⅛-inch thick circle 2½ inches larger than desired pie pan. Fit pastry into pie pan, leaving 1¼-inch overhang. Flute edges.

To bake, prick bottom and sides of crust. Bake in preheated 425°F **convection oven** on rack 2, 8 to 10 minutes (or bake in preheated 425°F **radiant bake oven** 10 to 12 minutes), or until light golden brown.

Double Pie Crust:
2½ cups all-purpose flour
    1 teaspoon salt
    ½ cup butter or margarine, cut-up
    ¼ cup vegetable shortening
    6 to 8 tablespoons cold water

Follow the recipe above, except divide pastry in half before rolling. Fill and bake as directed in desired recipe.

One 9 or 10-inch pie crust

Brownies

½ cup cocoa
⅓ cup butter or margarine, melted
1¼ cups sugar
¾ cup all-purpose flour
½ teaspoon baking powder
½ teaspoon salt
2 eggs
½ cup dairy sour cream
¾ teaspoon vanilla
½ cup chopped nuts

Frosting:
1¼ cups confectioners' sugar
3 tablespoons cocoa
2 tablespoons butter or margarine, softened
2 tablespoons hot water
¼ teaspoon vanilla

Grease 9 × 9-inch baking pan. Set aside.

In medium mixing bowl combine cocoa and butter. Mix in sugar, flour, baking powder, salt, eggs, sour cream and vanilla. Stir in nuts. Spread in pan.

Bake in preheated 325°F **convection oven** on rack 3, about 25 minutes (or bake in preheated 350°F **radiant bake oven** about 30 minutes), or until edges just begin to pull away from sides of pan. Cool completely. Frost, if desired.

For frosting: In small mixing bowl place confectioners' sugar, cocoa, butter, hot water and vanilla. Beat on high speed of electric mixer until smooth and creamy. Spread on cooled brownies.

Fudgy Brownies: Follow the recipe above, except decrease flour to ½ cup and omit baking powder.

16 to 20 bars

Apple Crisp

Filling:
5 cups cored, pared and sliced apples
¼ cup sugar
1 tablespoon water
½ teaspoon ground cinnamon
⅛ teaspoon ground allspice

Topping:
½ cup packed brown sugar
½ cup whole wheat flour
¼ cup rolled oats
¼ cup wheat germ
¼ cup chopped walnuts
½ teaspoon ground cinnamon
⅛ teaspoon ground allspice
6 tablespoons butter or margarine, softened

Grease 8 × 8-inch pan. Set aside.

For filling: In medium mixing bowl combine all ingredients. Spread in pan.

For topping: In medium mixing bowl combine all ingredients except butter. Cut in butter. Sprinkle over apple mixture.

Bake in 350°F **convection oven** on rack 3, about 35 minutes (or bake in preheated 350°F **radiant bake oven** about 45 minutes), or until top is browned and filling is bubbly.

Rhubarb Crisp: Follow the recipe above, substituting rhubarb filling for apple filling. For rhubarb filling combine 5 cups chopped rhubarb, ¾ cup to 1 cup sugar, 2 tablespoons all-purpose flour, 1 teaspoon grated fresh orange peel, ½ teaspoon ground cinnamon and ⅛ teaspoon ground allspice. Increase baking time by 5 minutes.

6 to 8 servings

Fruit Bars

Toffee Bars

Base:
- ½ cup butter or margarine, softened
- ½ cup packed brown sugar
- ¼ teaspoon vanilla
- 1¼ cups all-purpose flour
  Dash salt

Topping:
- ¾ cup semi-sweet chocolate chips
- ½ cup butter brickle chips

For base: In medium mixing bowl cream butter, brown sugar and vanilla. Add flour and salt. Mix until crumbly. Pat into 9 × 9-inch pan. Bake in preheated 325°F **convection oven** on rack 3, about 10 minutes (or bake in preheated 350°F **radiant bake oven** about 15 minutes), or until set and edges begin to brown.

For topping: Sprinkle chocolate chips over top. Return to oven until chips are softened, about 1 minute. Spread chips to frost bars. Sprinkle with butter brickle chips. Cool. Cut into squares.

16 to 20 bars

Rice Pudding

- ½ cup uncooked long-grain rice
- 2¼ cups milk, divided
- 2 tablespoons butter or margarine
- ½ teaspoon salt
- 2 eggs
- ¼ cup sugar
- 1 teaspoon vanilla
- ½ teaspoon grated fresh orange peel
- ⅛ teaspoon ground nutmeg
- ¼ cup dried currants or raisins

Lightly grease 1-quart casserole. Set aside.

In medium saucepan combine rice, 1 cup milk, butter and salt. Bring to boil. Reduce heat to medium low. Cook, covered, 20 minutes, or until liquid is absorbed and rice is tender. Stir. Cool 5 minutes, uncovered.

In medium mixing bowl beat eggs and remaining milk. Stir in sugar, vanilla, orange peel, nutmeg and currants. Add rice. Pour into prepared casserole. Place casserole in 8 × 8-inch baking dish. Add 1 inch of hot water to baking dish.

Bake in preheated 325°F **convection oven** on rack 3, 35 to 40 minutes (or bake in preheated 325°F **radiant bake oven** 40 to 45 minutes), until knife inserted in center comes out clean.

6 to 8 servings

Fruit Bars

Base:
- ¾ cup packed brown sugar
- ½ cup butter or margarine, softened
- 1⅓ cups rolled oats
- 1¼ cups all-purpose flour
- ½ teaspoon grated fresh lemon peel
- ¼ teaspoon salt

Filling:
- 1 can (21 ounces) blueberry pie filling
- ¼ teaspoon grated fresh lemon peel
- ¼ teaspoon ground nutmeg
- ¼ teaspoon ground cinnamon

Lightly grease 9 × 9-inch baking pan. Set aside.

For base: In medium mixing bowl combine brown sugar and butter. Mix in oats, flour, lemon peel and salt. Reserve 1¼ cups of mixture for topping. Pat remainder evenly into bottom of prepared baking pan. Bake in preheated 325°F **convection oven** on rack 3, 10 minutes (or bake in preheated 350°F **radiant bake oven** 10 minutes).

For filling: In small mixing bowl combine all ingredients. Spread filling over hot base. Sprinkle with reserved base mixture.

Continue baking in 325°F **convection oven** about 20 minutes (or bake in 350°F **radiant bake oven** about 25 minutes), or until golden brown. Cool before cutting.

Peach Bars: Follow recipe above, substituting 1 can (21 ounces) peach pie filling and ¼ teaspoon ground allspice for filling ingredients.

16 to 20 bars

Gingersnaps

    1 cup packed brown sugar
  ¾ cup vegetable shortening
  ¼ cup molasses
    1 egg
 2¼ cups all-purpose flour
    2 teaspoons baking soda
    1 teaspoon ground cinnamon
    1 teaspoon ground ginger
  ¼ teaspoon salt
  ¼ teaspoon ground cloves
  ¼ teaspoon ground nutmeg
      Granulated sugar

In medium mixing bowl cream brown sugar, shortening, molasses and egg until fluffy. Blend in remaining ingredients except granulated sugar. Cover and refrigerate at least 1 hour.

Form dough into 1-inch balls. Arrange 3 inches apart on two cookie sheets. Flatten with bottom of glass dipped in granulated sugar.

Bake in preheated 350°F **convection oven** on racks 2 and 4, 5 to 6 minutes (or bake in preheated 375°F **radiant bake oven** 5 to 6 minutes), or until edges just begin to brown. Repeat with remaining dough. Cool on wire racks.

4 dozen cookies

Oatmeal Cookies

  ½ cup vegetable shortening
  ½ cup butter or margarine
  ¾ cup packed brown sugar
  ⅓ cup granulated sugar
    1 egg
    1 teaspoon vanilla
    1 teaspoon almond extract
 1⅓ cups all-purpose flour
    1 teaspoon baking soda
  ½ teaspoon salt
    2 cups rolled oats
    1 cup raisins
  ½ cup chopped nuts

In medium mixing bowl cream shortening, butter, brown sugar and granulated sugar. Add egg, vanilla and almond extract. Beat until light and fluffy. Add flour, soda, salt and oats. Mix well. Stir in raisins and chopped nuts.

Drop by heaping teaspoons onto ungreased cookie sheets. Bake in preheated 325°F **convection oven** on racks 1, 3 and 5, 12 to 15 minutes (or bake in preheated 350°F **radiant bake oven** on racks 2 and 4, 12 to 15 minutes), or until light golden brown. Repeat with remaining dough. Cool on wire racks.

3½ to 4 dozen cookies

Peanut Butter Cookies

Peanut Butter Cookies

  ¾ cup peanut butter
  ½ cup butter or margarine, softened
  ½ cup packed brown sugar
  ½ cup granulated sugar
    1 egg
  ½ teaspoon vanilla
 1½ cups all-purpose flour
  ¾ teaspoon baking soda
  ¼ teaspoon salt
      Granulated sugar

In medium mixing bowl beat together peanut butter, butter, brown sugar, ½ cup granulated sugar, egg and vanilla until creamy. Blend in flour, soda and salt. Cover. Refrigerate at least 1 hour.

Form dough into 24 balls, each about 2 inches in diameter. Arrange about 2 inches apart on two cookie sheets. Flatten with fork dipped in granulated sugar to form crisscross pattern.

Bake in preheated 325°F **convection oven** on racks 2 and 4, 10 to 12 minutes (or bake in preheated 350°F **radiant bake oven** 10 to 12 minutes), or until light golden brown. Cool on wire racks.

Variation: Follow the recipe above, except omit salt. Add ½ cup chopped salted peanuts with flour.

2 dozen cookies

Oven Ideas

There are many creative and energy-saving ways to use your oven. By cooking two or more items at once, you can create a meal that's easy and efficient. We've suggested some combinations here. Other recipes which bake at the same temperature can also team up as meal partners. Elsewhere in this section you'll find helpful oven tips, plus directions for caramel corn, granola and dough art.

Beef Rib Roast, Potatoes and Grand Marnier Soufflé

3½ to 4-pound boneless rolled beef rib roast
6 to 8 baking potatoes
Grand Marnier Soufflé, page 166

Place roast on roasting pan. Calculate roasting time as directed from chart on page 109. Bake in 325°F **convection oven** on center of rack 2 or 3 (or bake in 325°F **radiant bake oven**), until meat thermometer registers desired doneness.

Place potatoes in **convection oven** around edges of rack 1 during last 1 to 1¼ hours baking time (or place potatoes in **radiant bake oven** during last 1½ hours baking time). Let roast stand 15 minutes before carving.

During standing time prepare soufflé as directed. Bake in 350°F **convection oven** (or bake in 375°F **radiant bake oven**), as directed.

Serve roast and potatoes with cooked green vegetable or salad, if desired.

Serve soufflé immediately out of oven.

6 to 8 servings

Pork Roast and Scandinavian Fruit Soup

3 pound pork roast
Scandinavian Fruit Soup, page 151

Place roast on roasting pan. Prepare fruit soup as directed. Cover casserole with foil instead of lid to assure both casserole and meat will fit into oven.

Bake roast in 325°F **convection oven** on rack 1, 15 minutes (or bake in 325°F **radiant bake oven** 15 minutes). Place fruit soup in oven on rack 4 or 5. Bake meat and soup an additional 1½ to 2¼ hours, or until meat thermometer inserted in roast registers 165°F. Stir soup once.

Let roast stand 15 minutes before carving. Serve with green vegetable or salad and rolls, if desired.

6 to 8 servings

Pork Roast and Scandinavian Fruit Soup

Rolled Meatloaf, Savory Carrot Pudding and Apple Crisp

Rolled Meatloaf, page 121
Savory Carrot Pudding, page 146
Apple Crisp, page 175

Prepare Rolled Meatloaf, Savory Carrot Pudding and Apple Crisp as directed.

Bake meatloaf in 325°F **convection oven** on rack 3, 15 minutes (or bake both meatloaf and pudding in preheated 350°F **radiant bake oven** on rack 3, 15 minutes). In **convection oven** add pudding to rack 3. In **convection oven** or **radiant bake oven** place Apple Crisp on rack 1. Continue baking another 45 minutes, or until meatloaf is brown, knife inserted in center of pudding comes out clean and Apple Crisp is bubbly and brown.

Serve with tossed salad and rolls, if desired.

4 to 6 servings

Stuffed Pork Chops and Lemon-Dill Green Beans

Stuffed Pork Chops, page 125
Lemon-Dill Green Beans, page 146

Assemble Stuffed Pork Chops as directed. Bake, covered, in preheated 350°F **convection oven** on rack 3, about 30 minutes (or bake in preheated 350°F **radiant bake oven** about 30 minutes).

While pork chops bake, assemble Lemon-Dill Green Beans as directed. Uncover pork chops. Bake green beans alongside pork chops in **convection oven** another 20 to 25 minutes (or bake in **radiant bake oven** another 25 to 30 minutes), or until pork chops are no longer pink and green beans are hot.

Serve with tossed salad and rolls, if desired.

About 4 servings

Baked Ham and Sweet Potato Puff

Baked Ham and Sweet Potato Puff

4 pound boneless fully-cooked ham
    Orange Raisin Sauce, page 100,
        or Brandy Peach Sauce, page 99 (optional)
    Sweet Potato Puff, page 149

Place ham in 9 × 9-inch baking pan. Bake in 325°F **convection oven** on rack 3, 1 hour 20 minutes to 1 hour 40 minutes (or bake in 325°F **radiant bake oven** 1 hour 20 minutes to 1 hour 40 minutes).

Prepare Sweet Potato Puff as directed and place in oven during last 45 to 50 minutes of cooking time. Glaze ham with sauce during last 30 minutes.

Bake until meat thermometer inserted in center of ham registers 140°F and knife inserted in center of puff comes out clean.

Serve with green beans or asparagus, if desired.

4 to 6 servings

Baked Chicken, Pilaf-Stuffed Tomatoes and Baked Curried Fruit

2½ to 3-pound broiler-fryer chicken
    Pilaf-Stuffed Tomatoes, page 148
    Baked Curried Fruit, page 151

Place chicken on roasting pan. Bake in preheated 375°F **convection oven** on rack 1, about 50 minutes (or bake in preheated 375°F **radiant bake oven** about 50 minutes).

While chicken bakes, assemble Pilaf-Stuffed Tomatoes and Baked Curried Fruit as directed. After first chicken roasting time, place tomatoes and fruit in **convection oven** on rack 4 and continue baking another 10 to 15 minutes (or bake in **radiant bake oven** another 15 to 20 minutes), or until meat thermometer inserted in thickest part of chicken registers 185°F, tomatoes are lightly browned on top and fruit is bubbly.

Let chicken stand 15 minutes before carving. Serve with tomatoes and fruit.

About 4 servings

Caramel Corn

- 1 cup butter or margarine
- 1 cup packed brown sugar
- ½ cup light corn syrup
- 1 teaspoon salt
- 1 teaspoon vanilla or imitation butter flavor
- 6 quarts popped popcorn
- 1½ cups salted Spanish peanuts

In medium saucepan combine butter, brown sugar, corn syrup and salt. Bring to boil, stirring constantly. Let boil without stirring 5 minutes. Remove from heat. Stir in vanilla.

In large pan or bowl combine popcorn and peanuts. Pour syrup over mixture, tossing to coat well. Pour onto three 15 × 10-inch jelly roll pans.

Bake in preheated 250°F **convection oven** on racks 1, 3 and 5, about 20 minutes (or bake in two batches in preheated 250°F **radiant bake oven** on racks 2 and 4, about 30 minutes). Stir corn and exchange racks after half the time. Cool.

About 6 quarts

Candied Citrus Peel

- 1½ cups citrus peel*
- 6 cups water, divided
- 2 cups sugar
- 1 cup water
- Sugar

In wok or medium saucepan place peel in 2 cups of water. Heat to boiling. Drain and rinse peel. Repeat process twice.

In wok or medium saucepan combine 2 cups sugar and 1 cup water. Heat to boiling, stirring occasionally. Add drained peel. Return to boil. Reduce heat to medium low. Cook, stirring occasionally, about 15 to 20 minutes until peel is translucent. Remove with slotted spoon.

Coat both sides of peel with granulated sugar. Place on wire rack over baking sheet. Let dry overnight (or dry in **convection oven** on rack 3, using fan only, 3 to 4 hours, until dry but not brittle).

*Use 2 large grapefruit or combination of 6 smaller fruits (lemons, oranges or limes) for 1½ cups peel. With sharp knife or vegetable peeler remove 1-inch wide strips from fruit. Cut into 2 to 4-inch lengths. Scrape away any white pulp from colored peel.

About 2 cups

Caramel Corn

Rich Croutons

Granola

   6 cups rolled oats
   1 cup shredded coconut
   1 cup peanuts
   ½ cup chopped dates
   ½ cup raisins
   1 teaspoon grated fresh orange peel
   ½ cup butter or margarine
   ½ cup honey
   ⅓ cup packed brown sugar
   2 tablespoons dark corn syrup
   1 teaspoon vanilla
   ½ teaspoon ground cinnamon
   1 cup dried banana chips
   1 cup plain candy coated chocolate pieces

Grease 15 × 10-inch jelly roll pan. Set aside.

In large bowl combine rolled oats, coconut, peanuts, dates and raisins. Set aside.

In medium saucepan place remaining ingredients except banana chips and chocolate pieces. Cook on medium heat, stirring occasionally, until butter is melted and mixture can be stirred smooth. Pour hot mixture over oatmeal mixture. Stir to coat evenly. Spread mixture in prepared pan. Bake in preheated 325°F **convection oven** on rack 1, 30 to 35 minutes (or bake in preheated 350°F **radiant bake oven** 35 to 40 minutes), stirring twice.

Let cool. Break apart. Stir in chocolate candies and banana chips.

10 cups

Yogurt

   2 cups milk (low fat or skim)
   ⅓ cup instant nonfat dry milk
   2 tablespoons unflavored yogurt

In medium saucepan combine milk and dry milk. Beat with a wire whisk or electric mixer until well mixed. Cook on medium heat, stirring constantly, until thermometer reads 180°F. Remove from heat. Let cool to 110°F.

Whisk in yogurt. Pour mixture into medium bowl. Cover with plastic wrap. Place in oven with only oven light left on. Let stand overnight or about 8 to 10 hours. Refrigerate.

Use as a low-calorie substitute for sour cream in recipes, a topping for fresh fruit, or stir in honey, jam or preserves.

Four 8-ounce servings

Rich Croutons

   8 cups stale bread cubes (½ to 1 inch),
        about 10 to 12 slices of bread
   1¼ cups butter or margarine
   1½ to 2 teaspoons Italian seasoning (optional)

In large mixing bowl place bread cubes. In small saucepan melt butter with Italian seasoning. Pour butter mixture over bread cubes, tossing to coat. Spread bread cubes in 15 × 10-inch jelly roll pan.

Bake in 250°F **convection oven** on rack 3, 1 to 1½ hours (or bake in preheated 250°F **radiant bake oven** 1½ to 2 hours), until dry and crispy, stirring several times. Spread on paper toweling to cool.

Bread Crumbs: Crush croutons with rolling pin or in food processor.

TIP: Bread left too long in freezer can make excellent croutons.

About 5 cups

Beef Jerky

Marinade:
½ cup soy sauce
½ cup water
¼ cup Worcestershire sauce
2 teaspoons salt
1 teaspoon onion powder
½ teaspoon garlic powder
¼ teaspoon liquid smoke
¼ teaspoon hot pepper sauce

1 to 1½ pounds flank steak

For marinade: In small mixing bowl combine all marinade ingredients. Partially freeze flank steak (about 1 hour) to ease slicing. Slice steak thinly across the grain (⅛-inch thick slices). Place slices in baking dish or small mixing bowl. Pour marinade over meat slices. Cover and refrigerate overnight.

Remove meat slices with slotted spoon. Drain excess marinade by placing meat on paper toweling. Arrange slices on two metal cooling racks or nylon net covered oven rack.

Bake in 150°F **convection oven** on racks 2 and 3, 4 to 5 hours (or bake in 150°F **radiant bake oven** 4 to 5 hours), or until jerky is dry and bends without cracking.

Place between layers of paper toweling to remove excess moisture. Let cool completely.

2 to 3 cups

Defrosting Frozen Cakes

Place frozen cake on serving plate. Put in **convection oven** with only fan and oven light on. Leave in oven until wooden pick meets little resistance when inserted in center. Time will be about one-third to one-half of that listed on package instructions for thawing at room temperature.

Proofing Yeast Dough

Use oven cavity as a warm place for proofing yeast dough. Place covered bowl or pans of dough on middle rack. Turn on oven light only. Proof as directed in recipe.

How to Make Cover for Oven Rack

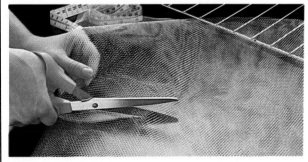

Cut piece of nylon net the width of a rack less 2 inches and twice the depth. Sew Velcro™ or snap tape to shorter ends.

Slip net through back support. Wrap around rack. Fasten snugly. Clean in washing machine. Store rolled up in drawer.

Dough Art

Start with the recipe below and let your imagination take over. Picture frames, magnets, clay pot decorations, candle holders, baskets and hanging mobiles are just a few of the possibilities.

Basic Salt Dough

2 cups all-purpose flour
1 cup salt
1 cup water

In medium bowl combine flour and salt. Add water, a little at a time, stirring to mix. Form dough into a ball (additional water may be needed). On lightly floured surface, knead dough until smooth, yet firm, about 7 to 10 minutes. Place dough in a plastic bag until ready to use. (May be kept in refrigerator up to 5 days.)

To shape: Roll dough to ¼-inch thickness on lightly floured surface. Cut with lightly floured cookie cutter shapes. Place on foil-lined cookie sheet. For a whiter baked product let cut-outs air-dry overnight. If a natural light brown color is desired, bake after shaping (without drying first). Bake in preheated 300°F **convection oven** on rack 3, about 1 hour (or bake in preheated 300°F **radiant bake oven** about 1½ hours), or until dry. Small pieces may bake more quickly than large ones. Check early. Cool completely.

• Paint with diluted water paints or acrylic paints.
• Use a wooden pick to write child's name on cut-out shapes.
• Use as place cards at birthday parties.
• Use a drinking straw to punch holes for hanging.
• Press a small amount of dough through a garlic press to form hair.

Index